The Integrative Family Therapy Supervisor

The Integrative Family Therapy Supervisor

A Primer

Robert E. Lee
Craig A. Everett

BRUNNER-ROUTLEDGE

New York and Hove

Published in 2004 by
Brunner-Routledge
29 West 35th Street
New York, NY 10001
www.brunner-routledge.com

Published in Great Britain by
Brunner-Routledge
27 Church Road
Hove, East Sussex
BN3 2FA
www.brunner-routledge.co.uk

Library of Congress Cataloging-in-Publication Data

Lee, Robert E. (Robert Ernest), 1943-
    The integrative family therapy supervisor : a primer / Robert E. Lee, Craig A. Everett.
       p. ; cm.
    Includes bibliographical references and index.
       ISBN 0-415-94558-5 (hardback : alk. paper)
       1. Family therapists—Supervision of.
       [DNLM: 1. Family Therapy—methods. 2. Family Therapy—education. 3. Mentors.
    WM 430.5.F2 L479i 2003] I. Everett, Craig A. II. Title.

    RC488.5.L44 2003
    616.89'156—dc21

                                                                            2003009531

Dedicated to William C. Nichols—teacher, supervisor, mentor, colleague, and friend.

Contents

Preface

We have developed this primer of relational and family therapy supervision to offer resources for the new generation of clinical educators and supervisors of marital and family therapists. There are other books on family therapy supervision that have been written over the past decade, but we believe this work will reflect the historical evolution of the field to its present focus on integrative clinical work in a variety of challenging clinical settings. Most family therapy practitioners today no longer follow singular models of intervention as did their mentors of one or two generations ago. The developments of the field and applications of family therapy to the full range of clinical disorders, as well as the mandates of managed health care, have changed forever the roles and expectations of couple and family therapists.

Our focus will be on a *personally developed integrative model* of supervision. We expect that this book can be used as a text for graduate courses in family therapy supervision as well as by supervisors in either academic or private training settings. We also have organized this in a sort of "workbook" format to offer practical steps and guidelines for Approved Supervisor Candidates of the American Association for Marriage and Family Therapy (AAMFT). A goal would be that when they have completed work in this book they would have reflected on and acquired, with the aid of their supervisory mentor, the basic ingredients and work products necessary to complete their application for that credential.

We have been teaching and supervising marital and family therapists for over three decades. We have done this in private practice and agency settings, graduate programs, and workshops and institutes. In all of our work we have followed the requirements of the AAMFT. Over the years, we have found that our teaching and training approaches have evolved in response to the changing practice of marital and family therapy—its professionals, its theories, and its settings.

The Changing Field of Family Therapy

Many of you in practice today may describe the way you do therapy and supervision as "eclectic" or "integrative." However, in contrast, the marital and family therapy (MFT) field 25 years ago was characterized by loyalties to major theories and theorists—the pioneers, if you will. The field at that time was rather fragmented and somewhat chaotic. Even as it was competing for national recognition as a profession among the established mental health providers, the family therapy profession itself was internally divided by competing orientations and theories. The notion of integration was foreign to most of these pioneers who, through a sort of sibling rivalry, believed that their own approaches and contributions were the most effective and systemic. Despite their similar systemic orientations, it would have been hard for these early pioneers to concede that there was actually a common foundation with specific systemic concepts that could offer a sense of integration to the emerging MFT field.

As occurs in family systems, beliefs and values often tend to change across generations. Competition today among the major theories gradually has been replaced by a sense of "equifinality"—that all therapeutic roads lead to healing— and consideration of common therapeutic factors present in all approaches. Much discussion now centers on generic aspects of treatment and the identification of central concepts like "therapeutic alliance," "loss," "life cycle," "isomorphism," and "differentiation" and interventions such as the use of enactment, ritual, reframing, and genograms. Many of you now use these terms and these techniques no matter what approach you first were trained in or from which these concepts and interventions arose.

Concurrent with this change in thinking about therapy with families, the number of MFT practitioners has increased exponentially; with this increase has come an enormous diversity of clinical practice settings. These developmental factors and growth of the field have created unique influences on how we all think about and do clinical work.

Many of you may continue to practice in traditional solo and group settings or in institutions of high learning. However, many family therapists now work in community mental health centers, psychiatric hospitals, family service agencies, and child welfare programs. Many others practice in residential programs for delinquent youth, medical settings, religiously oriented family counseling services, and hospices. Family therapists work in many programs with native-born U.S. citizens, first- and second-generation immigrants, and citizens of other continents. Some supervise in-home family therapy. Others work within demarcated communities such as military bases, Mennonite communities, Indian reservations, and Hmong or Mexican community centers. Family therapists today may have clients of all ages who are "straight," gay, lesbian, bisexual, and transgendered. Some of your clients are privileged in many ways. Others are not.

We could go on, but we want you to know that we appreciate that those seeking advancement as family therapy supervisors or Approved Supervisor status with the AAMFT bring diverse educational and career experiences, values, and needs. Because we have experiences with many diverse training and practice contexts, we recognize that the expectation of "one size fits all" is no longer a viable way to operate. Participants in traditional classes often tell us that they feel frustrated in their learning objectives, and they do not feel that their experiences and their unique stories are respected. They have reported that they would appreciate a collaborative learning experience that begins with their definition of who they are and their own unique learning objectives. They want their journey to be informed by the major family therapy theoretical influences and the best supervisory academic lore. They also want the conclusion of it to satisfy the requirements for the Approved Supervisor credential.

Accordingly, once you have reached the conclusion of this book, we expect that you will have accomplished the content objectives set forth in *Approved Supervisor Designation: Standards and Responsibilities* (AAMFT, 2002a). Our goals are that you accomplish the following:

1. You should be familiar with the contributions of the major models of family therapy to the supervisory process in terms of their philosophical assumptions and pragmatic implications.
2. You should have developed and articulated your own personal model of supervision that has been drawn from existing models of supervision and from your preferred styles of therapy.
3. Having considered the implications of the "intergenerational" supervisor–therapist–client system, you should be able to facilitate the co-evolving therapist–client and supervisor–therapist–client relationships, and be able to identify and evaluate problems in therapist–client and supervisor–therapist–client relationships.
4. You should be able to structure supervision, solve problems, and implement supervisory interventions within a range of supervisory modalities (e.g., live and videotaped, and individual and group supervision).
5. You should be sensitive to contextual variables such as culture, gender, ethnicity, and economics and be knowledgeable of ethical and legal issues of supervision.
6. You should be alert to and able to address adequately those distinctive issues that arise in supervision of supervision.
7. You should know the requirements and procedures for supervising applicants for AAMFT Clinical Membership.

Defining Integration

Craig remembers attending family therapy conferences as a doctoral student in the mid-1970s and being challenged by other graduate students and even leaders in the field to claim an identity with one of the pioneers or their approaches. Even at social events associated with these conferences, practitioners and students would expound on the "uniqueness" and efficacy of their "model," whether it be some-one studying with Bowen, Haley, Minuchin, or another pioneer. There was pressure to conform and become loyal to a certain narrow orientation much as today one might be asked, "Are you a Republican or a Democrat?"

However, collaborating with William C. Nichols (Nichols & Everett, 1986), Craig was among the few lone voices in the field who would advocate early on for an integrative model that appreciated the complexity of working with the entity that we call a family system:

> The challenge . . . is to steer clear of premature commitment to any single school or set of techniques and to continue the emotional and intellectual struggle to integrate what can be integrated from diverse sources into an ever-deepening understanding of the richly complex phenomena with which we are grappling. . . . We [want to] introduce . . . an integrative family therapy approach in which historical, interactional, and existential perspectives all have a place and blend into a coherent systemic framework for study and treatment. (p. 64–65)

Two generations have passed. The field of family therapy has evolved in its appreciation both of its subject matter and epistemology. The voices of Nichols, Everett, Feldman, Grunebaum, Gurman, Lebow, Liddle, Pinsof, and others have become the theoretical "negative space" out of which the image of contemporary family therapy is emerging. This is what Jay Lebow (1997a) described as the "quiet (integrative) revolution in couple and family therapy."

Given the diversity of contemporary clinical settings, including many that are nontraditional, it is not surprising that family therapists have developed their own personally pragmatic combinations of various concepts and techniques. However, we would call that approach "eclecticism," namely, "a pragmatic, case-based approach in which the ingredients of different approaches are employed without concern for theory" (Lebow, 1997a, p. 5). Eclectic clinicians like the idea of a range of choices in treatment, affording them greater flexibility, the potential for a high level of treatment acceptability among clients, and treatment efficacy. They are committed to a diversity of ideas and, in these postmodern times, shy away from those who espouse one "real" version of the universe.

Although we understand that this approach may be appealing to some clinicians, we believe strongly that an *overarching conceptual map* or theory is central to the practice of family therapy, and to the training of family therapy practitioners. Such a map would describe who we are and what we are about. This elevates a family therapy professional above a skilled technician who applies a bag of tools in a somewhat knowledgeable way. As integrative family therapists and supervisors, we have a map that can help us understand social phenomena and help us make decisions in a consistent way relatively uninfluenced by momentary states of heart and mind. In fact, even the most eclectic of us probably have an unconscious, implicit way of making sense of things that determines what tools one remembers and employs in any given situation. That being the case, we think it is important that such internal models be made explicit so that they can be subjected to the influence of reason and new leaning. These models will then grow in a cohesive and purposive fashion.

The integrative orientation will be described in detail in Chapter 2. At the minimum, an integrative approach to family therapy is founded in systems theory (Lebow, 1997a) and would include the following:

1. A blending of adjunctive theory and practice
2. The integration of historical, interactional, and existential data

However, from our perspective, and for the purposes of educating family therapy clinicians and supervisors, we view the actual integration process as much more complex. In essence, it is a process whereby the clinician moves from the bigger picture of the training system's overall functioning, symptoms, and dynamics toward an informed narrowing of choices to specific responses and interventions. The flexible use of conceptual and intervention tools is informed by a systems-based metatheory of relational change, the developmental levels of supervisor, therapist and client, the comfort levels and styles of all, and the clinical and diagnostic presenting problems of the family. On the one hand, all interventions are driven by a cohesive approach based on high levels of ongoing education and training. Consider this as quality control. On the other hand, many integrative approaches are collaborative and highly personalized. Therefore, an integrative approach—to supervision as well as to therapy—is both responsible and responsive.

Integrative Supervision

As you will see from Chapter 3's outline of a basic model, we view the value of this integrative model as providing supervisors with the orientation and resources to train therapists to cognitively and experientially blend the following:

For assessment
1. Recognition of systemic dynamics (from theory) that are observed and experienced in the clinical family.
2. An understanding of the clinical family's developmental stage, structure, process, and symptoms.
3. An awareness as a therapist of one's own personal resources, biases, and orientation that can color the perception of the clinical dynamics.

For treatment
4. An understanding of the clinical family's resources, balance (homeostasis), and potential for change.

5. Identification of the target symptoms and/or the target dynamics within the family's structure and process.
6. Awareness as a therapist of one's own level of training and experience, and skills to implement certain interventions.
7. The selection of an appropriate clinical intervention in response to all of the data. This selected intervention may offer structural, strategic, family or origin, narrative, and/or experiential feedback to the family; or, it may be an intervention that offers simply support and understanding.

For us, the product of integrative family therapy supervision should be a therapy practitioner who can cognitively and experientially integrate a systemic understanding of a clinical family's dynamics, using historical, interactive, and existential data, and blend these data into an informed, coherent, and reasonable systemic framework of assessment and treatment. We understand that the family is itself an integrative system for its members. It provides them with nurture and direction for their development within the family and after they have left the physical family. We view supervision as a similar integrative milieu and process that provides nurture and direction for therapists and supervisors-in-training to learn the skills of blending systemic theory with clinical practice in the context of personal and professional development.

Our Goals for Writing This Book

We want this work to be useful for supervisors both academically and clinically. However, we also want it to provide the basic ingredients for a supervisory candidate to experience a reflective and learning process from which she or he can develop models and philosophies of supervision to meet the AAMFT standards. To do this, we have tried to make this book friendly, integrative in orientation, practical and pragmatic, and filled with exercises resulting in the products necessary for the AAMFT Approved Supervisor credential.

To accomplish this, we begin with a discussion of "generic" family therapy supervision. However, because we respect who you are and what you ultimately need, we keep an eye on the unique context in which you are working. Chapter 1 explores some foundational ideas to get you started consolidating your own experiences if you are already doing supervision, or to get you started doing supervision if you are beginning. We describe the basic rules and methods that all family therapy supervisory settings require.

In Chapter 2 we present our own view of the role of integrative approaches in the history and development of the family therapy field. Then in Chapters 3 through 6 we provide the basic theoretical foundation for a working integrative model. This includes discussions of intergenerational theory and the dynamics of the clinical training program, a discussion of the importance of viewing the supervision process from developmental theory, and a review of the contributions of the major family therapy approaches to supervision. In Chapters 7 and 8 we discuss the practical tools of supervision, that is, live, videotape, and case presentation approaches, and the unique contributions of individual and group supervisory formats. Next, in Chapter 9, we ask our readers to consider the cultures that are therapy, supervision, and training settings by first taking a careful look at themselves as a cultural product. Who you are influences the entire training system of supervisor, therapist, and client. Chapter 10 reviews what research has discovered about the best resources that make supervision effective, and Chapter 11 discusses issues that can help the supervisor troubleshoot the supervisory relationship and process. Chapter 12 enumerates other supervisory responsibilities and reminds you of your administrative tools to help manage the requirements of your many roles.

Chapter 13 offers a practical approach to helping the reader through a solution focused process of discovering what one already knows from having been a consumer of supervision and through which one can construct a personal model and philosophy of supervision. We recognize that these will be dynamic constructs that will change over time and context, but the exercise will get you started and, if you so desire, credentialed! Chapter 14 is another practical chapter that presents two illustrations of working with family therapy trainees through several "phases" of training; it explicitly demonstrates our model of integrative supervision "in action." Finally, Chapter 15 reviews where we tried to go together, considers supervision-of-supervision, and discusses the lifelong process of becoming a family therapy supervisor.

Our goal is to create an ongoing dialogue with you about the practical, day-to-day application of scholarship in contemporary supervision settings. We see ourselves as facilitators who, based on our own years of experience, can provide a clear discussion and effective model from which the readers can learn and begin to build their own model. Of course, the integrative model that we will offer here remains a hypothetical construct. Its ultimate value will be the extent to which it becomes useful to you.

We think of your experience with us through this book as a journey. The departure point and destination will differ for each of you. The quality of the journey will depend on how involved and interactive you become with the content and suggestions. We hope you will find the exercises thought provoking and that they will assist you in compiling your own journal. We have tried to organize this so that your notes in the journal can be used to easily compile the Supervision Philosophy Statement and Case Study for your Approved Supervisor credential. We also hope that this book will be practical and friendly enough to be useful for supervisors in agency and other community settings.

Although this text has not been endorsed by the AAMFT, we have written it so that it could be used as the primary text for supervision courses approved by the AAMFT. These classes take place within graduate programs accredited by the

Commission on Accreditation of Marriage and Family Therapy Education, in some private training institutes, at AAMFT-sponsored advanced clinical institutes, and at the annual AAMFT conferences.

As we indicated, we have tried to write this work in a user-friendly and personal manner. So, before we begin the content, we thought that it would be helpful to give you a brief overview of each of our own backgrounds and experiences, much as you might learn from the supervisory mentor with whom you may be working.

About the Authors

Robert E. Lee

I have been clinical director of the marital and family therapy program at Michigan State University for about 10 years. Prior to that I was in clinical practice for 25 years. The settings in which 1 was professionally educated and trained will tell you a lot about my current family therapy orientation. Formal family therapy programs did not exist when I started out. If they had, I probably would not have noticed them. My master's degree and doctorate were in experimental social psychology and I was deeply impressed by Kurt Lewin's field theory, general systems theory, and Piaget's notion of assimilation and accommodation. Each described individuals transacting with their immediate environments and both being changed in the process.

I then entered a postdoctoral clinical internship in marital and family counseling where I tried to make sense out of what I was seeing: children in treatment but their behavior apparently a product of what their parents were doing; and families quitting treatment just when I thought progress was being made. Following that experience, I went to work in a large general medical and surgical hospital where I specialized in those conditions antecedent to, attendant upon, parading as, or subsequent to physical illness. I was intrigued by the "why now?" question. Why did people get sick when they did? Why did they seek treatment when they did? Why were many individuals noncompliant with their treatment regimens? Why did many not want to leave the hospital? And so on.

I had found psychodynamic theory only moderately useful in the counseling internship and less so in the medical hospital. I fell back on the theorists who had impressed me in graduate school. I quickly discovered that the answers to my questions in both settings involved appreciating the social contexts in which individuals and their families were embedded. As I was applying these insights, I discovered that the field of family therapy was developing apace and that my postdoctoral internship site and its faculty were prime players.

I subsequently went into private practice with one of my first supervisors, William C. Nichols, and he directed me to the emerging family therapy literature and the family science upon which we thought it should be based. As Craig will quickly agree, Bill has always been a scientist-practitioner and he eschewed gurus and therapeutic fads. He taught me family therapy as he believed it should be: carefully considered theory leading to goal-setting—those goals pursued by the technique most likely to accomplish those goals for that client family, at that time, in that setting. This orientation has served me, my clients, and my students well over the past three decades. As you will see, it guides this book.

I am a fully licensed marital and family therapist and an Approved Supervisor of the American Association for Marital and Family Therapy. Over the years I have been chair of Michigan's marital and family therapy licensing board, and president of the national Association of Marital and Family Therapy Regulatory Boards and the Michigan Association for Marital and Family Therapy. I also helped administer the national licensing examination for marital and family therapists in its early years.

In my current setting I teach graduate-level courses in marital and family therapy, and I have published extensively in various areas of marriage and family life, divorce, individual and family assessment, and professional training. My most recent research includes, among other things, children and families involved in the foster care system, and how families help children develop high "emotional IQs." I also have been active with a large child welfare agency since 1987.

Craig A. Everett

I have always viewed my early training opportunities as well-timed in terms of the development of the family therapy field. I was among the first generation of family therapists who were actually trained in an "integrative" family therapy doctoral program at Florida State University during the mid-1970s. This was unique because the majority of clinicians entering the MFT field in those years were coming from either prior training in psychiatry, psychology or social work, or from specific and rather narrow training experiences with some of the pioneers in the field (i.e., Minuchin, Bowen, Haley, etc.).

Before going to Florida State, I had the opportunity to work for two years in what were amazing inpatient clinical settings for a young and beginning therapist. The first was in a pediatric neurological center—I was the only graduate student to volunteer for this assignment—that provided desperate surgeries for hydrocephalic or other brain-damaged children. This was my first clinical experience that forced me to struggle to learn about families, how they worked, how they grieved, and how to answer their questions about their dying children. Because of the experimental surgeries being developed in those years and the severity of these children's needs, there was only about a 25% to 30% survival rate. The images of these grieving families and their dying children have never left me and that experience certainly propelled me into the family therapy field. I also credit that experience with grounding me early in my career with a sort of practical realism: Whether writing or teaching or practicing, I have always tried to remain focused on the basic and most practical aspects of clinical work.

Later I spent a year in training at a large state psychiatric facility where I worked primarily with children and their families, but also on geriatric, adult, and forensic wards. From there I moved to an outpatient mental health center where I worked with children and adolescents and their families. Although my focus in my early clinical training had been on families, I had not studied with the major theorists/pioneers; I taught myself about family dynamics through pursuing family therapy workshops and training opportunities. I am indebted to Chuck Kramer, M.D., the founder of the Chicago Family Institute, whose monthly seminars I traveled four hours to attend in the early 1970s, for his early formulations about the emerging family therapy field and encouragement to apply those principles to my work in the mental health field.

By this early point in my career, I needed more formal family therapy training and theory. Based on six years of what I thought were pretty powerful clinical training experiences, I wanted to study with someone who could help me gain a view of the entire family therapy field. I had enough prior experience, and I guess personal independence, that I knew that I did not want to become pigeonholed into someone else's orientation. Selecting Florida State at that time was the best fit because it allowed me to experience Bill Nichols as my mentor. I know that he will cringe or do something worse when he reads this, but it is my feeling that if anyone deserves the title of Grandparent of Integrative Family Therapy it would be he.

Bill Nichols stood out clearly among the other family therapy pioneers and educators of that decade in his advocating for a broad systemic understanding of the family. He consistently taught that effective clinical practice only evolves from good clinical theory. We learned the practical limitations with our clinical families of becoming too wed to narrow or singular approaches to treatment, or of trying to fit every case into a particular model or (worse) to some technique that we might have learned at a weekend workshop. We learned vigorously that we had to explain, theoretically, and defend carefully every clinical assessment and potential intervention.

All of these experiences have shaped my own orientations and roles in the field. I obviously adopted a similar integrative approach to my clinical work and teaching. Nichols and I co-authored the first text on integrative family therapy, *Systemic Family Therapy: An Integrative Approach,* in 1986. My other work has continued to reflect my early training experiences in inpatient and outpatient psychiatric settings. I have tried to continue to integrate the clinical wisdom of systemic family therapy in works on family therapy with the borderline personality disorders (Everett et al., 1989; Everett & Everett, 1998), divorce (Everett & Everett, 1994), and more recently with attention deficit/hyperactivity disorder (Everett & Everett, 1999).

Professionally I have had the unusual opportunities to teach and train family therapists in both academic and private settings. I taught at and helped to develop AAMFT-accredited marital and family therapy degree programs at Auburn University (master's level) and at Florida State University (doctoral level). Since I left the academic world in 1987, I have been in full-time private practice in Tucson, Arizona. My wife, Sandra Volgy Everett, is an AAMFT Approved Supervisor and was trained as a clinical child psychologist. In addition to writing together we have co-directed a private family therapy training program since 1987, The Arizona Institute for Family Therapy.

Acknowledgment

We would like to gratefully acknowledge the patient and insightful edi torial assistance of Michelle Crooks, Ph.D. She has worked hard to help us make this a reader-friendly text and as well as a pleasant creative experience for its authors.

Chapter 1

Basic Ingredients in the Supervisory Process

The Ground Rules of Supervision

L earning to be a supervisor, like learning to be a therapist, is a lifelong task. But you need to begin somewhere and the journey of a thousand miles begins with the first step. This chapter is meant to be that first step. We intend to build a foundation upon which everything that follows can be erected. We believe that it is important for a beginning supervisor to have a clear understanding of those principles that seem to be central to all effective family therapy supervision.

First, we will ask you to reflect upon positive and negative experiences you have had as a consumer of supervisory services during your own training and to consider what you have learned from them. Next, we will identify and review what others in the family therapy field generally consider to be foundational to family therapy supervision. In the course of our journey together we expect that you will give considerable thought to these and make aspects of them your own.

Appreciating What You Already Know

We want to begin a process of personal reflection on your own resources which then can be integrated into the clinical and theoretical issues we will discuss. We would like you to think about your best and worst supervisory experiences. We want to stir up those memories to make your reading of this work more relevant and remind you of how much you may already know about effective supervision.

As you cull your memories for things that will be helpful to your own practice of supervision, we would like you to be very systematic and behaviorally explicit. In each exercise that will follow, close your eyes and try to really picture an event or a relationship as it occurred. Try for detailed visualization, with an alert eye to tone of voice, facial expression, and other body language. It may help to picture the room, your clothing, and even the season. As you reconstruct the past, visualize actual behaviors that illustrate what you mean: "I am _____ing. My supervisor is _____ing." For example, if you are saying "My supervisor is being supportive," what does "being supportive" look like in that vision? If someone is being "critical," what demonstrates that? Finally, we recommend that you put the content that you construct in these exercises down in a journal or notebook so that you can integrate you insights when you begin to formalize you own philosophy of supervision in Chapter 13.

Exercise 1: Your Positive and Negative Models

Take a few minutes to close your eyes, think back, and visualize.

• What have your previous supervisors done that has been really helpful? What were their resources that you appreciated, at the time or in retrospect. Picture a supervisory session with a supervisor you really found beneficial. What was she or he doing in that session? And what were you doing?

After you have thought about this for a while, make a list of these ingredients. Then, prioritize them.

• Now think about when you were being supervised, and identify what sorts of things you would *not* want to experience again. What were the experiences at that time, or in retrospect, that were *not* helpful? If you can picture a really ugly session, do that. What was the supervisor doing and what were you doing?

Again, make a list and then prioritize these items.

Exercise 2: Supervisory Relationships

• Think of individual supervisors now or in the recent past who you value or have liked a lot. Think of your overall time together with these supervisors. Identify the supervisors who you really have appreciated in their overall relationship with you.

List and rank these with regard to their importance to you.

• Think of individual supervision now or in the recent past where you have felt dissatisfied, ill-at-ease, irritated, confused, or negatively tense. Think of the overall ambience of these relationships.

Make a list of those issues you have experienced as off-putting or unhelpful. Rank these with regard to their importance to your supervision experience.

Exercise 3: Developmentally Appropriate and Inappropriate Models

• Think of supervisors who you experienced as very helpful when you were first starting out. List their resources that you have really appreciated in the overall relationship.

List and rank these with regard to their importance to you at that time (and presently, too, if that would change your perceptions).

• Think of supervisors whom you experienced as not particularly helpful, or even as detrimental, when you were first starting out. List their traits or behaviors that you considered negative in the overall relationship.

List and rank these with regard to their importance to you at that time (and now, if that would change things).

• Think of specific episodes in specific training sessions with your first supervisors. What did you want from them during an episode and what did they do that you felt was unhelpful or detrimental?

Again, list and rank these with regard to their importance, if that is possible.

Exercise 4: Compiling Your Personal Lessons About Effective Supervision

Take a few minutes to reflect on what you have written. Go though your lists and highlight those items that strike you as very important to supervision at any stage and in any setting. Also identify those items that were sensitive to your developmental level or practice setting at the time. How do (or will) such personal experiences shape what you do as a supervisor?

We suspect that as you look at your two lists—the resources and dynamics that have typified good supervisory experiences for you and those that were toxic—a basic recognition of the nature of good supervision will start to emerge. We also suspect that as you complete these exercises, as with our own supervisors-in-training over the years, the issues you have identified have more to do with the process of supervision than with concerns regarding specific theoretical issues or schools of thought.

With all of these things in mind, the next step is to review what the supervision literature considers foundational.

13 Basic Principles of Clinical Supervision

We have identified 13 principles (Table 1.1) that appear to represent a core of theory and research about family therapy supervision. These have been derived both from the theory and research regarding clinical supervision in general as well as from our own experiences as training supervisors. We have found these principles to be essential to our own work over the years as clinical educators and family therapy supervisors. Each of these principles will be discussed in the ensuing chapters. We are listing them here at the beginning because they can provide a foundation upon which your own model of family therapy supervision will be built and evolve. However, we do not expect that this list is exhaustive. Over time, we expect that you will add to these principles from your own experiences.

1. Supervision Must Be Respectful

We must learn to look for, identify, and appreciate the unique qualities, resources, and constructions of reality of the many therapists and their clients we will supervise over the course of our careers. To do this successfully we must examine our own cultural views and values and become acutely aware of how they can influ-

---

TABLE 1.1 Basic Principles of Supervision

1. Supervision must be respectful.
2. Supervision, like therapy, must be a safe place.
3. A working alliance must be developed.
4. A supervisor does not offer therapy to the clinical family.
5. A supervisor does not offer therapy to the therapist in training.
6. Supervision operates within a clearly defined clinical training system that includes intergenerational subsystems and dynamics.
7. The dynamics of supervision involve hierarchy and power.
8. Supervision develops through predictable stages.
9. Supervisory interventions are driven by theory.
10. Supervision should be competency based.
11. The supervisor has simultaneous responsibilities to the therapist, the clinical family, the clinical setting/institution, and the self.
12. The supervisor, like the therapist, follows clear ethical principles of conduct and practice.
13. Supervision is unique within each training system.

---

ence our perceptions of those with whom we work (Anderson, J., 2000). Supervisors need to be attuned to and model sensitive and respectful verbal and nonverbal language and interaction (Corey, Corey, & Callanan, 1988; Haber, 2000; Isaacs & Benjamin, 1991).

2. Supervision, Like Therapy, Must Be a Safe Place

When trainees are unnecessarily anxious, or even fearful, learning will be inhibited. Personal security for all of us facilitates self-disclosure, openness to feedback, and the risk-taking behaviors necessary to learning and professional growth. Consider your own training experiences. When supervision did not feel like a safe place to you, what happened? Our guess would be that you felt defensive or cautious. We would also expect that, if you felt afraid of or intimidated by your supervisor, you also felt uneasy with some clients. When a supervisor pushes a therapist to perform in a certain manner to get results, the therapist often passes those expectations on to the clients. (This refers to the concepts of parallel process and isomorphism. These are revisited in Principle #6 and are discussed in Chapter 3.)

As supervisors, if we cannot create a safe place for growth in our supervisory roles, we can expect our trainees to present us with a variety of defensive behaviors, from resistant to deceptive. For example, they may "forget" to tape sessions with difficult families or they may only bring in "successes" for you to review. They may be overly anxious or stern with their clients.

Rest assured, we are not advocating for the maintenance of tranquility of trainees! Safety for personal learning and growth certainly does not preclude critique, challenge, and even confrontation. Just as the experienced family therapist knows how to carefully perturb a dysfunctional family system, we recognize that a certain amount of discomfort often can enhance growth. Perhaps it is shaped something like a bell curve: too little stress and individuals may remain complacent, too much stress and individuals may panic. Some amount of arousal is probably "just right." (In subsequent chapters we discuss this balance of stress and learning in the actual supervisory process.)

Emerson (1999) has suggested five elements of supervision that can promote and enhance safety for the trainee.

1. Supervisory sessions should aspire to be settings in which the trainees feel truly listened to, actively and attentively, by the other participants.
2. Supervisors should pay close attention to the trainee's words and the feelings behind those words, respecting and accepting the individual who is speaking.
3. There should be no hurtful remarks, humor in which someone is victimized, or acceptance of self-degradation.
4. Trainees should have "the right to pass" with regard to struggling with specific issues.

5. Both supervisor and trainee must honor and promote safe sharing through strict confidentiality. This recommendation goes beyond the AAMFT ethical standards (see Principle #12 and Chapter 12) that prohibit only supervisors from revealing confidential information about trainees. All participants in the training system must feel trust.

3. A Working Alliance Must Be Developed

From the earliest stages of interaction in the supervisory relationship there must be shared goals and enough of an alliance to support work on achieving those goals (e.g., Colapinto, 1988). Bordin (1979) observed that a working alliance includes mutual agreement about the goals, theory, technique, pairing, and bond. No matter what issues or dilemmas appear in the supervisory experience, maintenance of this working alliance with your trainee must continue to be your first concern.

An important aspect of developing this working alliance is the supervisor's ability to be open and available to the therapist while maintaining appropriate boundaries. Self-disclosure by the supervisor to the therapist is an important part of this process. However, all self-disclosure should be offered by design. Just as in our clinical work with families, in which we need to gauge an appropriate degree of connectedness and separateness, we need to be aware of the same dynamics with our trainees.

Williams and Dombeck (1999) discovered in their focus groups with supervisors and trainees that the use of self-disclosure by supervisors may be a good way to model openness and facilitate joining, provide reassurance, and educate about the therapeutic and supervisory processes. However, too much personal material or self-disclosure can make trainees uncomfortable by promoting intimacy or providing personal information that therapists do not wish to know. Therefore, self-disclosures by supervisors should be carefully considered interventions and include only material that has been thoroughly worked through by the supervisor. Supervisors should never use trainees as "sounding boards" for their own personal problems or conflicts with colleagues, and trainees should not be made the keepers of information that would be embarrassing for others to know.

4. A Supervisor Does Not Offer Therapy to the Clinical Family

It is the therapist's role to provide direct clinical work with the clients (Nichols, 1988). It is important to remember that one's proper level of focus as a supervisor is on the therapist–client subsystem, no matter how inexperienced or ineffective your trainee may appear (Liddle, 1988). Some beginning supervisors may succumb to the temptation to show off their own clinical skills or to rescue the therapist or the therapy situation. Many therapists themselves may look for an opportunity to shift the therapeutic responsibility to their supervisors or to be rescued! Remember: The therapist treats the *client* and the supervisor facilitates the *therapist*. Of course, issues of client welfare, family safety, and personal harm may arise in which a supervisor may need to intervene. We discuss these matters in Chapter 12.

5. A Supervisor Does Not Offer Therapy to the Therapist in Training

As clinicians we recognize psychological and psychiatric disturbances on the one hand, and personal emotional issues that inhibit education and therapy on the other. Unless a supervisor operates from a Bowenian point of view (see Chapter 6) supervision and therapy are typically viewed as two distinct roles and the AAMFT Code of Ethics, Principle 4.2 (American Association for Marriage and Family Therapy [AAMFT], 2001) prohibits combining them. Therefore, most of us will be concerned about recognizing and maintaining the boundary delineating one role from the other. We also need to appreciate when therapy, as an adjunct to supervision, will be useful and/or required. This issue regarding the potential referral of a trainee for therapy is discussed further in Chapters 11 and 12.

6. Supervision Operates Within a Clearly Defined Clinical Training System That Includes Intergenerational Subsystems and Dynamics

A clinical training system is a complex environment "with reciprocally influencing domains of conceptualization and action" (Liddle, 1988, p. 154). However, such a training system can be thought of in the same way that family therapists understand the intergenerational dynamics of family systems.

A training system includes at least three and often four generations:

1. The supervisory mentor/supervisor
2. The Approved Supervisor candidate
3. The therapist or trainee
4. The client-family

Of course, the relative hierarchy and various dynamics of this intergenerational system may be viewed differently through the lenses of different supervisory models (see Chapter 6). Nevertheless, the interaction between each of these respective generations (e.g., the supervisor and the therapist) represents a distinct clinical subsystem. Just like in a family system, there will be relational dynamics such as triangles and coalitions. This systemic perspective allows a supervisor to step back and more objectively view interactional dynamics, defensive behaviors, and stuck places in order to be able to understand one's training role.

The systemic supervisor expects that interactional patterns within the overall training system will replicate themselves within each subsystem (Liddle, 1988). This is called *isomorphism*. Isomorphism has been defined in a variety of ways

(White & Russell, 1997). Generally it is considered to be a *parallel process* wherein patterns that occur in the client's relationships may also occur in both the therapeutic relationship and the supervisory relationship. This dynamic can provide valuable insights for supervisors in understanding underlying dynamics with their trainees, and between their therapists and their clients (Lee, 1999a; Liddle, 1988; White & Russell, 1997). For example, if you and your therapist experience turbulence in your relationship, it may be a clue as to what may be happening downstream in the therapeutic relationship.

Isomorphism also provides clues to potential interventions (Liddle, 1988). For example, the supervisor's move to correct a dysfunctional relationship between herself or himself and a therapist may result in parallel changes between the therapist and the clinical family. By way of an embarrassing example from early in his career, one of us (REL) was flattered by a therapist under his supervision, lost his objectivity, and accepted her request to provide therapy to her son. Concurrent with this happening, the therapist allowed a mutual attraction to build between her and an amorous client who was separated from his wife. A supervisory mentor saw what was happening, laid down the law, and once the supervisor quit muddying the water with his own boundary problems, the therapist ceased her unprofessional relationship with her client. Isomorphism and intergenerational issues are discussed further in Chapter 4.

7. The Dynamics of Supervision Involve Hierarchy and Power

Concerns regarding safety often involve issues of power. For the beginning supervisor the various types of power in a training situation may not be easily recognized. To be sure, some issues of power are quite overt and in many settings institutionalized. As a supervisor you become recognized as an authority within your clinical setting, and you are also ultimately responsible, legally and ethically, for your trainees' cases (see Vesper & Brock, 1991). You will have the power to judge and, perhaps, even to punish (Emerson, 1999). The ultimate of these roles, of course, is your power to decide whether or not someone can even complete their training to become a therapist.

Trainees will worry about the extent to which your evaluations and recommendations will affect their careers and employment prospects (Todd, 1997a). They will care about how you view their work and also how you experience your relationship with them. Moreover, supervisors have covert power based on unchallenged assumptions about roles, gender (Carolan, 1999; Turner & Fine, 1997), race (Killian, 2000), sociocultural membership (Nazario, 2000), and combinations of these variables (see Chapter 9).

Of course, trainees have overt power to the extent that they have explicit rights and expectations in their training experience and supervisory relationship. Trainees have covert power to the extent that supervisors themselves have needs to be helpful, have been socialized to seek approval, may have not resolved some of their own personal relational issues (including many of those we have discussed), and otherwise may be unsettled in the presence of a given trainee.

Rambo and Shilts (1997) have recommended the creation of a "collaborative" supervisory setting in which the trainee's voice is explicitly privileged. In this regard they suggested that all parties make themselves aware of the diverse settings in which marital and family therapy is currently practiced and how this shapes that which is therapeutic. As we have discussed, supervisors and their trainees need to have a goal of paying careful attention to the language used and the listening process, and supervisors should consistently expose themselves to cultural diversity.

For example, a white male group supervisor was surprised when a normally reserved biracial female bluntly started a debate and tenaciously pursued it despite an apparent lack of interest in the issue by her colleagues and with no prospect of winning over the supervisor to her point of view. When he said that they would have to agree to disagree and move on, she was outraged, left the session, and proceeded to the department chair's office to complain that the supervisor had shown her disrespect. She revealed, among other things, that she had been raised in a small Zimbabwe hamlet where she had experienced a lifelong fear of white male authorities. Her confrontation with her supervisor was a very important personal step for her. The chairperson counseled the supervisor later that this therapist's risk-taking step may have been encouraged by the safe climate that had been created for supervision. This example indicates the importance of having mechanisms that explicitly recognize overt and covert power issues in the training system, empower softer voices, and allow redress of grievances. Sensitivity to power issues in the training system and in the supervisory relationship are discussed further in Chapters 3 through 5 and 9 through 12.

8. Supervision Develops Through Predictable Stages

The therapists we supervise will range from beginners to veterans. They will differ broadly in what they know and what they can and cannot do (e.g., Nichols, 1988). Those with previous experience will likely have diverse styles of doing therapy. They also will have differing exposures to and successes with specific presenting problems, clinical populations, therapeutic models, and intervention techniques.

The beginning stages of supervision may include a high degree of didactic education, prescribed reading, and therapeutic direction by the supervisor. Illustrated in Figure 1.1, the didactic and directive supervisory behavior should taper off over time and, in so doing, create a place for autonomy to grow (Dwyer & Lee, 1999; Nichols & Lee, 1999). Initial insecurity should gradually be replaced by realistic self confidence (Nichols & Lee, 1999). Developmental issues are more

Autonomy

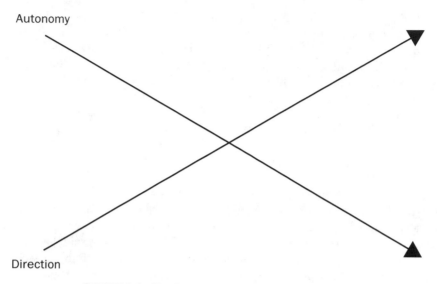

Direction

FIGURE 1.1. The Titration of Direction and Autonomy

fully discussed in Chapter 5. For integrative supervisors, thinking in developmental terms provides a crucial perspective and framework from which to track the professional progress and learning of their trainees. These trainees themselves may describe different needs and roles according to their own respective stages of professional growth.

9. Supervisory Interventions Are Driven by Theory

A supervisor, like a therapist, should always be able to explain whatever she or he is doing (Nichols, 1988). Integrative supervisors, like integrative therapists, should be guided by systemic theory and logical plans of intervention (Lee, 1999b; Nichols & Everett, 1986). Although many effective teachers of family therapy (e.g., Minuchin & Fishman, 1981; Whitaker & Ryan, 1990) have written eloquently about the practice of therapy as an "art" and a "dance," it is in reality an artistry informed by many years of education, training, and clinical experience. As supervisors we need to recognize that beginning family therapists need to employ carefully developed assessments and interventions that are derived from a solid foundation in systems theory, in lieu of more intuitive actions. Similarly, as integrative supervisors, we need to rely on our own understanding of systemic principles to inform our work with trainees (Liddle, 1988). These matters are discussed further in Chapters 3, 4, and 6.

10. Supervision Should Be Competency Based

Competency-based supervision is a corollary to many of the previous principles. Supervisors take the role of helping their trainees feel competent and the therapists, in turn, help their clients feel competent (Wetchler, 1990). Of course the flow of these issues can move in either direction. Clients can make therapists feel competent, and they, flushed with success, make their supervisors feel competent. Conversely, if a client finds fault with the therapist and the therapist does not manage this criticism effectively, it is likely that the therapist will look askance at her or his supervisor.

11. The Supervisor Has Simultaneous Responsibilities to the Therapist, the Clinical Family, the Clinical Setting/Institution, and the Self

In many clinical and teaching settings, supervisors occupy simultaneously a variety of roles—teachers, administrators, colleagues, supervisors, and friends. In academic settings the individuals concurrently may be supervisors, professors, employers (of trainees as teaching and research assistants), major professors, and dissertation chairs. However, regardless of the setting, supervisors maintain at least two specific roles: They are both teachers and cops (Goldenthal, 2000; Grant, 2000; Vesper & Brock, 1991). On the one hand, their job is to facilitate the professional growth of therapists. On the other hand, their job is to oversee the treatment process so that the client is well-served and the administrative needs of institutional settings are met. The client and the community must be protected from harm, and so must the institutions within which the supervisors and therapists work.

Some of these roles are simple. Ongoing administrative responsibilities may include auditing paperwork, confirming contact hours, and completing therapist evaluations. Others are more complex. For example, a supervisor's failure to insist on psychiatric hospitalization may be experienced as a vote of confidence by a client, may produce high anxiety in a therapist, and may put the therapist's agency and the supervisor's program at risk for a law suit or a poor public image. Well-conceived supervisory and administrative structures—including mutually conceived contracts, contingency plans, and checklists—may be helpful to supervisors as they take care of themselves and all of the other members of the training system (Storm & Engelberg, 2000; Stromberg, 1987; Vesper & Brock, 1991; Welch, 1998a). These tools are discussed in Chapter 12.

12. The Supervisor, Like the Therapist, Follows Clear Ethical Principles of Conduct and Practice

The American Association for Marriage and Family Therapy (AAMFT) has evolved clear ethical standards that involve supervision as well as clinical practice (AAMFT,

2001). Supervisors must learn to be aware of and sensitive to conflicts of interest with the potential to inhibit openness and behavioral flexibility within the training system or to allow exploitation of participants. The supervisor must be concerned that all participants within the training system have realistic expectations of their capabilities, even when appropriate stretching for growth is encouraged. The supervisor also must afford appropriate privacy. These standards are reviewed at length in Chapter 12.

13. Supervision Is Unique Within Each Training System

In Principles #1 and #8 we indicated that the manner in which the supervisor, the therapist, and his or her respective clients construct "therapy" (and therefore "supervision") depends on the personal traits and resources of supervisor and the trainee *and* on the contexts in which both are operating (Hoffman, 1997; Roberts, 2000). The cybernetics of cybernetics (Becvar & Becvar, 2003) reminds us that supervisors are an integral part of the supervision process. Supervisors uniquely shape each training system of which they are a living part (Liddle, 1988). Differences in personality, definitions, values, and expectations among supervisors, therapists, and clients may prevent working alliances, create divergent therapeutic goals, and misguide the choice and target of interventions. This includes everyone's ideas about what therapy is and how it is done, how people in relationships should be, what constitutes a "problem," and how important it should be considered relative to other matters.

Because of these issues, the beginning supervisor might find it beneficial to begin a new training relationship by doing a covert interview of herself or himself in the context of her or his expectations of the new therapist and anticipation of potential learning issues (Lee, 1999b). The interview of the therapist should focus initially on the trainee's own goals and aspirations in general, and the context of this particular training relationship, her or his expectations of the supervisor and, if she or he has completed previous supervision, and what experiences proved the most beneficial (Liddle et al., 1988a). Because you as the supervisor have been supervised yourself over the years, it is appropriate to disclose what sorts of experiences were helpful and what were not at various stages of your career. These interviews during the first meetings need to model openness, curiosity, and respect. They also provide a vehicle for interaction and a sample of behavior. While establishing rapport and moving on to other topics, the supervisor will be able to see how the two of you solve problems and negotiate openness and intimacy. You will be able to recognize social skills on the one hand, and respective values and biases on the other. Power issues may also be manifest subtly in various assumptions, unasked questions, or unquestioned privilege (e.g., Akinyela, 2001; Anderson, 2000; Killian, 2000; Lawless, 2002; Turner, 2000).

These initial exercises and the review of the 13 Principles have been intended to help the reader begin to think as a supervisor and to get started in doing supervision. Because these are commonly accepted principles with regard to family therapy supervision, they will provide a framework for understanding and learning in your training as a supervisor. Because they are accepted standards of practice, these principles also should be foundational to your own models. Once again, we would encourage you to complete the suggested lists from the exercises and perhaps make a copy of these 13 Principles so that you can add notes and additional thoughts as we begin to identify more theoretical and clinical issues in supervision.

Chapter 2

Understanding the Historical Influences of the Field on the Past and Future of Supervision

We begin with a chapter that almost was not written. Then it was written by Craig and set aside by Bob. Bob, impatient to get on with things, thought that the readers would be less interested in others' models and more eager to get on with the development of their own. He selectively remembered students "who always skipped Chapter 1 in texts." Craig demurred: "History is important. Without a solid base in the historical and theoretical development of family therapy, your journey can be seen as arbitrary and capricious. You need to carefully tie what is and will be to what was and is becoming. Our book will be more valuable if the reader sees her or his work as a systemic piece of the developing family therapy profession." Of course, Craig was correct, and our prepublication reviewers ended the debate. For this book to stand alone in a classroom it must include the historical base and development of family therapy supervision.

Writing any history is anxiety arousing. If you are conscientious, you recognize that what you put in, what you delete, and how you weigh things may shape someone else's reality. We are mindful that, for generations of young people, Richard M. Nixon, John F. Kennedy, and Vietnam will be viewed as Oliver Stone depicted them. For this reason we urge our readers to also consider the constructions offered by others who have recorded and lived family therapy history. (See Liddle, Breunlin, & Schwartz, 1988a; Nichols, 1992, 1997; Todd & Storm, 1997.) In our own review we emphasize the spirit of the times as we understood it.

The History

Family therapy supervision cannot be separated from the development of family therapy as a theoretical orientation and clinical profession. Thirty years ago the marital and family therapy field was characterized by two qualities: a pioneering fervor and a fragmentation of views and approaches. While competing enthusiastically for recognition among established mental health providers, family therapy as a discipline was internally divided by competing theories and the loyal disciples of the early theorists and pioneers. The notion of "integration" was largely absent. Instead, the diverse theoretical sects believed that their own approaches and contributions were the most effective and the most systemic. Despite their relative ties to systems theory, it would have been difficult for most of these early pioneers and their disciples to concede that there was a common foundation with specific systemic concepts that could offer a sense of integration to the emerging family therapy field.

As inchoate family therapy professionals in the 1970s we can remember being challenged by our peers, supervisors, and leaders in the family therapy field to claim an identity with one of the pioneering approaches. Even at social events, practitioners and students would enthuse about the "uniqueness" and "efficacy" of their model. These models, in turn, were identified largely in terms of the pioneers who developed them—Murray Bowen, Jay Haley, Salvador Minuchin, Carl Whitaker, Virginia Satir, and so on. There was much pressure to conform and become loyal to the unique orientation of one of these giants, much as one might be asked if one were a Republican or a Democrat. Professional status during these early years often came from being identified as a pioneer's disciple, and clinical decisions were argued in terms of "What would [Murray, Jay, Sal, Carl, or Virginia] do?" Supervision and training, of course, were at that time an extension of this discipleship.

Some outstanding family scientists worried about this trend. It seemed to them that the practice and development of family therapy was being shaped primarily by "gurus." Some thought that facts and science were sharing space with mysticism. William C. Nichols (1986) cautioned aspiring family therapists that "the first field to master is the family. Therapy comes second." (Contrast this with Minuchin and Fishman, who began their 1981 textbook by advising students that family therapy is a "dance.") Nichols and Everett were emphatic:

> The challenge we cast before our students is to steer clear of premature commitment to any single school or set of techniques and to continue the emotional and intellectual struggle to integrate what can be integrated from diverse sources into an ever-deepening understanding of the richly complex phenomena with which we are grappling. (1986, p. 80)

The Present State of the Field

The profession of family therapy has evolved substantially in the past three decades and, accordingly, so have the beliefs and practices of its supervisors. The domination of major family therapy theories or expected allegiance to a single orientation by practitioners may be a phenomenon of the past (Nichols, 1997). The competing loyalties to certain approaches have essentially disappeared, and many practitioners tend to view their family therapy orientation as eclectic or integrative (Lee, Nichols, Nichols, & Odom, in press). This may have resulted from increasingly sophisticated analysis and synthesis of theory. (See our later discussion of both the common factors model and integrative therapeutic approaches.)

However, this evolution in family therapy theory has also been informed and even driven by the increase in the numbers of family therapists and the diversity of their practice settings. Currently there are 46,000 family therapists identified in the United States (Northey, 2002), and they practice with a wide range of clients (Doherty & Simmons, 1996; Northey, 2002), in a wide range of settings (Northey, 2002). Many of these settings would be considered nontraditional relative to the private practice office. They include religious and community agencies, primary and secondary schools, homes, and medical centers. These settings shape and set limits on the methods and forms of family therapy offered.

A great deal of clinical family therapy practice involves clients from diverse subcultures. These subcultures also have their own constructions of what is therapeutic and how it is done. For their part, supervisors are expected to provide training relevant to these diverse practitioners in diverse settings. Given the number and diversity of family therapists and the number and diversity of the settings in which they practice, it is not unreasonable to expect that this would feed back into the profession of which they are systemic parts, influencing not just supervisory practices but what is taught. The latter represents both issues of content and an attitude (see Chapter 9, *Cultural and Contextual Issues in Supervision*).

Developing Family Therapy Models

At the present time, along with evidence of diminishing adherence to traditional theoretical schools (Lee et al., in press), there may be three emerging theoretical practice trends supervisors will need to be aware of:

1. Eclectic, atheoretical, intuitive practice
2. Espousal of a "common factors" model
3. Integrative therapeutic models

We decry the first—eclecticism—as an understandable but unfortunate development. We believe that responsible interventions are driven by information interpreted consistently based on clear clinical theory. We believe that the common factors model and integrative therapeutic models are the most promising of current family therapy developments. Although we will describe them separately, we believe that, in thinking and in practice, there may be much mutual influence between them.

The Common Factors Model

At conferences and in the literature we have been observing the cautious reconstruction of couple and family therapy. This reconstruction is largely focused on treatment issues and involves a restructuring of both theory and practice informed by what are considered to be the generic aspects of family therapy. This was perhaps foreshadowed by AAMFT's commitment in 1982 to develop a glossary of central family therapy terms (Foley & Everett, 1982). A sourcebook of family therapy concepts followed (Simon, Stierlin, & Wynn, 1985). Although in both works the origins of these words and concepts were tied to specific major schools of family therapy theory, the end result was for family therapists in diverse settings to comfortably use all of what was becoming identified as the core concepts, such as "therapeutic alliance," "triangle," "circularity," "structure," and "reframing."

Moreover, with the emergence of a national couple and family therapy examination process (Lee & Sturkie, 1997; Sturkie & Lee, 2001), those credentialed to practice family therapy are required to be able to apply concepts from the various theoretical models to a variety of clinical problems. The inevitable result has been for family therapists to become "multilingual" and less parochial.

Concurrently, others (Blow & Sprenkle, 2001; Sprenkle, Blow, & Dickey, 1999) began to identify empirically validated factors common to effective individual psychotherapies. They argued that family therapists should look for the same kinds of core factors and, once identified and found to be efficacious, teach them in lieu of lockstep allegiance to sole theoretical models. In a related development, new textbooks were produced (e.g., Midori Hanna & Brown, 1995) that taught family therapy with regard to key elements common to the various major models.

Integrative Therapeutic Approaches

Perhaps paralleling the consideration of generic therapeutic factors and concepts common to the major family therapy theories was the emergence of the integrative family therapy orientation. We increasingly see therapists in their many diverse settings using "some of this and some of that." It involves both theoretical constructs (e.g., incongruent hierarchy, differentiation, reciprocity, and metaphor) and interventions (genograms, restructuring, reframing, and assembling the family of origin). This development becomes even more interesting when we recognize that concepts originating from one early school of thought are being intertwined with interventions from what may have once been a competing school of thought. For example, a family therapist today may identify issues of differentiation (clearly from the Intergenerational/Bowen school) and life cycle (from developmental theory) in his or her initial clinical assessment of a family and propose interventions that might include reframing and restructuring (both clearly from the Structural school). Craig thinks of this as *pragmatic integration* but also admits that it may be simply a form of casual eclecticism. Lebow (1997a) believes that these are portents of a paradigm shift within family therapy; a "quiet revolution. . . . We have entered the era of integration in couple and family therapy" (p. 1).

Integrative theorists and supervisors believe that multiple lenses afford broader conceptual insights and more therapeutic degrees of freedom (Lebow, 1997b), but that there needs to be an underlying theoretical framework that allows clinicians to blend these "generic" ideas and actions *with clear intent and purpose.* Lebow (1997a) observed that, in articles, presentations, and clinical practice, "pure form practice of family therapy" is infrequent. In contrast, "the extent of [integrative models] is unprecedented" (p. 2).

What are integrated may be modalities of treatment, such as individual and family therapy, or various forms of family therapy, such as couples therapy preparing for family of origin sessions (Framo, 1976). In some cases, narrower theories may be knit into the fabric of a larger theory. Cognitive and behavioral interventions may be used to serve systemic ends. Some theorists think of "levels" of intervention, such as behavioral, psychodynamic, and systemic. Viable integrative approaches abound; Lebow (1997a) has done an effective job of categorizing them, and his article should be required reading for anyone interested in this orientation.

In contrast to eclecticism, integrative approaches involve the well-considered mixture of theory, assessment, and intervention. Some integrative approaches provide specific plans and strategies (e.g., Breunlin, Schwartz, & Mac Kune-Karrer, 1992; Pinsof, 1983) and offer a map from which supervisors can teach. Other integrative models (e.g., Lebow, 1987; Moultrip, 1986; Nichols & Everett, 1986) encourage therapists to develop their own models. Here, the supervisors' task is to help their therapists develop, articulate, implement, test, and grow their models (see Moon & Trepper, 1996).

But, prescriptive or therapist-centered, most integrative approaches are based on metatheory that involves the "essential elements of human functioning" and the human change process (Lebow, 1997a). Theory, assessment, and intervention are seen as transactively interrelated. Changes in one affect the others. An integrative orientation does not just describe systems but is itself systemic. For our purposes of educating family therapy clinicians, we conceptualize the integrative orientation as a *process* whereby the clinician moves from the "bigger picture" of understanding a family's overall functioning, symptoms, and dynamics, to being able to describe these patterns in basic systemic concepts, to integrating these with clinical data to form working hypotheses for assessment, and, finally, to integrating these data with an informed selection of appropriate interventions. This process is characterized throughout by multifaceted awareness, consistent intent, strategies appropriate to subgoals and goals, and recursive linkages between all of these.

A Look at the Future of Supervision

If we are in the midst of a revolution, our history perforce stops here. The readers of this work will write the next historical chapter by how they develop and where they practice. Although we have addressed this book to an integrative orientation, and specifically to a therapist-centered one, it will be useful to any individual in a family therapy supervisory training program pursuing the Approved Supervisor credential or who supervises relational therapy. However, because we believe—based on our professional experiences, including surveys of those who have participated in our supervision classes—that there *is* a revolution and because we eschew eclecticism, we give special attention to the integrative approach.

If this is where supervision is now, where are we headed? Lee and associates (in press) compared surveys of AAMFT Approved Supervisors from 1976 to 2001 and looked for trends. They discovered that the number of supervisors has remained a constant percentage of the AAMFT clinical membership. As membership has gone up, so has the number of Approved Supervisors. Furthermore, the demographics of Approved Supervisors have paralleled those of practicing family therapists. The number of females has increased—50% of Approved Supervisors are female. (Approximately 70% of those seeking family therapy credentials are female, according to Lee, 2002a.)

Unhappily, although family therapy increasingly is offered in diverse settings, the population of Approved Supervisors, as with family therapists in general, is predominantly White. One-half have a doctorate, which represents a drop from 67% in past decades. Overall, it appears that the membership of Approved Supervisors generally reflects the demographics of those whom they will be supervising. Given the importance of supervisors being attuned to the voices of therapists, this is a good development. However, given the diversity of practice settings and the increasing presence of international students (AAMFT, 2002b), it is clear that there are too many underrepresented voices among the ranks of Approved Supervisors and family therapists.

Because minority voices are continuing to be underrepresented among therapists and supervisors, although clinical practice will occur in diverse settings with diverse clientele, cultural competence must be a major component of everyone's training (see Chapter 9).

Increasingly, supervision will be provided by individuals with terminal master's degrees working with trainees with terminal master's degrees. In this regard it might be helpful to do a detailed comparison of the background preparation and supervision performance of masters and doctoral supervisors. It might also be helpful to compare in the same way state-credentialed therapists who supervise with those who have received Approved Supervisor training. However, our lifelong personal experience with a wide variety of family therapy supervisors leads us to be cautious with regard to hypotheses about any of these groups as a whole.

Chapter 3

Getting Started
A Basic Framework to Guide Integrative Supervision

Our illustrative model of integrative supervision is like most integrative models in its process. The integrative clinician begins by using a systemic lens to construct the "bigger picture" of a family's overall functioning, symptoms, and dynamics. The next step is to integrate these observed systemic patterns with the clinical data from the actual interview to form early working hypotheses for assessment. Finally, these data are integrated with an informed selection of appropriate clinical interventions expected to change the family system.

For most of us, our integrative models of family therapy and supervision were not explicitly taught but emerged over years of education and clinical experiences. However, both integrative and eclectic models use a broad range of resources to complete an effective assessment and intervention plan for clinical families. What make our models *integrative* as opposed to eclectic are the overarching theory and subordinate principles and concepts that inform the therapist in a consistent, sequential, coherent, and cohesive manner.

It has been our observation that a supervisor who focuses solely on the teaching of a single model of family therapy is functioning in a nonintegrative manner, and this role can deprive a therapist of learning to use the breadth and depth of the full range of family systems assessment and treatment resources. Similarly, the supervisor who focuses solely on teaching a selection of eclectic techniques from a toolbox is also nonintegrative and fails to provide the therapist with the theoretical means to understand and conceptualize her or his clinical interventions. In both of these cases, the crucial aspect of learning to integrate clinical theory with real-life assessment data with informed interventions can be lost.

Here are some basic principles for the beginning supervisory candidate to consider and to carry over from her or his earlier systemic clinical knowledge. These principles apply to your expectations for the trainee and your responsibilities as supervisor.

Clinical aspects of assessments by systemic family therapists

1. Appreciation of basic systemic family dynamics (from theory) demonstrated and/or experienced in the clinical family
2. Understanding of the clinical family's developmental stage, structure, process, and intergenerational features
3. Understanding of the clinical family's symptomatology in terms of systemic issues of homeostasis, balance, coalitions, and alliances
4. Development of specific working hypotheses that focus on the clinical family as a system
5. Awareness of the trainees' own personal resources, biases, and orientations that can color or distort their perceptions of the clinical family dynamics

Clinical aspects incorporated in treatment plans of systemic family therapists

1. The clinical family's unique resources, balance, and potential for change
2. The target symptoms and/or the target dynamics within the family's structure and process
3. The potential of the clinical family for first-order and/or second-order changes
4. The therapist's own level of training, experience, and skills to implement certain interventions
5. Selection of the most appropriate clinical interventions informed by all of these concerns

Goals of systemic family therapy supervisors

1. Deepen trainees' basic understanding of general systems theory (Von Bertalanffy, 1980) as it is applied to family process
2. Ensure that trainees have sufficient basic knowledge of family systems theory to apply this knowledge to live case situations
3. Increase trainees' sensitivity to these systemic dynamics and their ability to recognize these in the data of live clinical families
4. Help trainees use this systemic data to formulate reasonable, comprehensive, and objective clinical assessments
5. Help trainees integrate their theoretical and assessment data into making an informed selection of the most appropriate clinical intervention for each clinical family
6. Help trainees to step back and objectively learn from their successes and failures; help them gain the confidence to take new directions or try more creative approaches when one fails

TABLE 3.1. The Three Levels of Teaching/Supervising the Integrative Model

Level One: Learning basic systems theory and concepts.

Level Two: Integrating systemic theory with the recognition of clinical patterns in the live data and the organization of a formal assessment with the clinical family.

Level Three: Integrating clinical assessment data with the informed selection of the most effective clinical intervention.

We believe that the integrative process is never complete or final. All of us, whether beginning family therapists or senior educators, have progressed along our own developmental paths and have honed our own internal checklists of the most important dynamics and patterns to look for in clinical families. In our training experiences we have found that beginning family therapists appear to progress through three rather distinct levels which are described in Table 3.1 (see also Lebow, 1987; Nichols, 1995).

This progression moves from the *first level* of learning to conceptualize family behavior from a family systems perspective. The *second level* involves learning to recognize these systemic concepts in the live clinical data of a family interview and integrating them into a formal and accurate clinical assessment. The *third level* involves the integration of these concepts and the assessment of the family system with the informed and careful selection of appropriate clinical interventions.

Level One: Basic Systemic Theory and Concepts

Level one is the basic foundation of all systemic assessment and treatment. It involves the process that all of us as experienced family therapists have experienced first hand: *learning to think systemically.* This involves helping trainees immerse themselves in the literature of family systems theory, from the basics of Ludwig Von Bertalanffy's general systems theory (1980) to such works as Haley's *Changing Families: A Family Therapy Reader* (1971), Minuchin and Fishman's *Family Therapy Techniques* (1981), Watzlawick and Weakland's *The Interactional View* (1993), and Hoffman's *Foundations of Family Therapy* (1981). Many of your trainees will have already completed basic courses on these works and theory. However, the supervisor working with beginning family therapists who are also beginning clinicians has the responsibility to recognize these concepts during clinical interviews and to help them learn to operationalize the concepts by identifying basic clinical patterns in a family's behaviors. This process is basic to all systemic thinking, assessment, and treatment.

For example, if a beginning trainee cannot define for you the theoretical

TABLE 3.2. Basic and Practical Family Systems Concepts
That Every Beginning MFT Should Master

System	Subsystem	Structure	Process
Organization	Positive feedback	Negative feedback	Circularity
Reciprocity	Closed boundaries	Diffuse boundaries	Open boundaries
Open system	Closed system	Enmeshing	Disengaging
Communication	Balance	Homeostasis	Parentification
Spousal subsystem	Sibling subsystem	Parent–child subsystem	Power
Triangles	Alliances	Intergenerational system	Scapegoating
Coalitions	Family of origin	Internal boundaries	Emotional cutoff
Differentiation	Hierarchy	External boundaries	
Power	Myths	Secrets	
Centripetal	Centrifugal	Complementarity	
Fusion	Vertical loyalties	Horizontal loyalties	

meanings of a triangle and how this dynamic occurs within a dysfunctional family system, you are going to be frustrated and disappointed when you point out to her or him that a glaring triangle is present in the family being interviewed. Table 3.2 provides a listing of the basic systems concepts (Everett, 2000) that we believe every beginning family therapist must be able to define, give examples of, and recognize in clinical data.

We think that these basic concepts represent the most practical and observable systemic patterns and dynamics that the beginning therapist can observe in a clinical family. They also represent the primary clinical concepts that are used to describe the presenting symptoms and dynamics of a family (Lee, Emerson, & Kochka, 1999). The integrative supervisor believes that these concepts are the foundation upon which future family therapy effectiveness will be built. This conviction gives us our primary outcome goal for the early supervision process: teaching trainees to recognize and explain, verbally and in their clinical reports, *all* of the basic concepts. This early focus on recognizing and operationalizing systemic theory often helps beginning trainees who feel overwhelmed with their early clinical experiences. It also can provide them with a sense of mastery when they begin to recognize in the clinical data these patterns that they previously had only understood cognitively. This learning also provides them with a common language shared by their supervisors, peers, and, indeed, the pioneers of the field.

Level Two: The Integration of Systemic Concepts with Clinical Assessment

The second level of integration is more complex. It involves the actual integration process of learning to recognize the basic concepts, define them as patterns observed in the clinical interviews (e.g., a triangle between two parents and a child), and now organize and define them into a formal clinical assessment. We recommend quite detailed outlines for systemic assessment with beginning family therapists. However, whether this assessment takes the form of a verbal report or more detailed written report, the trainee must explain to you as her or his supervisor all of the following:

1. How the clinical family is structured, that is, subsystems, boundaries, triangles, coalitions, and so on.
2. What the specific symptomatology of this family involves, ruling out individual psychiatric diagnoses in the context of the overall family dysfunction.
3. How either the individual diagnoses and/or the family system's dysfunctions characterize the homeostatic balance of the entire system.
4. The potential developmental aspects of the family's life experiences, such as, a first child or the last child having left the home.
5. Potential intergenerational influences and/or potential stressors from nonfamiliar external systems such as the children's school.
6. Demonstrate the ability to diagram these factors effectively in a three- to four-generational genogram.

Level Three: Integrating Theory and Assessment with the Informed Selection of Interventions

The third level involves the integration of the evolving clinical assessment with the process of making a careful and informed selection of the most appropriate intervention based on what is known about the clinical family's dysfunctions and resources. This is the final step of the integrative process. It is also the most complex. The integrative therapist may choose an intervention, based on the previously discussed considerations, from the broad array of established clinical theories in the family therapy field. For those of us who are seasoned clinicians, this range of choices is an amazing resource. We have discovered that a well-informed selection often can make the difference in whether the outcomes for a case are successful or not. As supervisors, our task is to support our trainees' alertness to major family therapy theory as a source of interventions appropriate to their developing assessment of their clinical families. Because of the importance of understanding these resources for supervision, an entire chapter (Chapter 6) will be devoted to the use of these clinical models.

Within this third level of integration Breunlin, Karrer, McGuire, and Cimmarasti (1988, p. 198) have described a useful sequence to help the supervisor structure and follow the trainees' clinical interventions:

1. The trainee selects what should be attended to within the family—"picks a class of information from which to make observations."

2. The trainee organizes her or his own sense of this data—"organizes this information into some meaningful pattern."
3. The trainee decides if and how this pattern within the clinical family should change.
4. The trainee decides how to offer the proposed change to the family in the form of an intervention.
5. The trainee then makes her or his own sense of the family's response to the intervention.
6. The trainee decides what to do next, for example, continue with the intervention or gather more information.

This process, whether one follows this model or not, is clearly recursive in that the movement from the initial assessment and intervention should become self-correcting, depending on the effectiveness of the intervention.

In this chapter we have given you an overview of the meaning and value of integrative approaches historically in the family therapy field. We have also provided a straightforward introduction to our beginning model of integrative supervision. This has focused primarily on defining three levels of integrative supervision with practical suggestions of where to begin and what issues to focus on with your trainees at each level. The next three chapters provide more depth to this process. They describe the merits of intergenerational theory as a fundamental metaphor of the overall training system for both supervisors and trainees, the usefulness of understanding the learning issues of trainees from a developmental perspective, and the contributions of the major family therapy clinical models to the roles of supervision.

Chapter 4

Intergenerational Structure and Dynamics of the Training System

I n Chapter 1 we wanted to help the reader begin to think about becoming a supervisor and define some of the basic issues and ingredients of the supervisory role. In this chapter, and in Chapters 5 and 6, we lay the foundation of an integrative systemic model. This model will be used throughout this book as our example of a viable integrative approach to family therapy.

To implement an integrative model involves the ability to view clinical and training dynamics from a broad and objective stance (Lebow, 1987, 1997a). More specifically, an integrative approach requires the stimulation of a personal paradigm, assimilation of a range of scholarship, considerations of the person of the therapist, and consideration of the nature of diverse cases (Lebow, 1987). These processes then lead to the development of a personal integrative model, the most useful of which are "metaframeworks acknowledging the wider systemic context in which individuals and families live" (Becvar & Becvar, 2003, p. 51). Such an accomplishment involves stepping back from more narrow or idiosyncratic theoretical models, and learning how to embrace and use the resources available from throughout the theoretical and clinical aspects of the family therapy field.

The following integrative systemic model aspires to this stature. It goes considerably beyond efforts to integrate such orientations as structural and strategic forms of therapy (e.g., Liddle, 1984). There are many models of integrative supervision available. (The interested reader is referred to Rigazio-DiGilio, 1997.) We have chosen to focus on our own integrative model because it identifies the broader resources of contemporary intergenerational and developmental theories, and the specific theoretical resources of all of the major family therapy orientations, and applies these directly to the supervisory process. We believe that this framework for appreciating-but-managing complexity (Rigazio-DiGilo, 1997) is useful to the widest range of family therapy supervisors and trainees in terms of education and experience. We believe that it will get done for the reader what Lebow (1997a) has suggested such a model potentially can do: illuminate training system processes and how they fit together, cultivate the coherence of theory, strategy, and intervention, and help the reader develop pathways to integrative work. To do this, the integrative supervisor needs to keep the trainee aware of "different theories, therapies, and strategies [while providing] broad organizational schemata that clinicians can use to orchestrate assessment and treatment efforts" (Rigazio-DiGilio, 1997, p. 195).

In this chapter we define the elements of an *intergenerational* orientation to the overall clinical training system and identify specific systemic dynamics that can be used to manage and enhance the ongoing supervisory process. In Chapter 5 we identify the importance of recognizing developmental issues in the training process and use developmental theory to offer a specific model of learning stages and transitions. And in Chapter 6 we discuss the process of integrating these broader resources with the specific contributions of the various theoretical orientations from the family therapy field.

As a supervisor you will often see clear signs when both your trainee and their clinical family have become locked into a joint, limited, and too narrowly constructed sense of reality. For example, the family and the therapist may experience themselves as "stuck." They may not be able to see dynamics that are obvious to you. They may overreact or underreact to simple issues in the context of the therapy. They may pursue inappropriate relationship goals. When clinical families display these symptoms, effective therapists will learn to ask illuminating questions or act in ways to block the limiting dynamics. However, often therapists are not able to intervene effectively because they—like their clients—cannot see these clinical issues as part of a bigger systemic picture (Tomm, 1984), or perhaps they may experience the same feelings as the clients (Bowen, 1978; Colapinto, 1988). When this occurs the therapy process indeed becomes stuck and little progress is possible (Lee, 1999a).

This is an example of what Minuchin and Fishman (1981) have described as the therapist becoming "inducted into the family system" and becoming unable to function as a change agent. One of the most important roles for a supervisor is to help the trainees become alert and flexible observers of themselves in the context of their functioning and roles with their clinical families. These crucial issues of self-awareness for the therapist have been discussed extensively by Aponte (1994) and Friedman (1991).

We have found it useful to teach beginning supervisors how to conceptualize their clinical education experiences and the system in which they are training as an intergenerational family system with ongoing isomorphic features. This means that as a supervisor you can use your prior training in systemic thinking and systemic family assessment to gain insight into the dynamics of the training system—including your own contributions (Becvar & Becvar, 2003; Liddle, 1988) and the training system's accommodation to the larger environments in which it is embedded.

The Training System as an Intergenerational Family System

The training system as intergenerational family system is a useful metaphor. It allows us to appreciate the recursive complexity that is the training system, while also helping us manage it. Identifying the training experiences, for trainee and supervisor-in-training alike, in the context of an intergenerational system allows us to use basic systemic concepts such as structure and process to gain insight into the various interactional dynamics that occur among the participants. This orientation will help us identify both functional and dysfunctional elements of the learning process as it extends vertically through these interlocking subsystems, as well as other familiar systemic phenomena such as subsystems, coalitions, triangles, and hierarchy.

Just as we diagram three- and four-generational clinical family systems, we can easily construct a genogram that outlines the structure of most family therapy training systems. This genogram (Figure 4.1) will help us assess the implicit dynamics that occur between all of the training system members—the supervisory

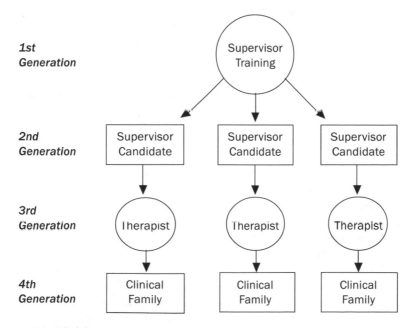

FIGURE 4.1. **A Four-Generational Model of an MFT Training System**

mentor, the supervisor candidates, the therapists, and the client families. When we look at Figure 4.1 and think of it as a "family system," our knowledge of family systems dynamics will lead us to recognize many potential interactional patterns in this training system. (Many of the fundamental systemic concepts familiar to both therapists and supervisors, and which can be used to describe the dynamics of this training system, appear in Table 3.2 in Chapter 3.)

The concepts of parallel processes and isomorphism, which we discuss later, are central to understanding and recognizing the implicit dynamics in this genogram. If we begin by looking for basic structural patterns we see dynamics such as alliances and triangles are present. When we look for process issues we see patterns emerge of scapegoating, parentification, enmeshment, and distancing. With more experience using this orientation, you will be able to see a broader range of these familiar systemic dynamics and even begin to integrate the recognition of other dynamics from broader family theories.

The Hierarchy

There is certainly some debate within the family therapy field as to the validity or value of identifying a hierarchy within either the therapy process itself or the training system. (The reader may wish to contrast Anderson, 2000, with Nichols, 1988, and Storm & Minuchin, 2000.) However, it has been our experience as training supervisors in both academic and private clinical settings that an implicit hierarchy not only exists within these systems but it is often necessary. The beginning supervisor needs to recognize that in most types of clinical training settings she or he becomes legally and often administratively responsible for the provision of competent and ethical clinical services (Storm & Engleberg, 2000; Vesper & Brock, 1991): The buck stops with you! In most training settings the supervisor will be expected to co-sign the trainees' assessments, treatment plans, and progress notes. As the supervisor you must recognize and understand your responsibility for your therapists' work and their provision of clinical services to the clients (Huber & Peterson, 2000).

Moreover, as a supervisor presumably you will be recognized among your peers and the trainees as a "senior" family therapist and considered as having more experience, knowledge, and training. Our construction of this integrative model of supervision as hierarchical is also based on its utility. There is an obvious element of power implicit to the clinical education and supervisory process (Nichols, 1988). Novice therapists who have never sat in a room with a dysfunctional family must learn from the therapists who know how this works and who have learned how to function in a helpful way with families. This relative power may be benevolent at times (Emerson, 1999), or it may be operationalized to enhance learning and competence (Grant, 2000). Understanding and managing this effectively and carefully is a central ingredient to becoming a competent supervisor. (We discuss this dynamic further throughout this book.)

Interlocking Dynamics and Subsystems

There are many transgenerational theories in the family therapy literature, each specifying a mechanism for complementary pathology within and across the generations. Early in the theoretical development of the family therapy field, Nathan Ackerman (Ackerman, 1968; Ackerman & Behrens, 1956) described the concept of "interlocking pathologies" that occurred with family systems. He noted that individual pathologies of a parent can spread into the marital and/or parent–child subsystems, and throughout the behaviors of the whole family system. He also observed that, as these interlocking dynamics spread across subsystems, they define a complex interactive process that may actually stabilize (homeostasis) and define an entire family system's interaction and life-style. These interlocking dynamics can characterize both the stability of some systems and the dysfunctional elements of other systems.

One of us (CAE) has described the significance of these interlocking pathologies in terms of identifying the interplay between psychiatric symptoms and other clinical phenomena, and family dynamics (Everett, in press). For example, in families with either a borderline personality disordered parent (Everett, 1989, 1998) or an attention deficit/hyperactivity disordered member (Everett et al., 1989; Everett & Everett, 1998) the interlocking characteristics integrated the symptomatology of each member into the ongoing interactive and homeostatic dynamics of the family's daily functioning.

The four-generation training system involves three interlocking dyadic subsystems:

1. The supervisory mentor and the supervisor candidate
2. The supervisor candidate and the therapist
3. The therapist and the clinical family

These three subsystems are linked in two ways. First, by the implicit definition of the *hierarchy*, the training supervisor, and in some specific settings, the supervisor candidate, has responsibility for all of the subsequent levels and subsystems. Second, the participants have membership simultaneously in more than one subsystem. This would be like a parent who has membership in three family subsystems: the marital, the parent–child, and the family of origin.

Because of these linkages, the relationship between these subsystems is *reciprocal* in that the information exchanged and the behaviors displayed will have a recursive effect that elicits or causes a response or reaction within the other linked subsystems. Whatever dynamics, emotions, or behaviors occur in one subsystem will influence those other subsystems linked with it. Each in turn will then be influenced by the others.

For example, in a family system, an ADHD child's behavior in school prompts a call to the parent, who complains to the other parent, who in turn is frustrated and reacts critically toward the other children, who in turn react negatively toward their ADHD sibling, who now acts out at home within the family by breaking things in his room. In a training system, if a supervisor scolds a therapist it is likely to influence what occurs between the therapist and her or his client family. And then what occurs within the therapy subsystem in turn is likely to influence what happens in the supervisory subsystem. And so on.

The relationship between these subsystems is also *circular* in that interactive patterns and information move from one subsystem to the other and back. This pattern serves to lock the particular subsystem into a routine, predictable, and homeostatic pattern of interaction. For example, a degree of aggression displayed by a trainee who has taken on a role of confrontation with a parent in the therapy process may be experienced as intimidating by the supervisor candidate, and she or he may actually avoid contact or appointments with this particular therapist.

These circular and reciprocal patterns in the training system may be less dramatic than their role with psychiatric disorders, but they can become insidious and jeopardize learning and clinical outcomes if they are not recognized.

Isomorphism and Parallel Process

Isomorphism is the process whereby the dynamics of the relationship between the supervisor candidate and the trainee may mirror similar dynamics that are present between the trainee and the clinical family (Liddle, 1988; Nichols & Everett, 1986; White & Russell, 1995). In the early literature on the training and supervision of psychotherapy, these dynamics were defined as *parallel process,* the interplay of dynamics between the patient, the therapist, and the supervisor (Doehrman, 1976; Ekstein & Wallerstein, 1958). The contemporary term of isomorphism connotes something more systemic than a parallel process. Because supervisors, therapists, and clients are conceived as transacting parts of a training system, the structure and even the content of the training and therapy subsystems are expected to be recursively replicated in one another (Liddle, 1988).

This is a central concept for supervisors to understand. It has both diagnostic and treatment value: If there is replication across the subsystem boundaries, then what the supervisor observes occurring between herself or himself and the trainee may suggest underlying dynamics that are present the therapist–client subsystem. That relationship, in turn, may reflect the relationship patterns in the clinical family. Therefore, when the supervisor recognizes this dynamic in a therapist and moves to alter it, one can expect to produce changes throughout the training system! However, if the supervisor does not see and change the potential dysfunctional dynamics in her or his relationship with the trainee, other aspects of the training system may remain stuck (Lee, 1999a).

Here is an example of a worst-case scenario, albeit one with a happy ending.

A professionally urbane supervisory candidate under the tutelage of an equally "sophisticated" mentor brought family therapy supervision to a new MFT graduate, also from a major city. However, she was practicing in a rural, conservative Christian agency. All of the parties involved—highly-educated, non-fundamentalist Christians—saw themselves as more sophisticated than the agency in which they were interacting. Their energies were focused on a single mother, unconventional by community standards, who complained of not being accepted by her family of origin or by her neighbors. The training system all shared and mutually reinforced the same narrow construction of reality. All participants condescendingly viewed the agency and its surrounding community as narrow, closed, and rigid. They therefore agreed that the therapist had no treatment options other than palliative emotional support. This precluded the possibility of change. Fortunately, the supervisory mentor smelled the coffee and wondered aloud, "Is it really true? Is it really true that the whole community is that closed and unsympathetic? Has the client ever exercised her voice and asked for help? The Christian church community is, after all, supposed to be a ministry." These questions made the supervisor aware of his assumptions and inactivity. He then put them to the therapist, and the rest is history. The therapist challenged her client. The client then brought her concerns to her family and to her church community. The client's family and church all responded in positive fashion. Both the therapist and the client experienced a dramatic increase in social comfort, self-esteem, and degrees of behavioral freedom.

Just as isomorphism may involve replication of structure and process, it also may involve replication of affect or of adaptive style (White & Russell, 1997). The supervisor and therapist may experience anxiety, anger, or depression concurrent with these affective states existing in the therapy session and in the client family's life. Conversely, there may be a lack of affect where emotion would be expected, or an inappropriate affect. Because isomorphism alerts us to the possibility that what is being created and experienced at one level is replicating what is being created and experienced at other levels, this provides the supervisor with important data as to what training issues need to be identified.

A training supervisor and a supervisor candidate were viewing a videotape that showed a relatively inexperienced family therapist passively watching a symmetrical escalation of conflict within a family session. Neither the supervisor nor the therapist perceived a problem. The mentor suggested that the supervisor watch the tape with the therapist during their next meeting and pause it at the height of conflict. The supervisor was instructed to ask the therapist, "What are you feeling now?" The supervisor reported to the mentor that, reluctantly, the therapist responded, "I felt like a little girl in there. I guess I was immobilized. This family just takes over. I didn't know what to do." On hearing this, the supervisor was aware that she herself felt immobilized too. "I didn't even think about the therapist doing anything. I don't know what happened." As it turned out, both the therapist and the supervisor were from highly enmeshing families of origin. Even as adults they felt helpless when their parents fought. This training incident was a revelation to both the supervisor and therapist. It helped them see how powerful their own family of origin dynamics could be in their professional work.

In this example, the isomorphic element was represented by the similarity of the enmeshing dynamic that occurred in the interlocking subsystems of the supervisor candidate–trainee and the trainee–clinical family subsystems. The example illustrates that such a dynamic was so subtle, yet powerful, that neither the supervisor nor the therapist recognized that it had actually immobilized them and restricted their ability to objectively assess and objectify the clinical process in front of them.

Identifying Triangles

The use of the genogram to identify elements of the overall training system can effectively assist the supervisor in identifying the presence of triangles among the interlocking subsystems. We know that triangular relationships occur naturally in social systems for purposes of support and self-protection on the one hand (Bowen, 1978), and coercion on the other (Nichols & Everett, 1986). Within family systems these triangles may define interactive patterns such as coalitions and the roles of scapegoated or parentified children. Although these triangles may have dysfunctional components, they may also serve to balance the family system by maintaining homeostasis. As clinicians we know that these triangular relationships in a family (e.g., between parents and a child) serve to lock the dynamics and subsystems into predictable behaviors (e.g., a scapegoated child).

Triangles in clinical supervision were identified early by Westheafer (1984) and can emerge at any location in the hierarchy and between the subsystems. For example, a supervisor candidate who is frustrated and struggling with an ineffective therapist may seek to induct the training supervisor into experiencing the same frustration and joining in a coalition to scapegoat the trainee. If the training supervisor participates with the supervisor by sympathizing and adding her or his own additional derogatory comments about the therapist, then the triangle has been formed. Such triangles can obviously disrupt and limit effective supervision.

A more common pattern may be observed when an ineffective or inexperienced supervisor feels overwhelmed or inadequate in her or his training experience and attempts to elicit from both the trainee and the training supervisor a sense of support, protection, and even the need to be rescued.

For example, a rather powerful and destructive triangle emerged between a therapist, his clinical family, and his supervisor.

> The supervisor had expressed some frustration and inadequacy with a particular male trainee. In her earlier reports she had praised his "sensitive side" and commented on some similar interests (a red flag, of course). Now she had begun to focus on his "unavailability" and "resistance" in supervision. She reported that he had been reluctant to bring files and tapes. When asked about her change of opinion about this trainee, she could only recall being critical of his "lack of boundaries" in a certain case. The training supervisor asked to view a tape of that case and immediately supported her observations about the lack of boundaries. The training supervisor asked the supervisor to fast-forward the tape to the conclusion of the therapy session. (Many supervisors fail to review this important clinical dynamic.) This supervisor had not reviewed it, and both the training supervisor and the supervisor were appalled at what they observed. The mother expressed some concern that they were not making more progress; the therapist appeared somewhat defensive and suddenly stated: "I believe I can help your family. I have really wanted to do some things with your son but my supervisor would not let me." Even the family seemed surprised at first by his remark. However, the mother then said to the therapist, "It's OK to do whatever you want to do. We won't tell your supervisor."

It appeared here that the supervisor had attempted, unsuccessfully, to solicit a closer alliance with the trainee. It had disrupted their supervisory relationship, and the trainee had pulled away and was now acting out by seeking to collude with the clinical family. The supervisor had been blinded by her own personal needs and disappointment such that she was unable to function objectively. She in turn tried to pull the training supervisor into a potential triangle that would have scapegoated the trainee. All of these dynamics illustrate the value of looking at the broader systemic aspects of the training system to recognize the complexities of these patterns.

A Word About Boundaries

Many of our examples highlight another structural feature that training systems share with family systems: *boundaries*. Boundaries in systems define the nature of interaction within subsystems and systems, and between the system itself and other external systems (Everett, 2000). Boundaries between two entities may be rigidly closed, in which case feedback is limited. Other boundaries may be rigidly diffuse and offer little protection from feedback. However, boundaries also may be flexibly permeable or open, a situation in which there is a balance of feedback and protection (Guttman, 1991; Nichols & Everett, 1986).

The dilemma in the triangle example in the previous section occurred, in part, because the supervisor did not have clear boundaries between herself and the therapist, and, of course, the therapist had rather diffuse boundaries between himself and the clinical family. The boundaries were either too diffuse or unclear because predisposing personal dynamics among the participants resonated with other dynamics in the supervision and therapy.

It is the responsibility of the supervisors at all levels of the systemic hierarchy to define their boundaries within and between each training subsystem. We have observed that such boundary weaknesses can manifest themselves across all four generations in the training system. Each supervisor must be clear about her or his personal and professional boundaries. Each supervisor must be able to define and maintain her or his boundaries appropriately within the training system and in the clinical setting in which the supervision occurs. (Further issues regarding boundaries in other areas and specifically with regard to ethical issues are discussed in Chapters 10, 11, and 12.)

The usefulness of our introductory integrative systemic model lies in the assumption that, if you are a family therapy supervisor, you have the ability to recognize and understand basic system dynamics that occur across the interacting subsystems of the overall training system. We believe this intergenerational view of the training dynamics provides a unique resource for supervisors to be able to become more objective and to step back and recognize core dynamics that may occur through the training system with differing participants and subsystems. It defines the various roles within the training experience and clearly aids in the recognition of both structural and process elements. Family systems knowledge is foundational to the practice and supervision of family therapy and to this model.

There is a second foundational issue to this integrative model: The implicit developmental aspects of the training process. These are discussed in the next chapter.

Chapter 5

Developmental Aspects of Supervision

A s family therapists we have been trained to recognize developmental stages that occur in the life experiences of our clients (e.g., Newman, Newman, & Morgan, 2002) and their families (compiled in Carter & McGoldrick, 1998). Much of our clinical work addresses those challenges almost universally experienced at each stage of life's development. We know to watch for a child's signs of independence and the parents' response to these from toddlerhood through late adolescence. We appreciate how parents may struggle to adjust to the "empty nest" when their last child leaves home.

Similarly, as clinical educators and supervisors we must learn the importance of recognizing our trainees' movement along their own personal and professional clinical paths. Their development involves variables ranging from personal maturity and differentiation from their families of origin to learning clinical theory and experiencing therapeutic successes (Nichols, 1988; Tucker, Hart, & Liddle, 1976). As we learn to recognize these developmental stages and trajectories for our trainees, our roles as clinical supervisors will involve, at varying moments, instruction, nurture, critique, prodding, and celebration (Nichols, 1975; Taibbi, 1995).

We can become more effective supervisors by recognizing that all of our trainees pass through a continuum that reflects their personal and professional development. For example, there are students in our master's programs who have never conducted a clinical interview of any kind. They may bring to this role the life experiences of only a 24 year old. There are students in our doctoral programs and training institutes who may have 5 to 10 years of clinical experiences in mental health and agency work, but with no focused experience on working with families. There are clinicians trained solely in traditional psychology or psychiatry who have never had more than one individual client in their offices at a time.

Craig remembers when he entered the doctoral program at Florida State University. He was 32 years old, he had attended many family therapy training workshops, and he had worked successfully in a mental health center for four years and in an inpatient psychiatric hospital for one year. He thought he was in great shape for this program with all of this experience, particularly when compared to the other incoming graduate students. However, upon completing an introductory assessment, William C. Nichols, his family therapy program director observed, "It seems to me that by working in a mental health center you have earned about one year of experience repeated three times!"

Just as we assess where a clinical family may be located along a life span developmental continuum, we need to learn how to place ourselves and our trainees along a similar developmental framework so that we can respond more accurately and objectively to their immediate needs and progress. The developmental aspects of family therapy supervision have been present since the first national supervision workshops (e.g., Nichols, 1975) and the earliest professional literature (Ard, 1973; Tucker et al., 1976). Experts (e.g., Liddle, 1988; Nichols, 1988) have discussed developmental supervision based on trainees' stagewise acquisition of competency in the tasks required by the sequential stages of therapy (initial, mid-phase, and end phase). Supervision educators have spoken about the various roles a supervisor performs (e.g., teacher, consultant) and the various "levels" of consultation within them (Nichols & Everett, 1996; Taibbi, 1995).

Whatever model is used, it is difficult to imagine a supervisor who would not agree that education and training in family therapy must be developmentally appropriate to the individuals involved. As we recognized in Principle #8 in Chapter 1 (see Table 1.1), fundamental to family therapy supervision is that the knowledge and skill training offered by the supervisor depends on the trainee's career stage and degree of personal development. (We will address this again in Chapter 11; see Figure 11.1.) We did not talk about the supervisor's developmental trajectory. Moreover, integrating developmental theory into a model of supervision has never been fully developed in the family therapy literature.

Before we discuss these developmental issues further, we would like the reader to complete a brief self-reflective exercise. Take a moment to sit back, close your eyes, put on your "therapist" hat.

• Picture what you want and need from a supervisor *now*. If you were to contract with a new supervisor *today,* what would you want from him or her?

List these things, and then prioritize them.

• How are your current wants and needs different from when you were just starting out? Picture your first supervisory experiences as a new therapist. What did you want and need *then*?

List these needs and wants, and then prioritize them, and save them with the other exercises in your journal or notebook.

With this developmental orientation in mind, we want to encourage you to think of the overall professional development of therapists and to see yourselves as "coaches," "gardeners," "teachers," and "mentors." What your therapists need and want from you differs according to their developmental level. One of us (Dwyer & Lee, 1999) conducted focus groups with family therapy clinical students ranging in experience from new (pre-master's) to advanced (all but dissertation). The results showed that *beginning* therapists reported that they expected their supervisors to be authoritative guides who were largely responsible for the well-being of both client and therapist. They saw their role as trainees in the supervision process as "coming prepared to present concerns" and "alerting supervisors to . . . crisis cases." In contrast, *intermediate* and *advanced* therapists increasingly emphasized self-organization and self-determination—"identifying one's own goals, needs, and issues that have been activated."

These students, while agreeing that they needed to be firmly grounded in major family therapy theory, also wanted to be able to articulate an evolving personal theory of therapy and change. The trainees were to come to therapy with both "prepared treatment plans, with interventions designed to meet the goals and objectives," and a "developing vision" of the therapists they hoped to become. They appreciated that they themselves had some role to play in their development. They universally viewed supervision as an active and cooperative learning environment (Anderson, 2000) wherein the trainees were committed to their own growth, listened with an open mind, and took risks. Taking risks in supervision included "sharing mistakes openly" and "speaking up when my needs are not being met." These issues reported by the students are supported by the 13 principles of supervision in Chapter 1, which included the importance of a working alliance and of supervision being a safe place.

The Developmental Continuum

As early as 1973, a two-stage process of supervision for family therapists was proposed: a mentor who provides preceptorships for beginning students, and an experienced therapist who provides an apprenticeship for advanced students (Ard, 1973). Similarly, Nichols (1988) emphasized the need to craft supervision so that it meets the levels and needs of each trainee. He recommended that the supervisor use close or intensive supervision in the early stages of a student's training and that the supervisor then move toward a "consulting role" with advanced students. These early recommendations match clearly the needs and expectations expressed by the family therapy students in the focus groups.

We have tried to identify several consistent variables that we believe will help beginning supervisors identify basic developmental issues for family therapy trainees. We recognize that these have become part of an internal checklist by which we evaluate all of our trainees as well as our supervisor candidates. Assessing these variables allows us to make our supervision developmentally appropriate to the unique circumstances of each trainee. We suggest that you add these elements to your journal so that you can incorporate them as you develop you own philosophy of supervision.

1. A trainee's years of overall clinical experience. (As mentioned, many years of clinical experience in some settings actually may represent just one year of experience repeated over and over again.)
2. The clinical settings in which the trainee has had experience (e.g., inpatient, outpatient, agency, private).
3. The clinical populations with which the trainee has worked (e.g., racially mixed, low income, chronically mentally ill, affluent).
4. The trainee's ability to recognize psychiatric symptoms and to diagnose psychiatric disorders.
5. The trainee's years of experience in working explicitly with families and marriages (i.e., can she or he stay in the interview room with a dysfunctional family?).
6. The trainee's theoretical knowledge of family systems.
7. The trainee's ability to assess the dynamics of family systems.
8. The trainee's prior supervisory experiences: How long did she or he work with each supervisor? Were those supervisors family therapy trained? Did the trainee work primarily in mental health settings or explicitly in family therapy clinics?
9. The trainee's chronological maturity (e.g., a 24-year-old master's student or a 45-year-old institute student).
10. The trainee's relative level of emotional maturity.
11. The trainee's personal interactive skills (e.g., openness, candor, genuineness, social comfort).
12. The trainee's relative level of intelligence (i.e., verbal, analytical, cognitive skills).
13. The trainee's relative personal differentiation from his or her family of origin.
14. The trainee's range of real-life experiences (e.g., other work experiences, travel, prior relationship history).

From developmental theory, as well as our clinical work, we know that personal growth is not always linear or consistent (Lerner, 1991). Likewise, we observe in our trainees spurts of rapid change that may be followed by periods of stagnation and discouragement. In supervision, as in therapy, we need to be patient and give learning time to develop. Beginning supervisors often try too hard to teach certain skills or techniques or to fix mistakes or inadequacies as quickly as possible. Other supervisors may simply sit back and let their trainees learn by experience—sink or swim.

As you begin your supervisory training, here are a few important principles to consider that will help you match your approach to the developmental levels and needs of your trainees:

- Supervisors need to take the time to look at the developmental levels and resources of their therapists.
- Supervisors need to understand how their therapists approach learning, how they make sense of things, and how they express anxiety and defensiveness.
- Supervisors need to be patient and look at the bigger clinical picture in which each therapist is working, such as the clinical setting and clinical population, and their experience in such a setting.
- Supervisors need to formulate strategies in their minds based on each of the principles before they take any action or plan any strategies with their trainees.

This developmental perspective will also assist supervisors in looking more carefully at the interplay between cognitive learning and professional growth for each trainee, as well as recognizing issues of the trainee's personal development. It will be easier to recognize when trainees become immobilized or defensive in their clinical learning. When we match our expectations to the trainees' levels of development, our interventions and strategies thereby become more realistic and effective.

Understanding Transitional Periods in Learning

As we observed previously, developmental theory, in general, alerts us to the fact that supervision may not proceed smoothly. Our trainees will not always develop or unfold in a seamless growth pattern. Human developmental trajectories include transitional periods wherein growth is discontinuous and life is stressful and even tumultuous (Lerner, 2001). As individuals move from one level of competency to another, they need to let go of old ways of knowing and doing things because these no longer work. Until competencies suitable to the new level of life complexity are solidly in place, the maturing individuals are expected to feel unsettled, and their distress will affect the ambience of their social network. Accordingly, parents, siblings, and care providers are cautioned to expect periods of disorganization. However, as family therapists, we can reframe these periods of disorganization as portents of new stages of positive growth.

Supervisors need to incorporate these same expectations in their roles with trainees who will experience transitions as they struggle to progress from apprehensive novices to experienced therapists. The supervisor who understands and recognizes when a therapist is in a transitional stage will be able to more effectively and competently operationalize resources within the training system and aid the trainee's movement through this phase.

Supervisors who do not recognize the implicit nature of transitions in learning may respond not only inappropriately but in a manner that actually inhibits growth. We have observed beginning supervisors identify certain therapists as "lazy" or "ineffective" or "off the wall" or "resistant," when in fact the therapists were displaying ambivalence or moodiness as part of their transition to a new level of skills. To react too critically to a therapist in a transitional phase offers no positive suggestions, creates anxiety, mobilizes defenses, and is destructive to the working alliance. Such negative products at best delay the individual's forward momentum, and they can even delay her or his completion of the prior stage of training.

Supervisors can recognize when therapists may be in one of these transitional stages by behaviors such as a display of an unusual or unexpected amount of ambivalence, vulnerability, anxiety, moodiness, or personal apprehension relative to how she or he normally functions. When these behaviors are identified as indicators of learning and growth, we can anticipate that the trainee may be about to move on, not that she or he is regressing. Again, the supervisor needs to be able to step back and look at each therapist in terms of progress along a developmental trajectory or continuum.

> A supervisor worked with one rather mature student who was gaining confidence in her work with some very difficult cases. All of a sudden she was 20 minutes late for a supervision session and missed the next supervision appointment altogether. The supervisor noticed over the intervening week that she seemed to be preoccupied and less available in the group supervision sessions. When the supervisor asked her about this during the third week, she was able to reflect on how a session with a large, enmeshing, and controlling family had reminded her so much of her own family of origin that she literally became nauseated after the session. However, she showed a tape of her next therapy session with that family and was able to demonstrate that she had recognized these personal feelings and was able to use them to maintain a therapeutic role.
>
> A few weeks later in supervision she shared that her experience with that family had been so disturbing to her that she had fantasies of giving up becoming a therapist. She actually considered leaving town and moving back to her family of origin. Her fantasy was that she would leave town in the night so as not to have to face her supervisor or her peers. She felt that they would regard her as a disappointment and a failure. (You are no doubt recognizing these as dynamics from her family of origin.) In subsequent supervisory sessions she discussed her sense of personal betrayal to the family she was treating because she had not been able to fit in or play the expected role with them just as when she was growing up. She was able to

see this awareness and her struggle to remove its influence as a significant transition to a new level of therapeutic competence. She even asked the supervisor for a referral for adjunctive psychotherapy, a suggestion the supervisor already had been about to make.

There are no clearly defined or accepted developmental models in the literature that explain the range of dynamics that a supervisor will encounter. However, we think it might be helpful to share with you aspects of our own model. As you become more experienced as a supervisor you will develop a model of your own that will tell you what to look for and what to be sensitive to at each developmental stage. We are offering our model here so that you can incorporate aspects of it and add this developmental dimension to your supervisory work.

A Model of Developmental Issues in the Supervisory Process

The developmental trajectories of trainees include their capacity to perform the tasks of therapy: joining a clinical family and acquiring a therapeutic contract, performing increasingly sophisticated assessments, selecting therapeutic goals, planning, administering, and evaluating interventions, and so on (Liddle, 1988). The developmental roles of supervisors include their capacity to assume the various roles of supervision (Taibbi, 1995), namely teacher, administrator, coach, consultant, and mentor. For both trainees and supervisors this professional development is inextricably interwoven with their trajectories of personal growth (Nichols, 1988). Our example of the mature student illustrates this complexity.

Our basic developmental model involves three stages and two transitional periods. We think that it is most lucid and useful in an outline format.

Beginning Level

The beginning level refers primarily to the beginning therapist who has little prior clinical experience of any kind.

Tasks for the supervisor
1. Screen for personal resources and deficits: maturity, communication/interactive skills, intelligence, skills at personal reflection, and so on.
2. Understand the trainee's ability to implement prior training, clinically and academically.
3. Concurrently, develop a working alliance with the trainee.
4. Teach basic interviewing/interactive skills.
5. Begin to integrate systemic concepts and theory with the trainee's clinical observations.
6. Teach basic diagnostic/assessment skills.

Tasks for the trainee
1. Develop a working alliance with the supervisor.
2. Develop a professional identity as a therapist that can be separated or differentiated from one's own personal needs. This involves redefining one's desire to "help" or "fix" into a professional role and skill.
3. Do no harm.

Issues the supervisor observes in the trainee's progress and learning
1. The presence of learning and performance anxieties.
2. A narcissistic preoccupation.
3. A variety of self-protective defenses and mechanisms.
4. Placing personal needs over those of clients.
5. Excessive intellectualization.
6. Occasional seduction into the clinical family's dysfunctional processes.
7. Clinical reports that may be distorted toward being "liked" by the family or the supervisor, or having "helped."

Transitional Period 1

The first transitional period is characterized by unsettled feelings and behaviors in which the trainee is trying to move on to gain more autonomy, confidence, and competence.

Tasks for the supervisor
1. Be patient.
2. Recognize the bigger developmental picture.
3. Be nurturing.
4. Provide clear and firm, but flexible structure.
5. Celebrate the therapist's experiences with success.
6. Provide a referral for adjunctive psychotherapy if the therapist becomes stuck here and cannot move on.

Tasks for the trainee
1. Completion of the differentiation of personal and professional roles.
2. Development of confidence in professional identity.
3. Development of confidence in professional skills.
4. A growing sense of mastery and presence while actually working with clinical families.

Issues the supervisor observes in the trainee's progress and learning
1. More frequent moodiness or even depression.
2. Fantasies of loss of personal control to the supervisor.
3. Efforts toward fusion with the supervisor, such as clinging behaviors.

4. Testing structural limits or actual acting-out behaviors, for example, missed appointments, failure to bring process notes/tapes, demanding more time, or requesting more "how to do it" techniques.
5. Ambivalence manifested through fluctuating periods of control versus distancing.

Intermediate Level

Beginning therapists with good resources and skills can move to the intermediate level within three to six months; students with poor personal resources or limited prior training may take six or more months to reach this place.

Tasks for the supervisor
1. Support growing independence with less close supervision.
2. Support personal autonomy.
3. Help the therapists develop their own assessment checklist.
4. Cultivate therapists' ability to more quickly identify clinical dynamics in live therapy sessions.
5. Teach the selection and implementation of appropriate advanced intervention models (see Chapter 6).
6. Require therapists to defend their selections based on the integration of theoretical and clinical data.
7. Help therapists improve their skills of objectively and reflectively evaluating their sessions for therapeutic success or failure.

Tasks for the trainee
1. Development of a clearer professional identity.
2. Increased trust of the supervisor providing hands-on guidance with cases.
3. Confidence building in actual clinical interventions.
4. Improved ability to reflect objectively on personal clinical role and interventions.

Issues the supervisor observes in the therapist's progress and learning
1. Less apparent anxiety.
2. Demonstration of a more settled presence with cases.
3. Greater openness and transparency in supervision.
4. Less resistance.
5. A need to please the supervisor.
6. Distortion of clinical notes or reports, for example, idealization of cases or family members, unusual diagnoses or assessments, use of clever interventions (whether successful or not), and efforts to emulate what the student believes to be the supervisor's own orientation.
7. Blurring of personal boundaries with the case or the supervisor.
8. Imitation of the supervisor with other therapists or in group supervision sessions.

Transitional Period 2

In the second transitional stage, the therapist is moving from reliance on the supervisor and the latter's instructions to more personal autonomy. There is a desire for more control of cases but still an underlying uncertainty or apprehension about being on his or her own. This is the beginning of the process we call individuation in families. Beginning family therapy trainees may reach this phase anywhere in the supervisory process, from between perhaps six months to two years.

Tasks for the supervisor
1. Move from nurture to supporting the therapist's growing autonomy.
2. Reinforce the therapist's growing clinical skills.
3. Encourage therapists' therapeutic creativity.
4. Support therapists' individuation process. Give them permission to "leave home."

Tasks for the trainee
1. Gain a sense of personal and professional autonomy.
2. Overcome underlying insecurities about one's personal role and skills.
3. Begin to look ahead and make plans for "leaving home."

Issues the supervisor observes in the therapist's progress and learning
1. Occasional moodiness.
2. Separation anxiety.
3. Self-doubt.
4. Emotional withdrawal from the supervisor or training group.
5. Testing the limits of supervision.
6. Preoccupation with techniques.
7. Testing independence by reducing data in clinical reports (at this stage, this is different from resistance).
8. Triggering of latent family of origin issues regarding separation and individuation for the therapist and the supervisor (i.e., leaving home, empty nest, etc.).

Advanced Level

At the final stage of clinical training, the supervisor begins to take a more consulting role and prepare the student, both emotionally and professionally, for termination.

Tasks for the supervisor
1. Identify a clearer consulting role in supervision as a means of reinforcing confidence and support for therapist.
2. Support emotional separation and autonomy.

3. Look to future professional roles for the therapist.
4. Deal with termination of supervision.
5. Watch your own issues with regard to separation and leaving home.

Tasks for the trainee
1. Recognition of new levels of confidence in personal preparedness.
2. A growing sense of autonomy in clinical skills in general and family therapy specifically.
3. Awareness of areas for improvement and the potential need future training and/or consultation.
4. Recognition of the need for appropriate separation, independence, and closure from her or his role as a trainee, and her or his relationship with the supervisor, the supervisory process, the peer group, and the overall training structure and environment.

Issues the supervisor observes in the therapist's progress and learning
1. The ability to request greater responsibility with cases.
2. Clearer personal boundaries with cases.
3. Clearer personal boundaries in supervision.
4. Lessening of former ambivalence about confidence and professional role.
5. Comfortable transition to being able to use and ask for consultation rather than expecting close supervision.
6. Identification of future professional roles.
7. Preparedness for separation from the supervisor and the training process.
8. Possible inadequate or incomplete separation from her or his supervisor, which may be evidenced by sudden clinging, dependence, or reactive isolation.

Reviewing the Initial Assessment of a Trainee

As supervisors, once we apply this developmental perspective to our trainees and our supervisory roles, we find that there is a new set of questions to review to make sure we are looking at the bigger picture and remaining on target. In prior chapters we suggested exercises that would help you focus on your own goals and experiences as a supervisor. Here we would like you to select a trainee with whom you have started to work and answer these reflective questions based on our introductory developmental model. Again, put your answers to these questions in your journal.

1. Should my present style of supervision with this trainee be "closer" or more of a "consulting" nature?
2. Can this trainee complete basic systemic assessments or do I need to focus on operationalizing additional theory?

3. Is this trainee ready to do basic structural interventions or do I need to focus primarily on basic interviewing skills?
4. Should I begin by reviewing primarily process notes and assessment data or can this trainee handle the anxiety associated with a video review or live supervision?
5. How aware and/or free of personal family of origin dynamics is the trainee? Is she or he stuck enough to warrant a referral for personal therapy?

Your responses to these questions will help you decide what the primary developmental considerations are with this particular trainee and what are the appropriate interventions. As we have reviewed, awareness of the developmental continuum along which your trainees are moving and the specific transitional stages they may experience will add a powerful resource to your integrative model of supervision. This awareness will also help you define specific supervisory strategies to assist students who may become stuck for no other clear reasons.

In Chapter 14 Craig offers two detailed examples of our entry-level model of integrative supervision. These examples incorporate the 13 principles and the intergenerational and developmental considerations we have discussed thus far. In Chapter 11 these same fundamentals are used for troubleshooting the training system. In the next several chapters, we consider some of the more generic aspects of family therapy supervision. First we look at the tools of supervision, namely, modalities and formats; then we consider the diverse contexts present in the training system. Finally, we review what supervision research suggests is most effective.

Chapter 6

Major Theoretical Resources
for Supervision

T he third foundation of our integrative model, after intergenerational and developmental resources, is the major theoretical orientations of the family therapy field itself. We know historically that many of these primary clinical theories evolved from the work of certain pioneering family therapists, such as Minuchin, Bowen, Whitaker, and Haley. Although each theory's basic view of family dynamics and the associated style of interventions may vary rather widely, they all have in common their own foundation derived primarily from systems theory. (Of course, these elements are also interwoven with the unique personal resources of these pioneers.)

Some of us may have trained with one or more of these early pioneers or with their first or second generation "disciples." Two decades ago the family therapy field appeared more fragmented, with a variety of competing orientations. Many of today's senior practitioners learned a singular model of family therapy and have had to learn through their own clinical experiences how to best use and integrate other orientations and styles to be more effective in their practices. The family therapy field has moved over the past decade or so toward further attempts to consolidate or integrate some of these orientations (Lebow, 1997a). This new direction has been, in part, due to a desire to have available a more holistic approach to working with families; but more practically, it has been to respond to the pragmatic clinical awareness of practitioners that a singular approach to treating the broad range of presenting problems with which family therapists work these days is simply not realistic.

We want to review the contributions of each of the major family therapy theories to the supervision process. Some of these theories have specific models for supervision and in others the approach to clinical training is implied. We believe that understanding these respective contributions will provide you with practical components that can be included in your evolving integrative model.

In this regard, we agree with Hoffman (1997) who observed the need to appreciate the "cultures" that exist for both therapy and supervision. The manner in which we think about therapy and supervision dictates how we view the therapist and the clinical families, as well as our training strategies. We also know that the family therapy theories with which we are most comfortable shape that which we see in our clinical settings and how we make sense of what we see (Wedge, 1996). Finally, we know that the efficacy of any one clinical theory depends on the fit between it and the practitioner (Pinsof & Wynn, 1995). Therefore, before we begin the review of the theories, we would like to propose this following exercise to help you identify the clinical models and approaches with which you tend to be most comfortable and on which you rely. As an experienced therapist you have been tailoring what you know theoretically to fit each unique clinical situation before you. How you understand human development, family dynamics, and change all come together in this process.

Before reading farther, sit back, close your eyes, and picture yourself in several recent therapy sessions where you were the therapist. As you watch yourself work and hear yourself speak, ask yourself these questions:

- What theoretical model or approach or approaches were you using?
- Can you rank these approaches in terms of their importance to your therapeutic work?
- Are there certain approaches with which you tend to begin most cases?
- If you are not making progress, what backup approaches do you tend to use?
- When you talk to colleagues at meetings, how do you respond to this question: "What type of family therapy do you do?"

We expect that you will build on one or more of these clinical and theoretical resources as you gain experience as an integrative supervisor. They will inform your overarching view of what supervision is about, what its goals are, and what strategies would be the most effective with your therapists. Your ability to select effectively from these multiple theories and methods will become the cornerstone of your role as an integrative supervisor. This skill will also parallel your goal of teaching therapists to make informed decisions regarding their selection of intervention models.

Lebow (1997a) has suggested that some of you will apply your theories in a straight line. You will use a fairly predictable sequence based on your theory of what is generally present and a triaging strategy of what requires the most attention. In other words, one basic strategy will determine how you organize your data search and your interventions. Lee's (1999b) minimalist model is such a schema. Other approaches can be characterized as oscillating. Here, the integrative supervisor, like the integrative therapist, has the freedom to move back and forth between various theories in response to the clinical dynamics of each case. It is understood that the movement between theoretical issues and models is guided by the supervisor's perception of the training alliance and the therapist's personal resources and professional development. Nichols and Everett (1986) described just such an integrative model for family therapists, wherein the family therapist makes informed moves back and forth between a range of clinical theories that might include behavioral, psychodynamic, and systems models.

In the following discussion, we would like to examine supervision from the orientations of several family therapy theories. Each theory addresses issues related to aspects of both the content and the process of supervision. We have selected the following theoretical models to review: solution-focused, structural, strategic, family of origin, objects relations, and postmodern. In the recently completed national survey of AAMFT Approved Supervisors (Lee at al. 2003, in press), supervisors were asked to identify the clinical family therapy model that they most commonly used in their training. These data are summarized in Table 6.1 and will be visited again when we discuss each theory's implications for training and supervision. The terms "eclectic" and "integrative" were used somewhat interchangeably and so are combined. Cognitive-behavioral was endorsed by 5% of the sample. However, we will not be discussing it because it is not a traditional, systemic family therapy theory. "Other," which included several family therapy theories (e.g., experiential, contextual, communication, Ericksonian), was identified by 2% of the sample or less.

TABLE 6.1. The Family Theory Identified as Most Representative of Approved Supervisor's Clinical Orientation

Orientation	Percentage of the Sample ($N = 330$)
Solution-focused	8%
Structural	5%
Strategic Approaches	
Milan Systemic	4%
Watzlawick and associates	3%
Haley and associates	2%
Intergenerational (Bowen)	7%
Object Relations	7%
Postmodern Approaches	7%
Eclectic and Integrative	32%
Cognitive-Behavioral	5%
Other	20%
Total	100%

Supervision According to the Solution-Focused Model

We begin with the solution-focused orientation because it is such a helpful and versatile contribution to supervision. What better place to begin than with an approach that does not focus on deficits and mistakes, but instead uncovers that which supervisors and therapists are already doing well? The solution-focused orientation to supervision can stand alone (Rita, 1998; Wetchler, 1990). According to the recent data, 8% of AAMFT Approved Supervisors identified primarily with this model.

The solution-focused orientation can also be an excellent adjunct to other forms of supervision. As a part of our integrative supervision model, solution-focused approaches can be valuable for setting behavioral goals, planning interventions, and helping therapists implement other major theories (see Selekman & Todd, 1995). This model is based on therapists' strengths and it can build early confidence for beginning family therapists. At the heart of the solution-focused model is that it makes no sense to dwell on things one is doing when supervision and therapy are not going well. One should think instead about what one is doing when supervision and therapy sessions are more gratifying to the parties involved and do more of the same. The model can be helpful even when it is reduced to a script. It can serve as a default position when a supervisor operating within another model feels momentarily at a loss for some reason. It can be used to provide a lift for discouraged therapists. It reminds them of their competencies and gives them an immediate sense of what might prove beneficial with a client.

One way to get a good feel for the solution-focused approach is to try this exercise adapted from Walter and Peller (1992).

- Visualize a time recently when you were supervising (or being supervised, if you have not yet been a supervisor) and things were going well. You were feeling good about the session. What was the therapist doing? What were you doing?
- So, the next time you get together with that therapist and you are probably on the right track, what is it likely you'll be doing?

If you found that exercise intriguing, picture yourself using this same script as you supervise a therapist.

- Think of a time recently with this client (or any client) when things were going well. You were feeling good about the session. What was the client doing? What were you doing?
- So, the next time you get together with the client and you are probably on the right track, what is it likely you'll be doing?

The solution-focused model is based on the cumulative work of many individuals, including several partnerships: O'Hanlon and Weiner-Davis (1989), Berg and DeShazer (1991), and Walter and Peller (1992). It claims to be largely atheoretical, does not believe that there is one right way to supervise or to do therapy, suggests that the language used to describe a situation may support problematic conditions, and seeks immediate behavioral changes that will be experienced as successful. Often something really is not a problem because it is serving certain heretofore unrecognized ends. If something *is* causing difficulty, the members of the training system need to give up their current "solution" (which is not working) in favor of something different. In the various forms of solution-focused supervision, as in solution-focused therapy, three goals are pursued with a careful eye on the language used by the parties involved (O'Hanlon & Weiner-Davis, 1989, p. 126):

1. Change the *doing* of the situation that is perceived as problematic.
2. Change the *viewing* of the situation that is perceived as problematic.
3. Evoke resources, solutions, and strengths to bring to the situation that is perceived as problematic.

In our opinion, a wonderful attribute of the solution-focused approach is the direction it offers supervisors, therapists, and client families with regard to immediate and long-term goal-setting. Adapting Walter's and Peller's (1992) instructions to the task of supervision, we arrive at the following principles for supervisors:

• Stay with positive actions in the here-and-now that are under the therapist's control: "What would you like to be doing?" and "What does it look like when you are doing that?"
• If the therapist is negative, ask, "What would you like to be doing instead?"
• If the therapist stays negative, ask him or her to envision a future when the problem is no longer present. In that wonderful event, what will the therapist be doing?

Supervisors would also do well to follow these principles as they consider their own supervisory behavior (simply substitute "supervisor" for "therapist" in the examples).

Supervision According to the Structural Model

According to the recent data 5% of Approved Supervisors identified primarily with the structural orientation. We indicated in Chapter 3 that we believe that all therapists will benefit from learning early in their training to conceptualize family dynamics from a structural perspective. We have found this orientation to be the most successful, particularly for young and beginning master's level family therapists, because it presents a clear, organized, and visual picture of the clinical family.

It also allows beginning therapists to experience success with regard to early assessment and recognition of dysfunctional family dynamics.

For example, a supervisor candidate was dealing with a three-generational problem situation with a trainee. The family system consisted of a controlling and capricious maternal grandmother, her daughter, and the latter's young children. In supervision, the therapist characterized the children's mother as an adult who was becoming more in touch with her feelings and beginning to emancipate herself from her controlling mother. The therapist believed that the mother was giving her children permission to rebel against the controlling grandmother and had praised the mother in the videotaped session, stating to the mother, "Challenge her authority!" The supervisor saw this and had some concern about hierarchical issues, such as "Who should parent the children?" This appeared to be a structural dysfunction within the clinical family, but the training supervisor identified a pronounced structural dysfunction in the session itself, namely, the mother consistently spoke for the children during the session when the therapist directed questions toward them. She had also enmeshed them into an excessively close relationship with her, using them as confidantes and peers.

Structurally, this clearly indicated diffuse boundaries between her parental subsystem and the child subsystem. The training supervisor also wondered if the training system were not being inducted into the family system's dynamics because the supervisor candidate appeared to be identifying with the therapist in the challenge to the hierarchy and the grandmother's authority. Colapinto (1988) has pointed out that the role of the structural therapist is to try to build something (not uncover something): "The structural therapist does not emphasize the pursuit of individual change or the prescription of specific solutions. Instead, he or she tries to modify, enrich, and make flexible the family structure. . . . The family (like a recovered ecosystem) is the healer. . . ." (p. 19). Both the supervisor candidate and the therapist appreciated this observation. They decided that, structurally, the first thing to be addressed was the weak boundary between the mother and her children.

The supervisor using structural resources acknowledges and respects the clinical family's immediate concerns with their symptoms, but teaches the therapist that, to remove the symptoms, the family's patterns (the way this family does business) must change. The training supervisor, the supervisor candidate, and the therapist can use these structural conceptual resources to view the dynamics of the entire training system.

If isomorphism directs us to think about parallel processes throughout the training system, what then do we conclude about the stance of the supervisor vis-à-vis the therapist? The value of this structural model for the supervisor is that it focuses on the presenting problem, it acknowledges and respects the therapist's immediate concern with these issues, and it helps the two of them focus specifically on the interactive patterns that are present and that they experience in the therapy room with the family.

When supervising from a structural point of view, what would you be trying to create as a *treatment system*? One would focus on hierarchy, boundaries, the interaction between the subsystems, and immediate ways to interrupt or reposition the dysfunctional interaction and roles in the family.

Perhaps pausing for a moment to reflect on the dynamics of working with a structural orientation would be helpful.

- When you are supervising structurally, what does it look like? What are you doing?
- Can you picture what structural techniques—challenging, enactment, blocking, unbalancing (by taking sides)—might look like at all levels of the training system?
- Can you apply them to the foregoing illustrative case? First, how would the therapist do each intervention with this family? At the next level, what would your equivalent intervention as a trainer look like?

Supervision According to the Strategic Model

The national data in Table 6.1 indicated that only a small proportion of Approved Supervisors identified the various strategic approaches as their primary model: Milan systemic, 4%; Watzlawick's orientation, 3%; Haley's orientation, 2%. Of course these models differ substantially in their application. However, Todd (1997b) suggested viewing them in this context because all of them—and he included structural-strategic and solution-focused approaches in his continuum—are models of supervision that highlight the instrumental roles of the supervisors in producing therapeutic change. From one stance, Haley (1976) stated that supervisors are experts who teach therapists strategies for treating specific clients.

Mazza (1988) observed that, according to Haley, the manner in which the hierarchy is implemented with both therapists and clients may be specific to the needs of every situation. Moreover, when we extrapolate from the Milan therapy model (Andersen, 1993; Tomm, 1984) of supervision, we find that the resources of neutrality, circularity, and hypothesizing seem to be central to the role of a supervisor. Therefore, even though Milan-strategic therapists will ultimately offer a prescription for change, it grows out of the information-rich supervisory setting that they conduct and may be jointly conceived by supervisor and therapist. If, however, the therapists are thought to be noncompliant for any reason, it is reasonable to assume that strategic supervisors would use directives based on hypothesized relational factors to move beyond the stuck situation.

Strategically informed supervisors focus on the supervisor–therapist relationship and what elicits and maintains problematic learning situations (Protinsky & Preli, 1987). Strategic supervision not only involves the planning and implementation of therapeutic directives but also the use of strategic interventions with therapists. Similarly, strategic-informed supervisors, perhaps more than most others, focus on teaching therapeutic skills more than analyzing the client situation or focusing on the therapist's personality and, accordingly, prefer various forms of live supervision (Todd, 1997b). As such, this model combines primarily didactic teaching with directives. Based on Todd's (1997b) assessment, the primary strategies include the following:

- Focus on the dynamics of the present interaction.
- Stay goal-directed in the here and now.
- Emphasize positive reframing.
- Emphasize simple and immediately useful hypotheses and case formulations.
- Identify, use, and build on existing strengths.
- Regard being stuck as well-intentioned problem solving (so as not to stimulate resistance).
- Function in an active, directive, interventionistic, opportunistic, and pragmatic manner.

Supervision According to the Intergenerational (Bowen) Model

The national data indicated that 7% of Approved Supervisors have a preference for the intergenerational (Bowen) model. There are three interrelated goals for intergenerational (Bowen) therapy, and therefore for supervision (Papero, 1988; Roberto, 1997):

1. Teaching clients to conceptualize emotional phenomena in terms of a multigenerational, emotional system rather than as categories of psychodynamics or personality.
2. Promoting in clients the capacity for self-regulation of the reactivity (anxiety) to others.
3. Helping clients work on their own differentiation, which involves the capacity to separate from their family of origin while remaining connected.

This model is effective in helping clients define their personal goals and beliefs as well as work on their own personal boundaries and autonomy. The supervisor using a Bowen-oriented model initially works toward keeping the therapist focused on these goals of therapy with the clinical families, and secondly, uses these theoretical issues as a model for coaching and maintaining a differentiated relationship with the trainees. The use of this model is particularly helpful for young and beginning family therapists who are often still working on their own personal issues of separation and differentiation from their own families of origin.

The primary concepts that are useful from this model include the following (Papero, 1988): differentiation of self, the projection process, triangles, distance regulation, and coaching. These concepts are easy to teach to therapists and to illustrate in the clinical assessment and interview. However, with regard to the use of these issues in therapy and supervision, Papero observed that "the single most important idea to be communicated in the clinical arena is that when the clinician can relate to an anxious family without becoming a part of the emotional process within it, the family will automatically grow less anxious and more thoughtful" (Papero, 1988, p. 69). Understanding these concepts intellectually is one thing; it is another to live one's professional life in a well-differentiated way (Aponte, 1994; Friedman, 1991). The intergenerational (Bowen) supervisor pays close attention to the trainee's differentiation of self in the presence of the family. Only as the trainee is increasingly differentiated relative to his or her clients can he or she be an effective therapist (Papero, 1988).

The role behavior of the supervisor according to this model is that of coach. The goals of coaching are to help the trainee (1) become a more accurate observer of herself or himself and of the family, (2) develop a person-to-person relationship with each member of the family, (3) increase her or his ability to control emotional reactivity to the family, and (4) make a sustained effort to remain neutral or detriangled while relating to the emotional issues in the family. Intergenerational (Bowen) supervisors encourage growth in these areas between themselves and their trainees as much as between the therapists and their clients.

In supervision, as in therapy, the goal is to coach differentiation, namely, the ability to be in contact with another human being, as close as desired, while remaining a separate, autonomous individual (Papero, 1988). The focus of supervisors is always on the level of differentiation of themselves, and that of the therapists, and not on particular techniques to aid the clients. Supervisors are monitoring clinical issues such as:

- Is there a loss of choice about or control over behavior in the interaction or in the family?
- Are overreactions or underreactions present?
- Are there distortions of perception?
- Are there patterns of overinvolvement or underinvolvement in relationship patterns?
- Are the goals of relatedness appropriate to the parties involved?

Thus, coaching attempts to focus on a mutual awareness between the supervisor and the trainee such that each is more differentiated and remains neutral and untriangled.

In Chapter 4 we gave the example of the urbane supervisory mentor and Approved Supervisor candidate, the sexually abused therapist, and the rural client, all immobilized in their fused relationship. The training supervisor asked the supervisory candidate, "Is that true? What evidence do we have for that?" Once that question was asked, progress was made immediately throughout the training system.

Thinking about supervision from this model has raised some lively discussions within the field. If effectiveness as an intergenerational (Bowen) supervisor is directly related to one's level of personal differentiation, as supervisors if we focus on the relative level of differentiation of those we are supervising, are we therefore engaging in therapy instead of supervision? Indeed, according to Friedman (1991), the role of supervisor and therapist are the same "not because the supervisor is doing therapy but the therapist is doing supervision" (p. 1). However, the AAMFT Code of Ethics (AAMFT, 2001), under Principle IV, "Responsibility to Students and Supervisees," states, "Marriage and family therapists do not provide therapy to current students and supervisees" (4.2).

What is a supervisor using these intergenerational (Bowen) principles to do? Friedman was clear about his methods:

> I tell them [trainees] they can bring in three kinds of cases: a client family, their work system, or issues from their own family of origin. . . . I believe all members of the helping professions are involved in these three systems simultaneously. . . . so that increased knowledge of one's functioning in any one usually brings about more differentiated functioning in the other two. . . . The focus throughout is on teaching a way of thinking and promoting differentiation of self rather than on learning specific techniques for particular symptoms. . . . If the goal is always to promote differentiation (which requires the supervisor and therapist being supervised to constantly work to maintain his or her own) then the context is irrelevant. Every relationship is grist for the mill. I actually see "dual relationships" as challenging opportunities for promoting self-differentiation (pp. 1–2).

Supervision According to the Object-Relations Model

In the national sample of AAMFT Approved Supervisors, 7% reported their orientation to be psychodynamic and object relations. The goal of psychodynamic, object relations–informed supervision is twofold:

1. Teach the basic principles of this orientation to the trainees in working with clinical families.
2. Monitor the basic clinical patterns of projective identification, splitting, idealization, and collusion that may occur between the supervisor and the trainee or between the therapist and the clinical family.

This model brings to family therapy the unique resources of looking at underlying issues of attachment and bonding as they occur in human relationships. When the theory of this orientation is incorporated into marital and family interactions, many often unrecognized dynamics can be explained. The reader who is not as familiar with this orientation would benefit from reviewing the works of Dicks (1967), Fairbairn (1963), Scharff and Scharff (1995), Solomon (1992), and Willi (1982, 1984).

According to object-relations theory, a relationship does not occur just between individuals but involves the interplay of both conscious and unconscious intrapsychic object patterns and attachments, often from each individual's family of origin (Scharff & Scharff, 1995; Solomon, 1992). The quality and patterns of interactions are often the result of distorted projections from the past of one or both members. Accordingly, the present "reality" of the other person to some extent is lost. Instead individuals react in their perceptions, expectations, and emotions as if the partner were like these inner images. Often these projections include rather basic needs for security and nurture and fears of loss, abandonment, or rejection.

With regard to supervision, the resources of this model help supervisors focus on a variety of potential types of distortion that may occur in relationships throughout the training system. Trainees may experience the training relationship in unrealistically positive or negative ways. Trainees also must learn to recognize the projection of distortions from client families onto themselves and learn their capacity to handle these projections while addressing the emotional issues of the clients.

The training system itself plays a role in helping trainees handle ongoing issues of anxiety, criticism, and potential loss. The supervisor's role is to maintain a safe (e.g., calm, nurturing, and rational) environment in which trainees can appreciate and take back their reactive projections toward a family or their supervisors. In so doing they then can deal with the reality at hand.

As an example, when a trainee with injured self-esteem first meets with her or his supervisor, the trainee's tendency may be to regress to a level of idealization of the supervisor and even dependency on the supervisor. However, if gradually the supervisor is not perceived as meeting this inner need, the trainee may project onto her or him the image of a critical, inadequate, attacking, or withdrawing parent. The trainee will then behave reciprocally in an angry or possibly withdrawn role with the supervisor. Solomon (1992) has suggested that some trainees may express a need for constant reassurance, have a tendency to idealize, devalue, or discard, be grandiose, gain absolute control, express rage, or experience shame and/or depression over minor events in their training. If their supervisors do not recognize when this is happening, they may react in ways that the trainees believe confirm their perceptions and the projective identifications are in place.

As a supervisor working with these situations with trainees, you will need to look for the immediate triggers in the content of the supervisory session, label the extreme response, translate toxic emotions into underlying feelings (such as fear), and ask if personal situations are being confused with professional training experiences (Langs, 1994). Projections can become seriously dysfunctional to the training process and must be identified and managed. Without an effective working alliance, you have no basis with which to work with your trainee. These psychodynamic conceptual resources may help you learn to keep the interaction constant and safe for the trainee by providing a model of "play" (exploring, opening up, risking, venturing out into the unknown) and an attitude of certainty that gives hope of healing (Reiner, 1997).

Picture an initial session with a supervisory group. You are asking the members about their caseloads, previous experience, and the like. One of the individuals is staying to the outside of the group. There is little eye contact with you, he volunteers nothing, and when you address him directly, wanting him to feel included, his reply is tentative and his tone weak. Prompted by your belief in active listening, you suggest that he might be feeling uneasy today. His response is an explosion: "What do you expect?" he demands. "You're critical beyond belief!"

You have no history with this person, and you know yourself well enough to recognize that his accusation makes no sense. "Time out," you say firmly. You suspect that further ventilation will not bring a diminution of the affect and will only create a situation requiring administrative action. "Everyone take a cleansing breath. Come on, take a deep breath, hold it to the count of five, and now let the tension out with your break, slowly, through semi-parted lips. Again. Now, one more time." You want the trainee to move from raw, irrational emotion to intellectual operation, and thereby get intellectual leverage while inhibiting emotional expression. You therefore ask the trainee to recollect the moment just before the reaction. What was said and done at that precise point? "You were attacking me!" says the trainee, rising out of his chair. "Sit," you say. "We are fine now. Let's all settle ourselves." You use the force of your personality and your confident calmness to contain the group affect. Then you say to the trainee, in a very calm and measured voice, "When I suggested you might be feeling uneasy, it really shook you up. You felt attacked and tried to defend yourself." The trainee replies more calmly. "I *told you*. You're a very critical person and you control my future." Your reply is, "We have no history together, and you are new to this program. I suspect you've had some really bad experience of being picked on and treated unfairly. What is this situation reminding you of? Who treats you that way, or used to treat you that way?"

To keep this example short, we will conveniently fantasize the trainee looking confused and then firming up: "My grandmother." "So, based on past experiences you are very cautious and you are reacting as though I am like your grandmother. In what ways do I remind you of her?" He tells you. You had asked this for joining purposes. But your next question is to get the trainee to begin to differentiate the reality of you from the toxic internal object of "authorities." "In what ways am I *nothing* like her?" If he cannot respond, or his list is too short, you can then ask, "Would your grandmother have talked to you like this?"

In this sequence you have not accepted the projection or acted critically and angrily and thereby confirmed his toxic expectations. Instead you have asked him to test the reality of you against his expectations. By your manner with him you have provided a corrective emotional experience through which you will become internalized as an influential benign object in his psyche.

Supervision According to Postmodern Models

Postmodern approaches to supervision were cited by 7% of current Approved Supervisors as their primary model in the national survey. This model offers two primary resources for supervisors:

1. Recognition of the underlying influence of language in shaping our personal and clinical experiences (Dwyer & Lee, 1999).
2. The awareness that the potential for multiple realities exists in the work we do (Carlson & Erickson, 2001; Lowe, 2000).

Here is an exercise that may help define some of the resources from this model. On a sheet of paper, write down in one or more compound sentences that define what you think "supervision" is. Next, write down what a "supervisor" is. Now, take a minute to explore your responses. What nouns and verbs have you used? Each noun and each verb that you have used to characterize supervision and supervisors includes certain attributes and excludes others. Each highlights some things and downplays others.

Supervision, like therapy and other human relationships, is shaped by the language we use to make sense of our experiences. The metaphors that we use, and their connotations, influence the course of our relationships. The manner in which supervisors, therapists, and clients characterize themselves and each other, including their needs, shapes their initial and ongoing expectations and also their assessment of outcomes. (See Friedman, 1993, for many contemporary approaches based on this understanding.)

Therefore these issues should be explored explicitly. If the metaphors (or their definitions) used by the therapists and their supervisors are incongruent or even contradictory, the therapy, supervision, and even morale may suffer. Even when metaphors have been mutually agreed on (e.g., supervision as "teaching"), a specific metaphor can become the training system's only reality. So there may be merit to considering alternative metaphors (e.g., supervision as "coaching"). Each construction of supervision shapes reciprocal role behaviors and attendant feelings. Consider the following illustration.

A therapist complained to his supervisor that he was feeling increasingly aimless in sessions with a particular couple. The supervisor asked if he might be invited to one of the therapy sessions so that he could interview all three parties. The therapist asked the couple and they agreed. They all met together and, after some initial pleasantries, the supervisor asked each person how she or he thought things were going. The husband said that he wasn't sure, but he was feeling vaguely unsatisfied. The therapist said that he too had that feeling and was also feeling both anxious and sad because he sensed that he was not being experienced as helpful. The wife expressed surprise at the responses of the other two. She thought things had been going well. The supervisor then asked each person to give a metaphor that, to him or her, captured what therapy was all about and the role of the therapist. The husband said that the couple was an "athletic team" and the therapist was a "coach." The team was capable of winning the championship if only the coach would drill them in fundamentals and come up with winning game plans. The wife said that she thought of their therapy as a "journey" and the therapist was their "tour guide." They themselves selected their destination and stopping points along the way. They paid for the trip and the tour guide was to ride along with them and make the experience more meaningful. A tour guide has special knowledge about the areas and good ideas about side trips. Perhaps influenced by the wife's metaphor, the therapist said that he thought the couple jointly wanted him to be a "bus driver." As such, they were to pick the destination, but he was supposed to know the route. But he did not feel that he really knew their destination and he kept wondering when they wanted to get off. The supervisor then explored the ramifications of these metaphors for the therapy in terms of disparate role and goal expectations. He wondered if things might be made more congruent.

In a similar vein, thinking in terms of this model helps supervisors recognize that their trainees may hold a wide variety of motives, expectations, and ideas about their own needs—all of which may be quite different from those held by the supervisor. In fact, the diversity of a trainee's needs may be the rule rather than the exception, depending on the overall context of the training system. Therapists are likely to vary according to experience (Dwyer & Lee, 1999; Pike-Urlacher, 1996), gender (Caust, Libow, & Raskin, 1981; Wheeler, Avis, Miller, & Chaney, 1986), and learning style (Perlesz, Stolk, & Firestone, 1990).

Other important factors that can influence the supervisory relationship may be related to culture (e.g., Falicov, 1988; Hardy, 1990), preferred theoretical style and epistemological stance (Liddle, 1982), and emotional maturity and differentiation (Papero, 1988). Such diversity favors an integrative approach on the one hand, and careful consideration of socially constructed realities on the other (Carlson & Erickson, 2001). If a trainee's expectations do vary according to a wide range of developmental and contextual variables, then the supervisory system needs to be open to all voices and encouraging of those that are less likely to be heard. The latter would just not be those of therapists under supervision (Todd, 1997a) but also of those trainees, which are most likely by reasons of personality or subcultural membership to be reserved.

This approach involves more than the notion that we, as supervisors, should be open to the possibility of multiple realities. It means that we should expect that these realities are likely to be in play, and we must actively try to learn about them. Everyone in the training system needs to elicit and listen to each other's beliefs about the culture that is supervision and therapy. This includes beliefs about the supervisory role and the relationship between the supervisors, therapists, and clients, the therapist role and therapists' relationships with clients and, finally, about the clients, and whatever is seen as needing to be repaired. We need to respect and honor the therapists' lived experiences and their knowledge, skills, talents, ideas, values, and beliefs. Through modeling and the dynamic of ismorphism, therapists carry their orientation to their client families. This is some of the wisdom from this model contributed by Harlane Anderson and the late Harold Goolishian (Anderson, 1993; Goolishian & Anderson, 1992) in their emphasis on the assumption of "non-expert" positions in supervision and training. They recommended the role of "discourse" as opposed to the "transmission of truth."

Postmodern models encourage supervisors to enhance exposure to multiple realities through the use of reflecting teams (Andersen, 1991), interviewing clients about their therapy during therapy (Dwyer, 1999), and using other such methods during live supervision (e.g., Montalvo, 1997). Because new realities lead to new connections which in turn lead to empowering effects, Hoffman (1997) advised supervisors to interview therapists just as they would have therapists interview each client: "What of your own experience leads you to ask that question? Will you focus on that piece?" "Is there something personal—cultural voices? family voices?—that leads you to focus on that?" "What is most convincing in what we have been about? Least convincing?"

Narrative practitioners also remind us that within the postmodern framework the techniques espoused by White and Epston (1990) can be useful in the resolution of supervisory impasses. For example, when clients and therapists feel stuck, narrative-informed supervisors recognize this as a story that is shared between clients and therapists that has the potential to lead all participants to lose hope for the possibility of successful treatment and to interact in ways that protect each from feelings of blame and failure. In such cases, one can suggest alternative stories by looking for exceptions to the characterizations and to the dominant storyline. One can also externalize/personify the "frustration," "anxiety," or other destructive descriptions therapists use for their feelings. Just as in narrative therapy, the supervisor can ask externalizing questions, and pursue the exceptions: "Are there times when anxiety did not put in an appearance on this case? How were you able to do that? What were you doing differently? What was the family doing differently? How did you get that to happen?" The supervisor can then proceed to help the therapist make sense out of the exceptions: "What about you has helped you to stand up to anxiety? Did you know before that happened that you'd be able to do it? How did you decide to do that?" Then the supervisor can become more future-oriented: "If you were to take the next step in keeping anxiety with this client in its place, what do you think that would be? As you do that, what will you learn about yourself? Which of your colleagues will be the first to notice that?"

In summary, we have seen that the role of the supervisor is determined by the theoretical school employed. The structural, strategic, and some narrative models rely heavily on live supervision and intervening directly into therapists' sessions. Most psychodynamic and family of origin approaches would never do that. The Milan model uses live supervision, but does not focus on the therapist; rather, the goal of supervision is for everyone to explore the family process, including the therapist. Strategic therapy does not focus explicitly on insight but rather looks for change in interactional processes. Supervision from this model would seek to change therapists' interactional sequences with families rather than giving therapists a broad theoretical understanding of why they are doing what they are doing. In contrast, contemporary structural therapy would focus on the clinical family gaining some insight, along with the changed behavior. Here, the supervisors would teach therapists techniques alongside of theory. In contrast to both of these approaches, the intergenerational (Bowen) model deemphasizes techniques and focuses primarily on the therapist's own personal growth.

Finally, as you have seen from our discussion, the status of a supervisory role within a training system parallels the status prescribed for the trainees. The strategic and structural models define therapists as "experts" responsible for producing change—so then are supervisors. The family of origin and narrative approaches would deconstruct that expert hierarchy at all levels of the training system.

It is important for the reader to recognize that from an integrative orientation to supervision it is not necessary to fully embrace any one of the above models. Rather, the unique benefit of the integrative model, for supervisor and trainee alike, is that you can take the best and most useful aspects of any or all of the above approaches and use them to enhance the effectiveness of your supervision. Of course, the goal here is to learn how and when to use these resources in the best informed and objective manner to help your trainee and consequently the clinical family. That is the focus of the remainder of this book.

Chapter 7

Modalities of Supervision

Live, Videotape, Audiotape, and Case Presentations

In the previous chapters we defined the foundations of an integrative model of supervision and identified both the supporting theories and a sequence to the training process. In this chapter and those that follow we begin to discuss the practical aspects of supervision with regard to the specific modalities, individual and group formats, culture, ethics, administrative issues, and troubleshooting. We expect that you will be able to take resources from each of these chapters to build your own evolving model and philosophy of supervision.

We begin by looking at the advantages and limitations of the primary modalities used in the supervisory process, live, videotape, audiotape, and case presentations. Each of these methods has its enthusiastic supporters among theoreticians, supervisors, and therapists. Sometimes the method selected is dictated by theory. For example, some supervisors who employ structural-strategic or a postmodern approach would expect to use primarily live supervision. Those supervisors using psychodynamic or family of origin approaches would rely largely on case presentations. From our integrative model, the supervisor is encouraged to employ aspects of each and all of these modalities with trainees, according to an informed choice as to what method would be the most effective and will highlight certain learning issues.

The other factor that may effect the choice of a particular method, besides the theoretical orientation, is the clinical setting in which the training occurs. Many settings, such as institutes that focus on a sole model, use one or two primary methods. Other settings, such as community agencies, may not have the resources or facilities for live supervision or even for videotaping of cases. Also, many forms of live supervision, as well as videotaping, are difficult to implement during in-home family therapy. We also recognize that some supervisors work with special needs families in a variety of urban and rural settings where family therapy may take place in the process of helping a family paint a room, pick a crop, or while driving a parent for grocery shopping. Others may work in court-mandated settings where videotaping might be prohibited and case presentations may be the only supervisory possibility.

No matter what modality you employ, if you focus your supervisory role only on the therapist, the clinical family, and/or their interaction, you are working with what has been described as "first order cybernetics" (Breunlin, Karrer, McGuire, & Cimmarusti, 1988). If you supervise primarily at this level, you will set goals with the therapist and then audit them. If you are using live supervision you may employ a "bug in the ear," a call-in method, or an inter-session. If you use an inter-session, you may talk about the clients and about the therapist, or their interaction. You may even ask the clients about the therapist, or about her or his techniques (Dwyer, 1999).

As you move to the latter type of issues, you are beginning to work on "second order cybernetics," namely, looking at the entire treatment system—client/therapist/supervisor—and the inherent interactive processes. As a supervisor you are now consulting to the whole therapy system and understanding that your presence has altered it into a "training system." Some modalities (e.g., live supervision) may seem to make second order processing easier than others (e.g., case presentation). However, second order cybernetics has more to do with the orientation of the training system. The modality only determines the scope of the picture being analyzed. The bigger clinical picture and long-term treatment plans constructed in case presentation sessions can validly be regarded as a joint product of supervisor, therapist, and client and their respective settings.

The following is a review of the strengths and weaknesses of each of the supervisory modalities. We want to invite your personal participation in this review and encourage you to make notes in your journal following the reflective questions that we ask about each method. We believe that this will help you construct your own evolving model of supervision.

Live Supervision

On the basis of your experience being supervised and doing supervision yourself, what do you consider to be the most helpful aspects of using live supervision? In live supervision, supervisors can be relatively active, even to the point of intervening in the therapy process itself. Other supervisors may choose to set goals, give instructions, and audit performances and outcomes. However, no matter what form live supervision takes, what does live supervision offer uniquely? What things does this method provide you that you will not get in any other way? Make a list of these things. Rank them from what you believe to be the most to least important. Next, make a list of those things you consider live supervision's limitations. Rank them, too. Finally, if you are doing live supervision at this time, think about this question: How can you make it go better?

Strengths of Live Supervision

The following is a summary of unique and important benefits and goals of live supervision. These issues have been collected from the literature (e.g., Jordan, 2000; Woodside, 2000) and from the remarks of participants in our supervision courses and institutes.

1. The supervisor must have first-hand knowledge about the therapy on the one hand, and the trainee's developing resources on the other.
2. Trainees are faced with complex clinical situations and beginning therapists may be in over their heads. Live supervision is a supplement that provides information they do not know, supports them emotionally, and ensures that their clients receive at least minimal care.
3. Some therapy skills with families can be best taught, demonstrated, and practiced in a live setting.
4. Trainees can benefit from relatively instantaneous corrective feedback from their supervisors or a reflecting team as they proceed with their live cases.
5. If necessary, this immediate feedback can help trainees change direction quickly when there is an impasse or crisis with their live family.
6. Trainees and supervisors observe together the effects of evolving and implementing a certain intervention from their integrative assessment.
7. Supervisors' credibility is enhanced when they are viewed as paying immediate and close attention to the trainees' work.
8. The supervisor has immediate access to the more subtle clinical emotional and situational features that are often lost on a videotape or in the written recollections of a session.
9. Constructive responses from a supervisor or team can be an antidote for therapist performance anxiety, self-denigration, and predictions of blame.
10. Other trainees who observe the live session behind the mirror can learn from both the supervisor's observations/interactions and the ongoing consultation with the therapist.
11. Supervisors often receive greater personal satisfaction by immediately viewing the fruits of their labors.
12. The supervision here parallels the therapy, namely, it is action-oriented and focused on "what is happening right now."

Concerns About Live Supervision

Despite the many benefits of live supervision, there are clearly some concerns. We are wondering what you have put on your own list. Here is our compilation of potential limitations of live supervision (see Liddle, Davidson, & Barrett, 1988; Nichols & Lee, 1999; Schwartz, Liddle, & Breunlin, 1988; Storm, 2000a).

1. Live observation may contribute to greater performance anxiety and higher levels of stress for supervisors, therapists, and clients.
2. The focus on live data may actually serve to distract therapists and clients.
3. The focus on a single session may cause the therapist to miss looking at the bigger clinical picture.
4. Suggested changes or interventions using this method often require immediate behavior changes on the part of the therapist with little time for substantial reflection. This lack of opportunity to reflect may also increase the possibility of supervisors and therapists isomorphically replicating dysfunctional patterns of therapist–client interaction.
5. With the supervisor watching over the shoulder of the therapist, the method may undermine the goal of increasing the therapist's level of confidence and self-sufficiency.
6. Trainees' skill development may be privileged relative to theory development and professional growth.
7. The presence of the observing and interacting supervisor, and possibly other therapists and team members, may dilute the therapeutic relationship between the clinical family and the therapist.
8. The presence of an observing and interacting supervisor, and possibly other therapists and team members, can dilute the overall trust of the clinical family in their therapy process.
9. Live supervision is not a time-efficient method because it requires the supervisor to spend an entire hour with one therapist on one session.
10. The focus on live issues may bypass the recognition of fundamental issues, such as completing a thorough assessment of the family.
11. Live supervision requires special equipment and space that may not be practical in certain training settings.
12. There is no instant replay available as with the use of videotaping, so subtle issues may be missed and future reviews limited.

What Makes Live Supervision Work Best?

Live supervision has been reported often in the literature to be the highlight or nadir of many family therapy trainees' supervisory experiences (Dwyer & Lee, 1999; Liddle, Davidson, & Barrett, 1988; Schwartz et al., 1988; Wark, 2000).

Here is a compilation of suggestions from therapists about how to make live supervision go best.

1. Supervisors, respecting the presence of isomorphism, need to attend to the immediate supervisory relationship and relate to their trainees in the way they would have the therapists relate to their clients.
2. Supervisors must listen actively to and validate their therapists, stay connected with them and what is going on with a case, and be flexible.
3. Supervisors should recognize that offering criticism in a live setting, particularly with other therapists watching and in front of a clinical family, can be emotionally devastating to a therapist.
4. Supervisors should not offer directions that are inappropriate to the trainee's level of development and should take into account her or his ability to tolerate risks in this public setting.
5. Supervisors should be personable, acknowledge supervisory mistakes, use concrete suggestions, explain the reasons behind their suggestions (both from the immediate and the larger theoretical pictures), and be open to therapist feedback.
6. Supervisors should demonstrate respect, humor, enthusiasm, support, and humility when appropriate.
7. Supervisors should remember that too high of levels of anxiety and criticism combined with disrespect can be toxic to the entire training system.

Even though we value live supervision and have used it extensively in our own training programs, we are concerned that some supervisors tend to idealize this method above all other methods. The use of this method appeared to reach a peak in the 1980s (Nichols, Nichols, & Hardy, 1990) when 68% of Approved Supervisors said that they used this modality. More recently it was reported as the preferred modality by only 15% of Approved Supervisors in the national sample (Lee et al., 2003, in press). This change may reflect the rise and decline in popularity of certain theoretical schools as well as the more diverse settings in which training takes place. When live supervision can be used, participants often enjoy the drama and interaction when it is done sensitively and with clear goals that have been developed and discussed. As a supervisor using this method, you and your trainees need to be sensitive to the many issues of ethics and privacy associated with this modality. Many of the issues are similar to those involved in the use of video supervision, which we also address. However, several standards of practice and ethical concerns do seem to apply uniquely to live supervision. Most of these concerns are a part of the 13 principles of supervision that we discussed in Chapter 1.

Supervisors need to be sensitive to the needs of the various members of the training system who may be present during the live supervision and to the needs of the training system itself. Supervisors also need to be sensitive to issues of personal power, and especially must not to do anything that undercuts their working alliance with their therapists and the therapists' with their client families. Finally, the needs of the clients come first, and the supervisor must remember that it is the task of the therapist to treat the clients and that it is the supervisor's role to empower the therapist. One way the supervisor can do this in live supervision is to pay attention to the quieter or inaudible voices in the therapy room (Haber, 2000). But the supervisor needs to be particularly careful not to interject her or his own ego-based needs to show-off in front of the trainees and the clinical family.

Consider the following example of a supervisor unable to constructively address issues of power and control throughout the training system.

> A live supervision session was observed as part of a program accreditation site visit. From behind a mirror, a supervisor watched a therapist in a verbal power struggle with the parent of a rebellious adolescent. Each party was proposing a different course of action, and they were actively arguing with one another. The supervisor watched the symmetrical escalation with increasing agitation and finally called the therapist out of the session. Instead of addressing the power struggle, the supervisor confronted the therapist in a highly charged manner that was similar to what had just been occurring in the therapy session. The supervisor scolded the therapist for not listening to the instructions given before the session and now instructed the therapist to confront the parent. The session rejoined, the symmetrical escalation continued. Seething, the supervisor turned to the site visitor and said, "This is a very controlling and rebellious therapist. I can't imagine how we let this person into our program."

In this situation we see a parallel process between supervisor and therapist, therapist and parent and, allegedly, parent, and child. The supervisor not only failed to interrupt this destructive circular interaction, but contributed to it.

Supervision Using Videotape

We suggest that you repeat the exercise from the previous section on live supervision, but this time reflect on your experiences when videotape was your primary method of supervision. What does videotape supervision uniquely offer? What things can you get in no other way? Make a list of these things. Rank them from the most to the least important. Next, make a list of those things you consider to be videotape supervision's limitations. Rank them. Finally, if you are presently doing videotape supervision, what sorts of things seem to make it go best?

Strengths of Supervision Using Videotape

When you have completed your notations, compare your list with the ones we have developed. Our lists are derived from the supervision literature (Breunlin, Karrer, McGuire, & Cimmarusti, 1988; Nichols & Lee, 1999; Protinsky, 1997) and from participants in our supervision courses and workshops. Videotape supervision, like live supervision, is based on the raw data of therapy. However, in contrast to live supervision, the use of videotape offers several additional resources.

1. Videotape supervision offers supervisors and the training system ongoing access to raw data. Supervisors and therapists do not have to be in the same place at the same time. It permits distance learning.
2. Videotape supervision provides economy of time. The entire session does not have to be reviewed to isolate patterns, touch on various topics of interest, and focus on specific parts of the session. Supervisors also can sample many cases by the same therapist, or sample cases from many therapists in one group supervisory session.
3. The supervisor's and the trainee's review of the therapy taped sessions can be conducted when there is time and opportunity for ample reflection while also being informed by continued access to the raw data.
4. During a tape review, supervisors and therapists can take time to look carefully at subtle cues, such as nonfluency in speech, tonal shifts, body language, verbal interaction patterns, and interactional synchrony.
5. Videotapes help therapists learn to look over their own shoulders and observe their interaction with their clinical families.
6. Tape playback can be used to freeze time so that a small event can be reviewed in detail; or, as a sort of time-lapse photography, it allows a recap of months of therapy.
7. Videotapes provide an opportunity to aid recall and correct bias by permitting dynamics that were missed by the therapist (or the therapy team, or supervisor if there was also live supervision) to be recognized during the review of the tape.
8. The supervisor can use the tape to focus selectively on those parts of therapy sessions that highlight special clinical concerns or the role of the therapist.
9. The videotapes can be muted to allow the supervisor and therapist to focus exclusively on visual data, such as body language and nonverbal interaction.
10. Videotapes can be stored and sessions can be revisited as needed. Archived tapes can also be used for before-and-after comparisons of therapists or clients.
11. Supervisors can collect examples of effective therapy, as well as of therapeutic missteps, and integrate them into teaching tapes. These tapes can be used to provide data to sharpen perceptual, conceptual, and interviewing skills.

These tapes can also become invaluable teaching resources for subsequent supervision, workshops, or classes.

12. Videotapes can be used to help therapists reflect on their personal and professional roles by observing their ongoing behaviors with selected clinical incidents or types of clinical families.

13. Videotapes provide distance from and objectivity for the emotional process of the actual session.

14. Videotapes document reality. By reviewing clinical sessions therapists may find that they only selectively remembered aspects of events during the therapy that they thought went well or did not go well.

15. Reviewing videotapes can be used to desensitize therapists to and prepare them for live supervision.

16. Videotapes are time-efficient because they can be used with one or multiple therapists, as needed.

17. Clients themselves can participate in the review of videotapes, including videotapes of the supervision session.

Concerns with Supervision Using Videotape

As we have seen, the use of videotape can be a powerful supervisory tool. However, there are certain limitations. Compare your list to ours.

1. While videotaped recordings capture the actions of therapists, they are removed in space and time, and thus do not allow direct access to the cognitive and emotional processes that guided and or affected therapists' decision making during the "real time" of the actual sessions.

2. Later reconstructions of the clinical interview by trainees may lack accuracy or an ability to capture the emotional dimensions.

3. Therapists report, for the use of videotaping as well as with live supervision, a sense of performance anxiety. The idea that they are being taped has made them nervous, particularly knowing that their supervisors and peers will review their performances later. Some therapists have even spoken of discomfort accompanying a fantasy that some of their worst moments will be archived forever and, even worse, might be used as negative examples for others in the training program.

4. Videotapes can lead to a focus on a single session rather than on the larger clinical issues of context (Nichols & Lee, 1999) and case planning (McCollum & Wetchler, 1995). In fact, Breunlin, Karrer, McGuire, and Cimmarusti (1988) remind us that, at the very least, supervisors using videotape and their trainees need to remember to put the dynamics observed in any one session in the context of issues observed in the previous sessions.

5. There are potential ethical dilemmas in the use of videotapes just as there are in live supervision.

One of our standards of practice for the use of videotapes has been "fully informed consent, freely given." This consent must be provided by *both* the therapists and their clinical families. That means that all parties need to know why taping is being done, who will watch the tapes, and what security measures are in place for both the watching of the tapes and their storage (Protinsky, 1997). For example, as the supervisor do you keep your trainees' tapes in a locked facility and location? Do you limit watching them exclusively to members of the supervisory team? Has the client met all of the participants of this team? Do you allow therapists or supervisors to take videotapes home for personal review? If so, how can you guarantee who is watching them, especially if they are lost en route? All parties also need to know when the tapes will be erased or destroyed. If tapes are archived, all parties need give permission for their future use in the training program, and they need to appreciate that they may be vulnerable to subpoena in certain legal cases.

It is also important to consider the issue of consent being freely given. Presumably clients uncomfortable with the use of videotape can choose to have treatment elsewhere, but as supervisors we need to recognize the probability that they may feel some subtle coercion to agree to the taping to work with your therapist or training setting. They may not want to continue their search for a therapist and they may need the reduction in fee attendant on being seen in your training setting. We also cannot overlook the fact that therapists in educational institutions rarely have the freedom not to be videotaped.

What Makes Supervision Using Videotape Work Best?

Many former trainees have reported that the use of videotape in their supervision was the singular most important part of their training, and currently 65% of all Approved Supervisors use them (Lee et al., in press). Positive outcomes result from the following principles.

1. Once the training system has agreed to the use of videotapes, supervision will fare best when supervisors set aside time to establish the context of using the tapes in the individual sessions.
2. In reviewing the tapes themselves, supervisors and therapists should discuss how the tapes will be used in the context of supervision. It has been reported by therapists that review of tapes is often less anxiety producing when it is informed by specific questions, most often raised by the therapists themselves.
3. The review of tapes should reflect the developmental levels of the therapists. We have found that it is best to select only those parts of a videotape that are relevant to the therapists' learning issues.
4. In viewing the tapes with trainees, supervisors do well to use their own powers of observation and diplomacy to counteract therapists' tendencies toward

anxiety, self-denigration, and doubt. It also makes sense to ask for examples that the therapists feel good about.

5. Supervisors need to use their executive functions to raise critical questions or visit segments of tape that challenge defensive or naïve therapists' clinical roles.

6. Supervisors should use their creativity and imagination in the review of tapes. They should try not just to sit there and comment on minute-to-minute dynamics. Instead the tapes can be used to explore the therapist's own issues or to challenge the therapist. For example, a particular impasse can be reviewed, the tape turned off, and the therapist be given space in which to explore thoughts and feelings. Or, having watched a segment, therapists can be asked to relate what they are seeing to theory or their original assessment.

7. Supervisors may find it helpful to look at the absence of tapes for the supervision session as an indicator of learning issues. Todd (1997a) has reminded us that supervisors and therapists may collude to avoid discomfort. Therapists may "forget" to tape a session or cue a tape in anticipation of the supervisory session, and supervisors may not call them on it. This may be because either or both parties are distracted or their energies are spread too thinly. There may also be of other interlocking dynamics between the supervisor and the therapist that would cause this issue to be ignored.

8. Quinn and Nagirreddy (1999) have created innovative ways, often employing the clients themselves, to use videotapes in family therapy supervision. Their methods seem ideal for when supervisors want therapists to discover and reflect on their internal processes while engaged in therapy.

9. With regard to the ethical issues, Protinsky (1997) reported that discussion of such issues may be reassuring to all members of the training system. However, comments from participants in our supervision classes and workshops have indicated that the opposite also may occur. Perhaps raising awareness also raises concern. The supervisor needs to recognize this, but she or he must raise such issues and process them thoroughly before moving on with training. This is based on our first priority (Chapter 1) of establishing and protecting the working alliance.

10. Many of the guidelines that we listed as facilitating live supervision—such as social acumen, support, and grace—apply equally well here.

Supervision Using Audiotape

It seems to us that most of the issues that we have discussed in the use of videotape as a supervisory modality also apply to the use of audiotaping. However, the value of audiotaping may be overlooked with all our technological advances in digital video. We believe that the primary benefit of audiotaping is in providing the supervisor or training program access to raw data in clinical settings where live or video resources are not available. Moreover, even though we intuitively think of audiotaping as a poor relation to visual access to therapy sessions, there are some things that an audio cassette recorder makes possible that are available in no other way. Perhaps that is why 53% of Approved Supervisors in the national sample reported that they still use this method (Lee et al., 2003, in press).

We know that as humans we are all heavily dependent on visual cues (Warr & Knapper, 1968). By removing those cues, audiotape allows us to focus exclusively on the audio components and how things sound in a clinical session. This difference in itself can provide special insights to the clinical process. For example, what may have seemed like belly laughter to the therapist in the session may sound more like distress on review of the audiotape. Similarly, the use of audiotapes allows one to hear and sense a certain *rhythm* of the therapy (Keeney & Ray, 2000).

In some settings the use of audiotapes in supervision may make therapists, clients, and administrators less nervous. Audiotapes provide greater anonymity for the participants and less of a privacy, liability, and security risk than videotapes. We also know many supervisors who listen to audiotapes of their trainees' therapy sessions while engaged in lengthy commutes to and from work.

Case Presentation Supervision

Once again, consider what you believe to be the value of using case presentations as the basis of supervision. First, make a list of those things you believe the case presentation approach uniquely offers. Rank them from most to least important. Next, make a list of those things you consider to be the limitations of basing supervision on case presentations. Rank them. Finally, in using case presentations, how can you make this process go best?

Advantages of Case Presentations in Supervision

The case presentation, in its simplest form, requires that trainees learn to describe in their own words the clinical dynamics that they experience with a clinical family. We have found that this process is crucial for beginning therapists because it helps them learn to objectify clinical data and present (and defend it) in a focused and organized manner. The most arduous version of the case presentation approach, requiring verbatim reports, requires therapists to provide a complete record of what happened in a session. The product approximates a transcript. Sometimes the detailed description is required only of those parts of a session that have particular clinical and/or training significance.

Several family therapy leaders have supported the value of the case presentation method, particularly with beginning therapists (see Nichols & Lee, 1999; Wetchler & McCollum, 1999). The data from the national sample indicated that

76% of Approved Supervisors currently use case presentation methods in their supervision, and a third of these use verbatim reports (Lee et al., 2003, in press). Some of the advantages of case presentation methods include the following.

1. This method of supervision requires no special equipment and no special settings. Therapists, however, usually have recourse to their process notes.
2. The use of case presentation and process notes require that therapists become familiar enough with theory and assessment procedures to be able to verbally explain and defend their positions with cases.
3. For the beginning family therapist, following either a case presentation outline or a process note outline requires attention to details and the cognitive exercise of preparing and presenting one's thoughts and observations. This is often much more demanding and difficult than simply reviewing videotapes and dialoguing with the supervisor. It is our experience that this develops clinical discipline.
4. This method is time-efficient in that it allows a supervisor to review and to stay current with a large number of trainees and their cases. This may involve case management in broad strokes, such as keeping up to date with the current events of clients' lives, therapeutic goal-setting, and the well-being of the therapists.
5. The case presentation approach provides a broader perspective than do modalities that highlight a single session (McCollum & Wetchler, 1995). It is much like dialing down the power of a zoom lens to see the bigger picture.
6. The case presentation approach provides the opportunity to examine the broader contextual issues of the therapy, the clients, and the therapist. The supervisory team can work on what Wetchler and McCollum (1999) have called the "architecture" of therapy. The team considers what it knows about therapeutic process and about a case, and comes up with a master plan for the therapy with intermediate goals and strategies.
7. The case presentation modality is a way to look slowly and appreciatively at clients and therapists, and to use one's best systemic tools (e.g., ecomaps, genograms, and timelines).
8. The case presentation approach provides an opportunity to pay attention to person-of-the-therapist variables. The supervisory team can be alert to what is being talked about and how, and what is not being talked about.
9. The case presentation approach provides supervisors with opportunities to teach didactically and experientially.
10. The case presentation provides supervisory teams with opportunities to talk, ventilate, and explore questions at length during the supervisory session itself. It may involve conversation about the client family as it is embedded within larger systems. Such conversations could be entryways for consideration of contextual issues such as gender, ethnic membership, and religious involvement.

11. The case presentation approach provides a setting in which participants can explore how major family therapy theories would regard the therapeutic picture and a practical setting for evolving careful integrative approaches. In so doing, the therapists can experience what the various major models might highlight and miss. They can explore their own comfort levels with regard to the various models, and be in a position to gradually articulate their own integrative models of therapy.
12. The case presentation approach is an opportunity for substantial didactic teaching and experiential learning with regard to theory, technique, and contextual factors. Supervisors and therapists can consider what "therapy" represents in various settings and explore postmodern insights with regard to power, hierarchy, radical constructivism, and social constructivism (Hardy, 1993).
13. Proponents of the case presentation approach observe that it may be the least intrusive to the therapy process itself. Essentially, for good or ill, therapists are on their own with their clients. Montalvo (Storm, 2000a) and Nichols (1988) believed that this feature was necessary if therapists were to develop professionally, that is, to become self-sufficient and confident clinicians. Participants in supervision classes and workshops have also observed that the case presentation approach is the least invasive to clinical families.
14. Proponents of verbatim supervision have pointed out that, although it can be laborious, it requires "sustained, intense reflection." They observed that verbatim supervision goes beyond other case presentation methods in the depth to which it raises person-of-the-therapist questions and elicits answers. *Why did I do that? Why did I say that? Why then?* They observed that it might be the best approach to interpersonal process recall as first described by Elliot (1986), namely, comprehending individuals within their own experiential worlds.

Concerns in the Use of Case Presentations in Supervision

1. Supervision using this method must rely on therapists' reports of session content and process. Live data are not being compared to what therapists say is happening. This especially may be of concern given supervisors' ultimate responsibility for cases under their supervision.
2. In summarizing the therapeutic process, important details may be lost.
3. The therapist and the supervisor can become too focused on written details and fail to look carefully at the broader clinical process and dynamics.
4. Case presentation approaches are heavily dependent on therapists' written and verbal skills. Supervisors should always be aware that students with weak skills in these areas or those with culturally derived limitations need special attention.
5. The validity of the data that are written may be inversely related to the amount of time that has transpired between the actual session and the writing. *Process notes more than a day old are fiction.*

6. Case presentation approaches privilege conceptualization at the expense of skill training.
7. Although case presentation approaches allow reflection away from the fray, they do not help therapists learn to think on their feet.

What Makes Case Presentation Supervision Work Best?

Our recommendations for facilitating case presentation methods are similar to those we have offered for the other supervisory methods. There is a need for social acumen and grace (Anderson, Schlossberg, & Rigazio-DiGilio, 2000) on the one hand, and proper use of supervisors' executive function on the other. This involves developmentally appropriate short-term and long-term goal-setting for the training, and careful monitoring of the content of the individual sessions (Anderson, Schlossberg, & Rigazio-DiGilio, 2000).

Therapists have reported that case presentation supervision can be frustrating when it is turned into an administrative exercise, namely, when files are reviewed for completeness and signatures are provided but little case consultation takes place. Experienced supervisors generally believe that the sessions should be devoted to a developmentally appropriate mix of case management, theory and skills development, and exploration of the self of the therapist (White & Russell, 1995). Of course, we believe that the use of this method is essential for helping trainees develop integrative approaches to their clinical work.

What Modalities Will You Be Using?

Each of the modalities that we have discussed has certain advantages and disadvantages, indications for when to use them and contraindications for when not to use them. We hope you will incorporate these factors into your own developing supervisory awareness and models. We expect that most of you will learn to use the thoughtful integration of these methods depending on the needs and developmental levels of your trainees, and contextual and pedagogic factors. We find ourselves agreeing with Montalvo when he observed, "Each method is a window to help supervisors and supervisees gain information to understand families and to refine the tools of the therapist. Supervisors should think about using a variety of methods. . . . All windows are needed [to tap] what therapists think [and] to access what they do" (Storm, 2000a, p. 109).

Chapter 8

Formats of Supervision

Individual and Group

We have heard the story of an accreditation team's site visit to a family therapy program where the team expressed surprise at the high percentage of individual supervision provided to the therapists. There was a sense that they were displeased. The faculty members were taken aback by that. The faculty had always taken pride in the individual attention each student in their program received. They considered individual supervision, whether it was live or face-to-face using videotape and case presentation, as an expression of that personal care. They believed that the intensity and intimacy of individual tutorials was the way to go and that group supervision was something to be used for reasons of economy and convenience.

Ironically, this family therapy faculty recognized that group therapy and individual therapy are both valuable treatment methods with unique things to offer. Moreover, although individual family members were often seen in the campus clinic, whole family systems were preferred. Somehow there was a disconnection between how the faculty viewed treatment processes and training.

In this chapter, we want you to consider the unique contributions and the relative strengths and concerns of individual and group supervision formats. We also want you to consider the best ways to blend each method in your supervision and, if relevant, in your training program. We will also briefly discuss reflecting teams as a special case of group supervision.

Individual Supervision

Take a minute to close your eyes and picture a one-on-one, face-to-face session with a favorite supervisor. Can you articulate what it was about that experience that made it especially good? Was it the personality and style of the supervisor, or did the one-on-one format itself add something special? If so, what?

In the recent national survey of AAMFT Approved Supervisors, 91% indicated that they provided individual supervision as part of their training (Lee et al., in press). This percentage has not changed much over the past 25 years: Individual supervision was reportedly used by 89% of Approved Supervisors in 1976 (Everett, 1980a) and 92% in 1986 (Nichols et al., 1990). Supervisors typically provided trainees one to two hours of supervision a week.

Benefits of Individual Supervision

Although the Commission on Accreditation for Marriage and Family Therapy Education (COAMFTE) (2002) accepts the presence of two trainees as constituting "individual" supervision, most of us restrict the term to a dyadic relationship: a supervisor one-on-one with a trainee. Individual supervision may be a format of convenience that results when individual therapists privately contract for supervision in the process of doing internships, satisfying postdegree regulatory requirements, or acquiring new skills. However, in reviewing the written and oral comments of supervisors and therapists, there are certain benefits that one-on-one supervision is expected to provide to enhance the experience of live, taped, or case presentation sessions. These issues involve privacy, time available for the needs of the individual therapist, and intensity in the supervisory relationship.

Privacy

Value to the therapist   The relative privacy of one-on-one supervision, as compared to group supervision, may facilitate more open and profound reflection on evaluative issues, interpersonal dynamics, and self-of-the-therapist.

Value to the supervisor   The privacy afforded by individual supervision may provide the supervisor with a broader range of possible interventions. You may feel freer to challenge and/or to nurture certain trainees in this individual context rather than in a group setting.

Time Available for Individual Needs

Value to the therapist   We believe that the hallmark of individual supervision is individual attention. One-on-one supervision is focused solely on the unique training needs of each individual therapist. This includes both the content and process of the supervisory sessions. Certainly, the various topics addressed in individual supervision (i.e., family theories and dynamics, assessment and clinical interventions, the self-of-the-therapist, and career development) can also be addressed in group supervision. However, in group supervision time and energy need to be distributed among the members and their respective caseloads. Some therapists may struggle with insecurity or anxiety, perhaps exacerbated by the group setting, and thus may take refuge on the fringe of the supervision group. Such individuals may feel less anxious in individual supervision, and they may find it easier to talk and listen to the supervisor.

Value to the supervisor   Beginning therapists often say that they are confused by the multiplicity of perspectives with regard to theory and intervention that they experience in a group. Individual supervision may permit the supervisor to more carefully and thoroughly address each therapist's developmental needs and learning style. Here, the supervisor does not have to feel responsible for meeting all of the needs of the group members. In working with one therapist the supervisor can use a slower pace that facilitates attention to and organization of the complex data of the training system. Many therapists need this kind of time to develop and apply their own integrative models.

Intensity

Value to the therapist   Beyond what a dyadic training relationship offers for learning, this method may also afford a quiet and nurturing haven from the stresses of clinical work wherein trainees may lick their wounds, express their doubts, and recharge their batteries (Holloway, 1995). Perhaps this has more to do with privacy factors or positive transference for the trainee from other significant past and present relationships.

Value to the supervisor   Individual supervision has been the method of choice for clinical theories that highlight the value of the supervisory relationship, such as the psychodynamic, Bowenian, and many postmodern schools. From these perspectives, individual supervision provides an opportunity for relatively intense interpersonal relationships to develop quickly between the supervisor and the trainee so that these relationship dynamics can inform the treatment process. Personal and interactive dynamics for the therapist can be experienced, identified, and processed more readily in individual supervision and then applied directly to the therapist's ongoing interaction with clinical families. The supervisor also can use the potentially greater intensity of dyadic supervision to assess therapists' abilities to set and manage personal boundaries.

Concerns in the Use of Individual Supervision

For all of the attributes and popularity of individual supervision, we believe that it has some weaknesses. On the one hand, the dyadic supervisor–trainee relationship may not provide the training system the relational richness afforded by the presence of several therapists (see Figure 4.1, Chapter 4). On the other hand, because the relationship intensity is not diluted in this format by the presence of other therapists, dyadic supervision may encourage a more intense supervisory relationship with which some trainees may not be comfortable. Some therapists may experience a greater sense of intimidation relative to the supervisor than if they are part of and supported by a group. Other therapists may experience more anxiety in this setting. Some supervisors may feel freer to be more critical in a one-on-one relationship than in a group setting. Some supervisors have reported experiencing more boredom in individual supervision, particularly with certain types of trainees, than in a group setting. Supervisors who prefer more active and directive roles often prefer the interactive audience of a group setting.

A more subtle dynamic that may develop in individual supervision is a form of defensive collusion between a supervisor and a therapist (Nichols & Everett, 1986). The intensity of the dyadic relationship, just as in individual therapy, can foster transferential and projective dynamics that may originate in either the supervisor or the therapist. For example, a particularly vulnerable or dependent trainee may elicit a protective (and even parental) response from the supervisor. This dynamic can effectively erode the objectivity of both such that the protective collusion camouflages clinical errors or learning issues.

Similarly, individual supervision has the potential for blurring the boundaries between the supervisory and therapeutic relationships (Anderson, Schlossberg, & Rigazio-DiGilio, 2000). Additionally, because there are no witnesses to this process, supervisors must be especially sensitive to their power relative to trainees with regard to the handling of matters related to gender, sociocultural identification, evaluation, and privacy (Haber, 2000).

Individual supervision works best when all parties involved are sensitive to its limitations. These can be addressed explicitly in initial conversations and in formal training contracts that seek to address the needs and expectations of your therapists as well as your own (Todd, 1997a). However, such initial care needs to be reinforced by ongoing mutual attention to the working alliance. In this way, supervision continues to address the needs and wants of both parties, and you learn more and more about the process of supervision (Lowe, 2000).

Group Supervision

Repeat the experiential exercise that we suggested but for individual supervision, but this time think of a rewarding session of group supervision. What aspects stand out as especially meaningful? Of these, which are only possible because supervision occurred in a group format?

Group supervision may provide a correction factor for many of the concerns regarding individual supervision. However, the group format is an important supervisory resource in its own right. In fact, given the benefits we will attribute to group supervision, it is somewhat surprising to us that it is not more widely used in many training settings. Group supervision's highest reported usage by Approved Supervisors was 75% in 1986 (Nichols at al., 1990). Only 60% of Approved Supervisors reported that they used group supervision in 1976 (Everett, 1980a). In 2001, the most recent national sample, 68% of the Approved Supervisor reported using the format (Lee et al., in press). These data may be somewhat misleading in that they do not indicate how many supervisors use one format and not the other. It is probably safe to say that currently two-thirds (68%) of Approved Supervisors use both methods.

It is interesting to note that current accreditation for marital and family therapy programs ([COAMFTE], 2002) consider supervision in which two trainees are present simultaneously to be a form of individual supervision. We understand that this "in between" format was developed some years ago for reasons most likely of economy, but we believe that is a confusing method that diminishes some of the benefits of the one-on-one format.

Benefits of Group Supervision

Group supervision provides a rich environment for learning. The following summary of the benefits of group supervision is based on the literature (Bernard & Goodyear, 1998; Holloway, 1995; Proctor, 2000; York, 1997) and the oral reports of participants in our supervision classes and workshops.

Economy

Value to the therapists   COAMFTE and AAMFT membership regulations allow up to six trainees to be present in a supervision group. If the supervision is privately contracted, the cost savings can be significant when shared by two to six group members over the course of a year (York, 1997). The limitation of six per group certainly keeps the group process manageable.

Value to the supervisor   Group supervision is considered to be more economical in the use of supervisor time. This is particularly true in academic settings or large training institutes with many trainees at differing levels of training.

A Diverse System

Value to the therapists   Group supervision is an open system as opposed to a closed system (Proctor, 2000). As such it makes available to its participants a diversity of therapists, clients, presenting problems, and contexts. The trainees in a group are diverse in who they are professionally as well as personally. They are often at different stages of development. Their cases differ from one another, both in their presenting problems and in how they are conceptualized and treated. The members may represent practices in diverse clinical settings.

Some in the field would argue that supervision groups ought to be homogeneous with regard to all these factors (e.g., York, 1997), but others believe that there is an optimal mix wherein diverse individuals open themselves and their work to others. This experience provides insight into contextual issues that cannot be obtained from books. The group can also influence therapists to become more open and flexible in their clinical roles. Group members also learn to tolerate and appreciate differences in styles, conceptualizations, emotions, and techniques.

Value to the supervisor   Many supervisors value the richness of education and training afforded by the simultaneous presence of multiple trainees in a supervision group. We have found that supervisors who use the integrative model especially appreciate the relationally rich educational opportunities afforded by a training system with such elaborate "third" and "fourth" generations, namely, a system with many therapists and their respective clinical families.

Shared Consultation and Responsibility

Value to the therapists   Supervision groups give the participating therapists opportunity to assume several roles important to their own learning and professional development. In group supervision there may be significant shared responsibilities. The group, including the supervisor, is responsible for the supervision. Some members of the group may practice leadership roles.

Value to the supervisor   When the group shares responsibility for the training process, the supervisor may not need to be the ultimate authority or be aware of all therapist issues at all times. The supervisor also may not have to do all of the leadership work, be it executive or emotional.

Group Learning

Value to the therapists   Group members have observed that their learning was improved when issues were processed by the entire group. When group members comment on each other's work and are sought out and heard, they can feel more empowered. This experience builds confidence as well as professional and personal bonding. Members also are able to clarify and consolidate what they themselves know by teaching it to someone else, whether that be by answering questions about their own cases or consulting with another group member about her or his case.

Value to the supervisor   Once again, as a supervisor this format helps you to feel that you do not need to be the expert with regard to all things at all times.

Direct and Indirect Learning

Value to the therapists The group format allows both direct and indirect learning. A therapist may ask to have a specific case or issue considered by the group. Beginning therapists may wish to remain on the periphery. However, as the case is discussed, the more peripheral trainees can take what is said and apply it to their own cases. This experience may help them to be prepared when something occurs in their own professional lives because they have already learned from the experience of other therapists. Moreover, by observing more experienced therapists, the other group members can gain a sense of what is realistic in terms of expectations, mistakes, and skills on the one hand, and a sense of hope about where their training will take them on the other.

Exposure to the variety of models discussed in a group will also help in the learning of therapeutic and critical thinking, and professional socialization (Nichols & Everett, 1986). Group members may also have the corrective emotional experience of discovering that they all have the same concerns about professional work, their educational experience, and the often conflicting demands of their many roles (Lee, Eppler, Kendal, & Latty, 2001).

Value to the supervisor Again, many supervisors value the richness of education and training afforded by the variety of potential learning experiences in a group environment, especially one characterized by personal and professional diversity. They recognize that they cannot provide all of these lessons themselves.

Social Laboratory

Value to the therapists A group is a social laboratory in which one experiences the group process itself. One can seek feedback about oneself in this social and interactive context. Group members can seek and receive multiple perspectives about how they are coming across. They can also practice therapeutic communication and interviewing techniques.

Value to the supervisor The interactive nature of the supervision group provides a rich resource for the supervisor. She or he can use the group to teach social and therapeutic skills, reenact family dramas, portray family roles, challenge the defenses of a therapist, struggle with authority, celebrate successes, defend hypotheses and perceptions, and plan strategies.

Cooperation and Support

Value to the therapists Group supervision potentially has a restorative, refreshing function (Holloway, 1995). Trainees spread thin by professional and personal requirements have spoken appreciatively of the social support and networking provided by their regularly scheduled participation in a supervisory group. They reported a sense of common mission, concern, and caring. We also know how confident and stimulated participants feel when they emerge from a group session in which they feel heard, are reminded of their strengths, and perhaps are given a good sense of immediate direction.

Value to supervisors   Like our trainees, we appreciate the stimulation and excitement of a cooperative enterprise. We all have memories of how well supervision group members have taken care of us as supervisors or as therapists during tense times in our training, and how a group has provided a setting in which we could recharge our batteries.

Concerns in the Use of Group Supervision

There are limitations to group supervision. One of them is the limited amount of time and detailed continuity, relative to individual formats, that can be consistently offered to one case or one member's needs and wishes. Some group supervisors may ration, as equally as possible, the amount of time available to each member in a session. Others, in the absence of emergencies, may rotate therapists and cases each session. Some therapists prefer individual supervision because of performance anxiety that they may experience in a group. These therapists may covertly compare themselves unfavorably to other members' roles or skills demonstrated in the group. Some beginning supervisors also experience performance anxiety in providing leadership to a group.

Group members have also spoken of their concern with safety issues, including confidentiality and acts of consideration. The management of these privacy issues in a supervision group over time or in a singular session depends on the motivation and trust of both the supervisor and the group members. Others have commented that the development of strong group ties tends to dilute the one-on-one supervisory relationship.

As a supervisor, the use of group supervision will be most effective to the extent that you attend to the ambience of the setting, the group process, and the many supervisory tasks. For each therapist, these tasks include:

- Developmentally appropriate case conceptualization.
- Integration of theory, assessment, and technique.
- Increasing emotional awareness.
- Learning self-evaluative skills.
- Gaining emotional support.
- Social learning.
- Professional socialization.

Moreover, because the quality of group supervision is a shared responsibility, all of its participants need to bring courage and self-discipline.

Blending Individual and Group Supervision

We hope that this discussion of the relative strengths and weaknesses of these two supervisory methods will help you consider both the developmental needs of your trainees and how the respective use of these formats will enhance their long-term and short-term goals. We encourage you to think about the optimal proportion of individual and group supervision that you will offer your therapists and how to move back and forth between them. You will want to consider the best ways to carry personal issues discussed in individual supervision appropriately into the trainee's group experience. Similarly, there will be issues raised or observed in the group setting that you will want to pursue individually. If you work with a team of supervisors who divide time between either individual or group formats, it will become critical that you establish protocols for consultation and feedback methods to share training information between both settings in your training system.

As you think about the relative merits of each format for supervision, given your own emerging supervisory model, here are some practical questions to consider:

- Should beginning family therapy trainees receive more group supervision than individual supervision? If so, why?
- Can therapists struggling to learn assessment skills benefit more from the individual attention and intensity of individual supervision as compared to the interactive dialogue of a group?
- What is the benefit of group supervision for advanced family therapists about to terminate their training?
- Could there be an advantage of individual supervision over group supervision for therapists providing services in inpatient settings as compared to a community agency?

A Word About Reflecting Teams in Supervision

Reflecting teams are a special type of group supervision. They exist uniquely as an aspect of both the training process and simultaneously as an integral part of the treatment process (Andersen, 1991; Tomm, 1984). Some regard reflecting teams as an ideal way to acquire second order appreciation (and change) within the training system (Perlesz, Young, Paterson, & Bridge, 1994).

Roberts (1997) reviewed the various ways in which reflecting team supervision has been structured in various training settings and recommended that supervisors operate in a way that maximally highlights the various voices of the group. Supervisors should make sure that each member has input into discussions, avoids jargon, and uses the language and metaphors of the client. Supervisors should encourage the training system to consider why individuals have constructed things as they have, and emphasize the hypothetical nature of reflections. Supervisors should encourage positive, as opposed to negative, connotations, explore how the contributions of team members are similar and different, and inquire into the possible meanings of this. Finally, supervisors should ask the clinical families to comment on the ideas that have been generated.

To the extent that these recommendations are followed, reflecting teams can be regarded as live group supervision that strives to incorporate the views of family members, therapists, and supervisors in an equitable, recursive, and empowering way (Young, Perlesz, Paterson, & O'Hanlon, 1989). All parties have access to new information about behavior and its linkages. Within the postmodern framework, this awareness increases the relative degrees of behavioral freedom on the one hand, and awareness of contextual influences on the other.

In the next chapter we broaden the discussion of these practical matters of supervision. Having addressed methods and formats, we consider cultural issues within the training system.

Chapter 9

Cultural and Contextual Issues in Supervision

I t has been our impression, albeit a generalization, that many supervision classes tend to assume that supervisors belonging to the majority culture are supervising therapists who belong to the majority culture, and they in turn are treating clients who are members of the majority culture. These classes may include a token session, often toward the end of the course, wherein the instructors discuss supervision of therapists from the majority culture who are providing clinical services to clients who are members of a minority group. We have found that occasionally there may also be a discussion of majority culture supervisors' work with therapists who are members of a minority group. However, we have not seen a course that, from the beginning, recognizes that the training system may include any combination of majority and minority culture individuals at all levels of the training system.

A Native American supervisor recently described his work with a Latina therapist who had been providing services on a reservation with a tribal culture different from his own. As marriage and family therapy moves out of the middle-class offices of cities and suburbs, and as training programs become more effective in recruiting international students (e.g., AAMFT, 2002b), we can assume that such complexity in the training experiences for all of us will become the rule rather than the exception. As supervisors and leaders in the field, we need to anticipate and address these needs carefully, and help ourselves and our trainees gain a level of cultural competence.

As supervisors and educators we need to become culturally competent and be able to facilitate culturally competent training and therapy. With that in mind, consider your personal answers to the following questions.

- What does "being culturally competent" mean to you? What makes a person culturally competent?
- Do you believe you must have shared life experience with individuals and families from a different culture to be culturally competent in your dealings with them? Some individuals have advocated for strict client–therapist matching. How does that strike you? Other minority culture individuals have angrily called attempts at matching condescending. They have wondered "whose choice is it?" and "who does the matching?"
- Do you believe that taking on an alternate role to become more compatible (e.g., being "one down") is necessary in dealing with a person whose life experiences have been different from your own?

Some persons in the field have defined cultural competence in terms of "knowing what there is to know about individuals of various cultures." For example, Boyd-Franklin (e.g., 1989) has discussed aspects of the "Black family in therapy" and Bean, Perry, and Bedell (2002) culled the family therapy literature to compile a list of "the most common expert recommendations for family therapy with African Americans" (p. 153). Similarly, Szapocznik and his associates (e.g., 1997) have considered family therapy approaches for Cuban and other Hispanic families.

Others in the field have suggested that cultural competence is a matter of appreciating that individuals differ in terms of mores, norms, values, and interpretive frames of reference. They have observed that there may be more variations *within* any culture than *between* cultures (e.g., Allen & Olson, 2001; McAdoo, 2002) and that our cultural identities are a dynamic and fluid experience (Di Nicola, 1997). Cultural competence has also been defined, not in terms of what we know about others, but by what we know and keep trying to know about ourselves. Even if you have explored carefully your own potential biases regarding racism, sexism, homophobic attitudes, and economic privilege in your own training, and continue to explore them, it is important for you to appreciate the interplay of all these variables and the complexity of your privilege if you are a member of the dominant culture (Lawless, 2002).

To become culturally competent, professionals in general need to have a relatively sophisticated understanding of what they know and how they know it, appreciate what they do not know, and have sense enough to ask. In so doing, they create settings for discourse attuned to issues of justice and power (Grunebaum, 1987). Others (e.g., Akinyela, 2001) demur. They point out that asking with the intent to listen is not enough. Culture includes issues of power and voice. Cultural mistrust—a lack of faith in society's institutions—may create an unbridgeable chasm. Therefore, with the added argument that there may be some things about members of other cultures that we can never know because we have not lived their lives, and because these issues are often invested with great emotion, some professionals have called for a moratorium on doing supervision or therapy with someone from a culture other than one's own. They have argued that treatment systems need to be composed of "matched" individuals (e.g., Akinyela, 2001).

The trouble with such a matching proposal is the practical difficulty of doing it. Postmodern theorists have educated us that reality is personally constructed (what events are included and what interpretation they are given) and therefore matching really is not possible. Moreover, we ourselves have worried that when all parties to supervision or therapy think that "like is sitting down with like," there is much opportunity for important information to be lost. For example, one party leans forward and says, in a knowing way, "You know what it's like being ————" (e.g., female, gay, Mexican) and the other party nods in agreement. The other party rarely says, "I know what being ———— has been like for me (or I have been trying to know what it has been like for me), but I don't know what being ———— has been like for you. Tell us about that."

Recent research has suggested much disagreement among the family therapy leadership about what constitutes cultural competency in clinical practice (Nelson et al., 2001). However, we believe that the following traits are associated *jointly* with cultural competence in training systems (Corey et al., 1988; Isaacs & Benjamin, 1991). These traits need to become descriptive of family therapy supervisors who, in turn, will strive to make them descriptive of their trainees.

- Acceptance and respect for cultural differences, and comfort with the differences that may exist between yourself and others.
- Possession of cultural knowledge, including awareness of one's own values, attitudes, biases, and ways of understanding, and recognizing how these are likely to affect clients who are not of your culture.
- Demonstration of continuous cultural self-assessment, including monitoring one's functioning through consultation, supervision, and continuing education.
- Attention to the dynamics of cultural differences to better meet the needs of both the training experience and the clinical family.
- Adaptation of service models to match sociocultural contexts.
- Solicitation of advice and consultation from culturally diverse mentors and groups.
- Personal commitment to policies that enhance services to diverse clients.

Cultural competence must be a goal toward which all supervisors aspire. We recognize that this is probably more of a process (Hastings, 2002) than the actual possession of specific content. We want to be respectful to our therapists and their clinical families in a way that elicits their voices and that values what they know and what they do. We want these resources to characterize and become embedded within our entire training system (Haber, 2000). Unhappily, current research suggests that family therapy clinicians who are most racist may be less aware than others of the cultural issues involved in consultation (Constantine, Juby, & Liang, 2001). Clearly we must begin by coming to terms with ourselves (Hardy & Laszloffy, 1995).

Integrating an Appreciation of Cultural Diversity in Supervision

It is important to know what you, your trainees, and their clinical families consider normative. Differences in definitions and values among supervisors, therapists, and clients may hinder working alliances, create divergent therapeutic goals, and misguide the choice and target of interventions. This includes such basic issues as the truths of the therapy culture (Hoffman, 1997), namely, everyone's ideas about what therapy is and how it is done. This also includes beliefs about family organization, for example—where power should and does lie, and what dyads (e.g., mother–child, father–mother) should be given prominence over others.

The training system may include different constructions of the family life cycle. For example, a supervisor may be concerned by what appears to be parent–child enmeshment whereas in certain ethnic, religious, rural, and poverty cultures a longer period of interdependence between parents and children may be normative. These family systems may not envision young adults leaving home for a self-sufficient life. In some cultures there may be no empty nest syndrome or midlife crisis. Diverse cultures value diverse behaviors, for example, emphasizing the bond between a son and an aging mother, privileging life within the family as opposed to achievement outside the home, or valuing feminine chastity or the need of female children for protection.

Here is an exercise to help identify some of these cultural concerns. Picture a specific training system where you are the supervisor, a specific trainee, and a specific clinical family. Although this exercise works best in a group, take a moment to brainstorm all of the potentially different values that are present—yours, the therapist's, and the family's that could influence the training system. If your list is on the meager side, consider everyone's potentially unique ideas about mental health services on the one hand, and seeking help on the other. Think of their socialization to therapy. Think about the kinds of information each participant considers to be important to the therapy. Consider preferred and valued interaction styles, family life cycle location, and everyone's experiences at previous stages. Think of kinship bonds; male and female roles; male–female, female–female, and male–male relationships; and ideas about the expression of feelings. Think of beliefs and action tendencies related to age, gender, authority/hierarchy, religious orthodoxy, and socioeconomic status.

Given the complexity of these cultural issues, where do we begin? Falicov (1995) warned family therapists not to try to make things simple by assuming that "at the heart of things, we are all alike" or by reducing others to cultural stereotypes. We are all unique combinations of influences and orientations at particular stages of our lives. Falicov described "simultaneous memberships" and "participation in multiple contexts." Social scientists (e.g., Bronfenbrenner, 1992; Lerner, 1991) have described unique developmental trajectories of human systems embedded within increasingly larger social systems.

Because we believe that cultural competence is at once a value *and* a process, and given the cautionary observations of Constantine and her associates (2001), we need to continue this discussion by looking first at the components of our own culture.

Identifying the Ingredients of Your Own Culture

It has been said that "culture is something that someone else has" (Kostelnik, 1999). When we think about studying culture, we often consider it something sociological or anthropological—something "out there." We rarely think of ourselves as having a culture, because it is what we are given as our "natural" way of thinking, acting, and viewing the world (Leaf, 1975). You may not pay attention to aspects of your own culture until you bump into a situation that you do not recognize or that does not fit your way of thinking (Lev S. Vygotsky, described by Daniels, 1996). Still, we often react to that culture shock by negatively focusing on what others are doing. Nevertheless, those bumps potentially can raise our consciousness and understanding of our own culture. By considering our discomfort we become aware of things about which we are vigilant, things we talk about, things we don't talk about, things we do, things we don't do, things we believe, and so on. One supervisor, despite supposed sophistication about such things, remained fairly oblivious to the notion that he had a culture until a supervisory mentor had him review a list of dominant cultural attitudes compiled by Kohls & Knight (1994). We thought that it would be helpful to share these items with you. Do many of these items strike you as how things "actually are" or "should be"?

- People control their lives and their environments, and should reject the idea of fate.
- Change is inevitable and desirable.
- Equality and egalitarianism are social ideals.
- The individual is more important than the group.
- Self-help is preferable to dependence or interdependence.
- Competition and free enterprise are best for economic development.
- The future is more important than the past.
- Action is better than contemplation.
- Informality is desirable in social circumstances.
- Directness and openness are virtues.
- The practical is more important to deal with than the abstract, ideal, or intellectual.
- Improving material existence benefits human beings more than spiritual improvement.
- Problem solving is the best approach to dealing with reality.

Such ideas are often unquestioned by many of us socialized to the dominant culture in this country, but would be found unacceptable to someone socialized to another culture, for example, someone socialized in the Far East. The existence of such generally unquestioned truths is evidence that we do, indeed, have our own cultural lenses. As supervisors and therapists we need to be aware of and sensitive to our own cultural heritage because this self-of-the-therapist variable affects what we see, feel, think, and do clinically (Breunlin et al., 1992; Watson, 1993).

Self-Exploration Exercises

Do you feel comfortable asking someone else—especially without a well-established relationship—about his or her sexual orientation or feelings about race? In the past an African American therapist said in her supervision group, in a relaxed way, that she never thought about race and that it has not made a difference in her life. Her supervisor did not challenge that statement because it was comfortable not to do so. If you were her supervisor, would you have challenged that? When? Can you tell a member of a minority culture that she or he is too insensitive or, conversely, too sensitive?

Participants in our supervision workshops have shared the following exercises. They have found them helpful in sensitizing supervisors and therapists to their own cultural features, including assumptions, values, and biases.

- Think of the supervision of a therapist of the opposite gender, perhaps with a client of the same gender as the therapist. Make a list of any concerns you might have. Pick one concern. What do you imagine happening if you were to raise that concern? (Don't edit your internal voices. Be totally open to where your imagination might take you.)
- If any of the following were not your own contemporary subculture, think about the first time in your life when you met a gay/lesbian individual; an African American, Native American, Latino, or Asian individual; a lower or higher socioeconomic class individual; or an aged person. Consider the ramifications of how you experienced these individuals.
- If you are visually inclined, put together a collage to describe yourself. If this is too much physical effort, simply picture a collage that you would create and make a list of the pictures you would collect. The more details you provide about these personal images, the better. For example, if a flower were to be included, what kind of a flower? What color? What stage of bloom?
- Picture you and your colleagues on a winter retreat, away from your home. Give yourselves the following task. "We must decide what to do on December 25." What requests, concerns, and rationales emerge from the group?
- You have been abducted by aliens in a UFO. Backing away from their rectal probe, you promise to describe your "people" as completely as you can. Do that!

- Think of a time when you were having difficulty understanding the words or ideas of an international student, colleague, or professional. How did you respond cognitively, emotionally, verbally, and behaviorally?
- Describe yourself from a developmental/contextual standpoint. Draw a diagram of you and your immediate family as a system. Embed this system within a larger system that includes your extended families, schools, occupational organizations, churches, and whatever other systems you and your family transact with on an intimate basis. Place these diagrams within a larger concentric circle representing your community. Finally, place all of these within an even larger circle representing the national zeitgeist. Think of the developmental levels of all of the entities. Now, using this diagram and the multiplicity of mutual (if not equal) influences, describe yourself.
- Based on your influence diagrams, what situations might prove most troublesome for you?

We have emphasized that cultural competency begins with an awareness of one's own cultural heritage. From this we expect to obtain an increasing awareness of the cultural heritages of others and, in optimal situations, an appreciation of those other ways of being. Hardy and Laszloffy (1995) offer the *cultural genogram* as a training tool to promote both cultural awareness *and* sensitivity. This is an elaborate exercise expected to be done as a group. The developers offer questions to be asked in preparation for constructing the genogram and to be considered by the group as the participants' genograms are reviewed. Keiley and her family therapy students (2002) give a detailed description of the actual implementation of this tool within their graduate training program in marriage and family therapy and share the participants' experiences with it.

The cultural genogram itself was embedded in a larger curriculum in which ground rules for safety were negotiated, definitions of race, ethnicity, gender, sexual orientation, class, and culture were discussed, and participants' symbols representing their personal experience relative to these definitions were explored. Just as Hardy and Laszloffy (1995) suggested, the participants said that they gained "a first-hand experience of issues of gender and culture and how those issues cognitively and affectively influence the everyday lives of all people—including our client and ourselves . . . an opportunity to experience the intensity of actual cross-cultural interactions with our classmates in a nonclinical context" (Keiley et al., 2002, p. 177).

The cultural genogram is a tool for considering a wide range of cultural influences including gender. It can be adapted to dyadic training experiences, but the experience presumably would not be as rich. At the very least, Killian (2000, p. 190) asks supervisors and therapists to consider the following two exercises:

1. To what extent do you possess cultural knowledge of groups other than your own in terms of race, nationality, ethnicity, and sexual orientation? What groups

would you feel most and least competent to supervise and why?
2. To what extent are you familiar with current literature (journals, books, and conference proceedings in the last five years) on multicultural therapy and contextual issues in supervision?

If, after completing these inventories, the reader feels that more exposure to culturally relevant supervision and therapy are needed, she or he might consider participating in a cultural genogram experience concurrent with a good literature review.

There are other tools available for more limited consciousness raising. For example, the *Feminist Family Therapy Scale* (*FFTS,* Black & Piercy, 1991) and the *Feminist Family Therapist Behavior Checklist* (Chaney & Piercy, 1988) encourage supervisors and therapists to consider a feminist-informed perspective. The *Feminist Family Therapist Behavior Checklist* is very useful for raising training teams' consciousness of feminist issues in therapy and supervision, teaching feminist interventions, and recording the extent to which such skills are actually employed.

Cultural competency is a necessary aspect of integrative supervision. It is a core area that must be taught in our supervision classes and discussed daily in every context throughout our training systems. In the next chapters we discuss other practical issues in supervision, identify some consensual best practices, and offer some troubleshooting.

Chapter 10

Effective Practices
in Supervision

Participants' Views

As part of our integrative and systemic supervisory model, we believe it is important to process feedback from our trainees and their clinical families. In fact, we would hope that this process would become an integral element of your own supervisory model. In this chapter we review feedback collected from clients, trainees, and supervisors. These issues should inform training goals and methods for all of us.

What Clients Report They Have Valued in Their Therapy

We begin with clients' observations about their therapy. We know from the principle of isomorphism that what exists between therapists and their clients is likely to exist between the therapists and their supervisors. If a certain relational ambiance is expected to be valuable at the client–therapist level and we want to be sure it is created there, then it must also exist at the therapist–supervisor level. Isomorphism also suggests that, if it exists in these relationships, it also will characterize the relationship between the clients within their family relations and the relationship between you and your supervisory mentor.

Reimers' (2001) review of the literature indicated that some clients preferred a directive therapist while others preferred a more collaborative one. However, we believe that this issue of style is secondary to something more basic, namely, the therapeutic climate. Post-therapy debriefing by Quinn and his students (Quinn, 1996) revealed that three factors were experienced as crucial by clients:

1. The social relationship (shaped and maintained by the social skills of the therapists).
2. The therapists' ability to listen and also to provide of direction at times when it was needed.
3. A climate of discovery.

Laszloffy (2000) reported similar findings based on a sample of "extremely satisfied" and "extremely dissatisfied" clients. Those who considered themselves "very pleased" with their therapy experience described a positive social relationship with their therapists, wherein the therapists listened, the clients felt heard, and they felt empowered to successfully pursue clear, mutually agreed on therapeutic goals. In contrast, "dissatisfied" clients spoke of the lack of a positive relationship with therapists who did not accept the presenting problems as the clients experienced them, did not seem to care what the clients felt or thought, lectured the clients, and responded in critical and judgmental ways. The lack of shared goals and a relationship sufficient to support work on them were exemplified in a common complaint: "We weren't going anywhere."

If our trainees are to be able to construct such a therapeutic climate, we should create a similar climate in supervision. In our training roles, we are often modeling what a therapeutic agent looks and feels like. Through this experience we are creating a relationship climate that isomorphically will be re-created throughout the training system. Therefore, our trainees will be able to share and model the benefits of this climate in their clinical work.

As supervisors we should make our therapists feel both supported and heard. We should make our supervision a safe setting in which we carefully and sensitively explore the concerns of our therapists as they themselves experience them. Where appropriate, we should promote new skills and behaviors that actively help them successfully challenge their problems. We should carefully monitor how much we do that is didactic and be careful that it is relevant to the therapists' concerns and ways of conceptualizing things. Supervisory goals must be clear and mutually agreed on. We must find ways to be assertive and to offer criticism that is not aggressive and is clearly in support of the mutual supervisory goals. Finally, because parallel processes are expected to occur at all levels of the training system, relationships between supervisory mentors and Approved Supervisor Candidates also should incorporate these guidelines.

What Therapists Reported They Have Valued in Their Supervision

It is interesting to observe how closely therapists' descriptions of their best supervisory experiences match clients' descriptions of positive therapy. A national survey (Anderson, Rigazio-DiGilio, Schlossberg, & Meredith, 2000; Anderson, Schlossberg, & Rigazio-DiGilio, 2000) asked therapists about their best and worst supervisory experiences. The good memories involved four dimensions of supervisor behavior:

1. A sense of openness in the supervisory environment (supervisors who welcomed mistakes, were open to feedback, and explored new ideas).
2. A focus on strengths while communicating respect, encouragement, and support.
3. Encouragement of personal growth issues and a willingness to confront blind spots and resistances.
4. Conceptual and technical guidance and direction (e.g., supervisors providing useful conceptual frameworks for understanding clients, and teaching practical skills).

In contrast to such empowering supervision, therapists also described closed, rigid, and critical supervisors who were not open to divergent viewpoints, adhered to traditional gender role stereotypes, and who focused on their mistakes. Other exemplars of worst supervisory experiences involved behaviors we would consider socially gauche, namely, vulgar language, inappropriate sexual behavior, and pushing therapists to disclose more personal information than the therapist was comfortable providing.

Some investigators have asked therapists to maintain diaries based on their training experiences in the hope of getting a broader look at what constitutes a positive training environment. For example, one of us (Lee, Eppler, Kendal, & Latty, 2001) asked a cohort of first-year family therapy students to keep diaries during their entry into clinical practice. Their daily entries were intended to describe thoughts and feelings with regard to events that, for them, captured something important in terms of their professional development. They later reflected on what they wrote, individually and as a group, and decided that the preeminent source of gratification and aggravation in their daily lives was their multiplicity of roles. They performed concurrent roles as therapists, students, graduate assistants, and employees of various types (receptionist, administrator, clerical worker, nurse, etc.). In addition, they had responsibilities as parents, spouses, lovers, friends, colleagues, and children. They reported that the demands of all of these roles were a constant source of stress.

However, the trainees wanted their supervisors to appreciate that these disparate roles could be uplifting as well as depleting. They reported that these relationships promoted feelings of belongingness, confidence, self-worth, and enthusiasm. The outcome depended, they said, on whether their supervisors and significant others appreciated the complexity of the trainees' lives and the demands of their education and training experiences. When the significant people in their lives forgot how complex the therapists' lives were and the importance of things relative to the needs and wants of *all* the participants in the therapist's lives, they produced or exacerbated loyalty conflicts and abetted feelings of isolation, self-doubt, and failure.

What Supervisors Reported as the Most Important Aspects of Supervision

White and Russell (1995) collected data from a national sample of AAMFT Approved Supervisors describing their thoughts about effective family therapy supervision. Because these supervisors were systemically oriented, they commonly agreed that positive supervisory outcomes must be considered a joint product of the "person" of the supervisor and the therapist, their relationship, their work together, and the setting in which the supervision takes place. They reported that in their data 61 supervisors generated a list of 771 variables important to supervisory outcomes. The variables could be collapsed into the following beliefs regarding the best supervisory outcomes:

1. Interactions with therapists are characterized by clear expectations with regard to procedures, methods, and performance evaluation.
2. There is a solid working alliance.
3. A balance of attention is paid to details of case management, theory and skills development, and the self of the therapist.

From this review, it appears that clients, therapists, and experienced supervisors are remarkably consistent about the ingredients of the best training and treatment experiences. All participants in the training system are likely to feel most gratified by a process of enthusiastic discovery that is facilitated by positive personal relationships wherein therapists, supervisors, and supervisory mentors listen in such a way that the other parties feel heard, and wherein they feel empowered by the relationship, the climate, and the skills and behaviors taught to successfully pursue clear, mutually agreed on goals.

Feedback-Centered Supervision—Open Ended

We want to continue our emphasis on eliciting and hearing the voices of your trainees and their clients. However, beyond this research process, it will be helpful, as a beginning supervisor, to develop your own methods for eliciting and processing feedback from the training system. There are several helpful approaches. For example, you can have clients respond to paper-and-pencil surveys (Lee, Emerson, & Kochka, 1999). You can consult with clients before, during, or after a session, or at some point in the course of therapy (Dwyer, 1999). Some training programs use these techniques continuously to inform a feedback-centered orientation to therapy and supervision. Others use these tools to solve problems and as an interesting change of pace (Quinn, Nagirreddy, Lawless, & Bagley, 2000). These techniques have in common a basic respect for the voices of others and using these voices to keep supervision relevant to the concerns of the therapists and their client families while modeling a sense of openness and fair play (Schwartz & Baer, 1991).

There are different methods of having clients consult in their own therapy. One can use an open-ended approach, and let clients and therapists report their own observations (see Bischoff, McKeel, Moon, & Sprenkle, 1996; Quinn, 1996; Sells, Smith, & Moon, 1996). In contrast, one might wish to be more directive and ask the therapists to assess matters that you, or major theorists, consider important to their therapy or to supervision (Lee at al., 1999).

Whatever the techniques and processes employed, feedback-centered supervision values, and sometimes privileges, the opinions of clients about their experiences in therapy. Rather than supervisors and therapists being viewed as the origin of clinical observation, insight, and therapy agenda, the clients' self-expressed needs and priorities, problems and frustrations (revealed through feedback mechanisms) provide the context for and the goals of the supervision process. This approach can be a useful adjunct to supervision when supervisors and therapists have different theories, prefer different interventions, or envision different outcomes for the client (Quinn et al., 2000). It can also be useful when supervisors want to move away from a more authority-oriented supervision to a more collaborative approach.

For example, in a worst-case scenario, picture yourself becoming engaged in what appears to be an adversarial process with a therapist. Seeking client feedback to provide direction for the therapeutic work is one way to move on while you work on the supervisory issues and alliance. In so doing, you will be able to maintain the therapist's active cooperation in the process of supervision and the implementation of more effective interventions.

> When the supervisor and the supervisee have the benefit of feedback from clients about their priorities, needs, reactions and interpretations, the supervision process can become focused on the clients' concerns. The supervisee's learning goals and the supervisor's instructional goals now can be in the service of explicit goals for the client, thus rendering the supervision process responsive to the clients' needs. When the therapist's developmental goals emerge in the context of the stated needs of his/her clients, learning can be more exciting." (Quinn et al., 2000, p. 98)

Gaining Feedback About the Therapy Process

We recommend that therapists simply ask families, as a routine matter of course, "How do you believe things are going? What progress do you feel we have made?" However, believing that clients may talk more openly to someone who is not their therapist, special interviews for this purpose may be scheduled intermittently, or at set points in the course of therapy, in which the clients are interviewed by a third party. We have found that this is best done by someone other than the supervisor. When a supervisor does the interviewing, we have had clients interpret these sessions as evaluations of their therapists. Out of loyalty they declared themselves utterly satisfied with their therapy while being hostile toward the supervisor!

For example, the clients can be asked, "Can you share your thoughts and feelings about your therapy session so that your therapist can better understand what has been accomplished and what needs to be accomplished?" In less structured versions of this open-ended approach, the interviewer can take notes to share with the training system. A less haphazard approach would involve the videotaping of the interview so that supervisors and therapists have an opportunity to review and reflect on the entire verbal and nonverbal data reported by the family.

A more structured form of this kind of interview is described by Quinn and his associates (2000). These interviews were completed by neutral third parties and videotaped. Subsequently these tapes were reviewed in supervision. The therapists controlled the playback and paused the tape whenever they had a need to express thoughts and feelings. The supervisor's role was to facilitate the therapists' processing—help them articulate their thoughts and feelings—of the clients' feedback.

Quinn and his associates also have developed the Interpersonal Recall Interview (Quinn & Nagirreddy, 1999). Here, the clients review a videotape of one of their therapy sessions. The sessions selected typically are ones in which there is some obstruction of a constructive flow. In this case the clients control the playback and pause wherever they would like to express thoughts and feelings. These sessions—the clients reviewing the videotape of their therapy session—also are videotaped so that the therapists can benefit from the clients' review process.

Dwyer (1999) suggested that all parties could benefit when supervisors provide live consultation during the therapy sessions themselves. This requires a compatible training system atmosphere. The participants need to be open to procedural flexibility, there has to be mutual respect and mutuality of goals, and all parties have to be able to work together. When this atmosphere exists, supervisors can enter therapy sessions, typically at midpoint, to interview the clients and therapists: "How is this session going? What things are you experiencing as helpful? What do you think it might be helpful to talk about?" The interview may focus more broadly on the course of therapy: "What are your impressions of therapy so far? What has been most helpful? What has your therapist said or done that has been most helpful? How could therapy be changed in some way to better meet your needs? If you could change one thing about therapy to better meet your needs, what would it be?"

A supervisor also could interview the therapist in front of the family: "What are some of the things you have been particularly impressed with about this client? What do you find enjoyable (or challenging) about working with this client?" And, if there is a good therapeutic alliance, the interview might continue: "What thoughts or images do you have when you are preparing for a session with this client?"

As one can see, the interviewing of clients and their therapists offers the training system a review of current and longer-term training goals in the context of therapeutic goals. "Is there something you'd like your therapist to do more of? What would you experience as helpful?"

We have found that therapists and clients initially feel anxious about such interviews. Moreover, we recognize that some clients and some therapists are more flexible, curious, experimental, and "playful" than others. However, almost all participants have said in retrospect that this consultation was a gratifying experience. Clients described the process as keeping things "relevant" and "moving along." Therapists saw it as a method for handling impasses. Supervisors have described it as a way of demonstrating the safety of the training setting with regard to openness to feedback and "doing things differently." Supervisors and therapists also have reported that live consultation provided an opportunity to model vulnerability, openness, welcoming disagreement as a source of information, and collaboration. Other therapists in supervision who were privy to these interchanges because they viewed them from behind a mirror or on tape have said that they learned to be less anxious. Therapeutic alliances might become more robust, clients less critical, and therapy and supervision more creative than these anxious trainees had thought.

Gaining Feedback About the Supervision

Some time ago, a creative and useful manuscript arrived for review (Keiley & Piercy, 1999). It came at a time when many of us were trying to think of better ways to evaluate therapists' progress in supervision and were convinced that any such method should be collaborative. This manuscript did not offer an assessment device but rather an interview process wherein the teachers consulted their prospective graduates at the conclusion of their program of study. We realized that this interview format could be adapted to therapists and their supervisors at the end of their training together—or even be used as a marker to be completed periodically in the course of supervision.

Extrapolating from Keiley and Piercy, we explored the process whereby supervisors could ask therapists to carefully and systematically think about what they initially brought to the supervision, what they had learned, how they had or had not changed, and what aspects of the training experience were of the most value. The benefits of such a procedure were obvious. The therapists could take the time to reflect profoundly on their experiences and to consolidate their knowledge. The supervisors and their trainees would benefit from their experience and feedback. By being asked to be our consultants and being respectfully heard, therapists would find the power inequities reduced and they would feel an increase in their professional identities. We would all learn which knowledge, competencies, training experiences, and pedagogic processes were useful for them and which ones were not. We suspected that the consultation process might be most meaningful if prospective questions were considered in private by the therapists and their observations committed to paper. Subsequently these notes might inform the interview session(s). Extrapolating from Keiley and Piercy, some questions that might be useful to this process would be:

• What were your most meaningful learning experiences? How were you able to integrate this new learning into a theory and practice of family therapy consistent with your own resources and previous knowledge? What experiences got in the way of this process?
• What personal and relationship qualities did you bring with you or discover here that were important in achieving your goals?
• How would you describe your approach to therapy? How did you arrive at this formulation? What resources did you find here that helped in this process? What was less helpful? What has become more apparent to you about yourself as a therapist and your preferred way of being in the therapeutic context?
• When you think of the ideas, information, and skills you've learned here, which do you think will be most important to you in the future? How will you keep these ideas, information, and skills alive once you leave here? Which ideas and skills did you find less useful to you and you might leave behind?

Feedback-Centered Supervision—Theory Directed

Open-ended questions are designed to elicit the variety and richness of human experiences (Newfield et al., 1996). When these are used to influence therapy and supervision, they can empower clients relative to therapists, supervisors, and even major family therapy theorists. Clients can provide their personal constructions of their therapeutic realities, and specify what they think may be important as they construct these for the resolution of their concerns. We can also ask clients to provide feedback about the status of therapeutic variables held to be important by acknowledged experts in family therapy.

For example, clients' outcome optimism, perceived progress, and resourcefulness are thought to be associated with positive outcomes in family therapy (Dumka, Martin, & Sprenkle, 1995). Based on this, we could ask clients to tell us about the relative presence of these attitudes and what can be done to enhance them. In addition, major family therapy theorists and process-outcome researchers have specified interventions that are expected to be therapeutic relative to a specific family therapy theory. Here, supervisors and therapists would find the Michigan State University Family Therapy Questionnaire (MSU/FTQ; Lee et al., 1999) useful in asking clients about these interventions (see the appendix to this chapter).

The MSU/FTQ is a relatively exhaustive list of 74 family therapy interventions translated into everyday language for clients. It asks clients what interventions they remember having occurred in their therapy and to estimate each intervention's importance to them. In training, the MSU/FTQ is meant to assess the extent to which accepted family therapy practice is occurring. Moreover, when clients indicate that certain therapeutic techniques are important to them, we as supervisors and therapists need to take note. The MSU/FTQ is also a mechanism for recursivity that can be used throughout a course of supervision, with one or multiple clients. In contrast to other surveys of clients' experiences which assess the more "macro" process of therapy (i.e., relationship factors, climate of discovery, and appropriate agency), the MSU/FTQ deals specifically with family therapy "micro" process interventions.

What Is Needed for Effective Feedback-Centered Supervision

Experience has taught us that seeking feedback to inform our supervision should not come as a surprise to either our therapists or their clients. It should be something that we have all thought about and for which we have planned as an important component of our training programs and our philosophies of supervision. It should be seen as a collaborative endeavor that is expected to advance both therapeutic work and the training experience. Trust suffers when clients are not asked for feedback in a well-considered and collaborative way. Therapy and supervision risk being experienced as capricious and the training system may not feel safe. However, when all participants to the training system step back from the therapeutic work to mutually discuss and evaluate its process, this process clearly promotes trust building. The process of talking about therapy with the clients "underscores the humanity of all participants and validates the risk that everyone takes in therapy" (Dwyer, 1999, p. 143).

What is required for feedback-centered supervision to be effective is for the relationship between the supervisor, therapist, and client to be open and supportive. Supervisors, therapists, and clients must understand that "they will work, share ideas, solve problems, and negotiate change together" (Dwyer, 1999, p. 134). In addition, all participants in the training system must view the others as ethical and be aware of the larger context and system in which the therapeutic work is occurring. All parties also must be respectful of each other, and supervisors and therapists must be open to multiple realities, including differing therapeutic philosophies, values, and beliefs.

In the next chapter we focus explicitly and practically on troubleshooting specific and common dilemmas with which all experienced supervisors have had to work.

The Michigan State University Family Therapy Questionnaire

MSU/FTQ   Family Therapy Questionnaire*

Please provide the following information about yourself: ( ) Female   ( ) Male   — Age

Problem for which your family entered therapy: ( ) Marital Issues   ( ) Parent–child Issues   ( ) Other (brief description): _____

Please help us learn more about (your) family therapy. The following are things therapists sometimes do in family therapy.

Please go through the list and indicate (X) if you remember that your therapist did this. (If you don't remember, leave the item blank.)

For each action you remember, mark the portion of the line showing its importance to YOU.

Did
This: Importance:
X   None   Great

—   — — — — — —   1. Was both caring and firm.
—   — — — — — —   2. Encouraged humor.
—   — — — — — —   3. Used stories and examples to make a point.
—   — — — — — —   4. Respected silence.
—   — — — — — —   5. Kept his/her personal problems to self.
—   — — — — — —   6. Really knew how to listen.
—   — — — — — —   7. Stayed calm in emotional situations.
—   — — — — — —   8. Appreciated how each of us is different and special, and accepted us as we are.
—   — — — — — —   9. Helped us know and talk about our feelings and ideas no matter how uncomfortable.
—   — — — — — —   10. Identified and reinforced good things about the fanmilv and family members.
—   — — — — — —   11. Helped us to rethink our thinking.
—   — — — — — —   12. Helped us define the problem clearly.
—   — — — — — —   13. Asked each person to share his/her view of the problem.
—   — — — — — —   14. Asked what led up to the problem.
—   — — — — — —   15. Asked who had already tried to solve the problem and what he/she had done.
—   — — — — — —   16. Asked about ways we handled other problems.
—   — — — — — —   17. Helped us to understand how the problem was a normal thing and gave us hope it could be solved.
—   — — — — — —   18. Showed us how our problems might actually do good things for us.
—   — — — — — —   19. Showed us how everyone's behavior was connected to the problem.
—   — — — — — —   20. Helped us figure out what we could change, and which changes were most important.
—   — — — — — —   21. Helped us figure out specific things to do to make things better.
—   — — — — — —   22. Insisted parents be parents and children be children.
—   — — — — — —   23. Helped us be a more effective family.
—   — — — — — —   24. Helped each of us to sort out our rights and responsibilities.
—   — — — — — —   25. Stopped the shifting of blame to others, and made change the responsibility of every family member.
—   — — — — — —   26. Predicted reactions to change.

— —————— 27. Gave each person credit for his/her efforts for positive change.
— —————— 28. Helped us get together or apart (whichever was needed).
— —————— 29. Told us something concrete we could do to mark the end of something bad, and make a fresh start.
— —————— 30. Helped us face and handle important issues.
— —————— 31. Spoke in a way that matched our moods and experience.
— —————— 32. Checked that we were each understanding what was being said.
— —————— 33. Explored how we treated each other during therapy and at home.
— —————— 34. Helped us determine what is typical about us.
— —————— 35. Interrupted interactions (harmfuul or otherwise) and explained why.
— —————— 36. Separated what we said to each other from what we actually did.
— —————— 37. Explained behaviors differently from how we had understood them.
— —————— 38. Suggested better ways for us to relate to each other.
— —————— 39. Helped family members speak only for themselves.
— —————— 40. Discussed ways in which we might be loyal to our parents and other members of the family in which we grew up.
— —————— 41. Helped us learn to be more fair toward each other.
— —————— 42. Helped us to learn from our disagreements.
— —————— 43. Taught us to "fight fair."
— —————— 44. Encouraged discussion of family secrets.
— —————— 45. Focused therapy on our lives here and now.
— —————— 46. Helped us play together.
— —————— 47. Helped us with our sex life.
— —————— 46. Helped us be more affectionate.
— —————— 49. Worked with family members individually and together.
— —————— 50. Involved in therapy other family members and/or other persons connected to the problem.
— —————— 51. Insisted family members treat each other with respect.
— —————— 52. Discussed each member's background including experiences of growing up.
— —————— 53. Drew a diagram showing three generations of our family.
— —————— 54. Asked about family beliefs, rules, and customs.
— —————— 55. Discussed future plans of individuals and family.
— —————— 56. Asked which family members stick up for each other/join together/ are allies, and which do not.
— —————— 57. Described how what we learn as children connects to our problem.
— —————— 58. Helped us separate our present problems from things that happened in the past.
— —————— 59. Taught as things to do when we have a problem we need to solve.
— —————— 60. Used demonstrations, limit-setting, and teaching to keep sessions safe, under control, and focused on therapy.
— —————— 61. Didn't take sides.
— —————— 62. Took sides with one of us when it was needed.
— —————— 63. Gave us special things to do during therapy sessions.
— —————— 64. Had us set out real and imaginary situations during therapy sessions.
— —————— 65. Made homework an important part of our therapy.
— —————— 66. Kept us on track from week to week.
— —————— 67. Discussed our progress and asked our opinions about how therapy was going.
— —————— 68. Prepared us for the time therapy would end.
— —————— 69. Was professional, honest, trustworthy, and reliable.

— —————— 70. Worked wish other professionals, as appropriate, to help our family.
— —————— 71. Opened and closed sessions well.
— —————— 72. Helped us understand the normal growth stages of families.
— —————— 73. Asked about things we hadn't thought of.
— —————— 74. Assigned homework to help us develop healthier interactions with
the families we grew up in.

75. Please finish the following two sentences:

a.) Our therapist helped most by . . .

b.) It would have been helpful if our therapist had . . .

Chapter 11

Managing Issues That Interfere with the Supervisory Process

I n this chapter we focus on certain issues and dilemmas that can disrupt a constructive process in the intergenerational training system. These issues involve the relationships existing between supervisors, therapists, and clients. In previous chapters we focused primarily on learning positive, constructive, and supportive skills in becoming a supervisor. Here we focus largely on problems that may occur in the training system interactions and relationships, and we discuss methods to resolve them in a constructive fashion.

Recognizing Glitches in Supervisory Relationships

The relationship goals of supervisors are the same as the goals for therapists. As supervisors we want to be able to:

- Think and intervene systemically, while remembering that the system contains individuals.
- Stay in the room with a client (therapist and/or family unit) physically, emotionally, and intellectually.
- Attend adequately to the structure and dynamics of the training system (and subsystems).
- Adequately access client problems and resources.
- Plan and implement intervention plans consistent with training system resources and goals.
- Continue to assess and flexibly change strategies as needed.

Recognizing and Dealing with a Trainee's Baggage

It is important to recognize that problems, conflicts, impasses, and other glitches will occur during the course of a normal supervisory relationship. Sometimes these impasses may even may be signs of impending positive growth. However, when they are not, common sense suggests that we first look for deficits and idiosyncrasies in relationship skills and attempt to resolve those if present. However, sometimes impediments to the supervisory process come from major relationship boundary dynamics. We recognize that occasionally the supervisory relationship may become distorted by internal unresolved needs and even preconscious or unconscious distortions in the history of either the trainee or the supervisor. We have observed that some trainees bring a certain, and often unrecognized, emotional baggage to their training process. These issues may range from immaturity and lack of differentiation from their families of origin to specific forms of psychopathology. Many young trainees are often looking for a comforting and safe relationship with their supervisor. This often represents a need for emotional dependency. In contrast, another trainee might be hypervigilant for signs of danger in the relationship. Both of these examples suggest how this baggage can disrupt the supervisory alliance and process.

> A young therapist who was geographically but not psychologically emancipated from an abusive stepfather became highly reactive and combative in his first session of group supervision with a middle-aged male supervisor. The therapist had been reserved, and then replied to a question in a hesitant tone. Wanting to work on the alliance from the start, the supervisor said, "You seem a little uncomfortable. Tell me about that." The therapist erupted in a diatribe centered on the fact that he knew the supervisor to be overly critical and punitive. Because they had no previous history, the supervisor decided he would identify the distortion. "What evidence do you have for that?" The therapist became even angrier and abruptly left the room. Given the expectations this therapist carried into supervision with him, he was vigilant for maltreatment from the outset. He expected to be criticized and belittled. The therapist subsequently transferred to a female supervisor who was pulling into a collusive relationship with him. This triangle reinforced the distortion and impeded personal and professional growth. He later dropped out of training.

How long *should it take* in a new relationship to *really care about* what the other person is thinking and feeling about you? William C. Nichols (personal communication) once opined that 10 sessions plus or minus two, would be normative for therapists and clients (and supervisors and therapists). At that point one could expect the availability of more personal dynamics from most trainees reflecting their relative anxieties, fears, or sense of vulnerability.

It is important for supervisors to be careful about pathologizing issues raised in working with trainees. However, there will be times when it becomes clear that a trainee is experiencing you in an unrealistically negative way or is inappropriately idealizing you. This is similar to times when clients experience their therapists in unrealistic ways. Supervisors and therapists must be aware of these dynamics and act in ways appropriate to the others' psychosocial growth.

Negative circumstances perhaps capture our attention most. In contrast, idealization by our therapists often makes the training relationship easier: It feels good, it facilitates role modeling, and it may support therapeutic courage. But that idealization can get in the way of self-sufficiency. When trainees model themselves too closely after their supervisor, boundaries can be blurred and constructive learning can be blocked. By copying their supervisors, trainees avoid the anxiety of making their own clinical decisions. Trainees may become hypersensitive to your concerns and focus on seeking (and expecting) your approval. These trainees may attempt to hide what they feel are mistakes. In so doing, they may begin to view you as a punitive parent. If you respond negatively, this displacement from their families of origin will have been made real in the training relationship. Whatever the inappropriate relationship dynamics, it is the supervisor's responsibility to recognize these distortions, appreciate how they are problematic to the supervisory (and/or therapeutic) work, and help the therapists accept them as problems and resolve them.

Contextualizing Glitches with Trainees

An important question to be asked, both of the supervisor and the trainee, is the following: How does who you are, including how you have constructed your life experiences (and what lessons you have taken from these constructions), affect your current experience of others? This issue of "who we are" as individuals involves four knowledge bases in simultaneous operation at all levels of the training system. These four knowledge bases (outlined in Figure 11.1) belong to the supervisor, the therapist, and the client:

1. Life experiences (family of origin, extended family, other social systems).
2. Developmental stages (family and marital life cycles, individual developmental stage).
3. Education (substantive knowledge base, theoretical underpinnings).
4. Training (skills and techniques).

Case Example

Here is an interesting case that will help illustrate these four factors. Let's begin with the climax, an ugly and destructive symmetrical escalation.

> A young doctoral marital and family therapist is called into the office of his supervisor at a large Veterans Administration medical hospital and, as he hears it, is condescendingly being told how to treat a case. He protests

Supervisor	Therapist	Client Life
	Experiences	
	Family of Origin	
	Extended Family	
	Other Social Systems	
	Culture and Subcultures	
	Developmental Stages	
	Family Life Cycle	
	Marital Life Cycle	
	Individual Developmental Stage	
	Education	
	Substantive Knowledge Base	
	Theoretical Underpinnings	
	Training	
	Skills and Techniques	

FIGURE 11.1. Four Knowledge Bases Operating Simultaneously in the Training System

the authoritarian tone of his supervisor and issues escalate. The supervisor, face flushed, states, "You'll do as I say! You're acting like a two year old!" The therapist responds, "You're utterly inappropriate and I'm leaving!" The supervisor blocks the door and angrily orders the therapist to sit down. The therapist, momentarily unable to escape the situation and overwhelmed by negative emotion, tells the supervisor to perform a vulgar and impossible act. Subsequently, the supervisor filed a formal reprimand. The higher powers in the hospital did not respect the supervisor and tacitly affirmed the therapist. From then on, the supervisor and therapist dealt with each other in only the most perfunctory way.

This is a good systemic example of supervision gone badly. To better appreciate it, we will evaluate it from the view of the four knowledge bases. The therapist was the only son of a middle-class family. He was a WASP. He had taken his doctorate at an extraordinarily young age from an elite program and was ambivalent about the speed with which he went through the program. He joked that his mother had said, "Anything you get that fast can't be worth much!" This was his first job. He got it right after he completed a postdoctoral program in which he resented having had to take additional classes and do a term project.

The supervisor was a middle-aged Jewish psychologist. He felt very unfulfilled, unappreciated, and underpaid working in a medical hospital where the "real doctors"—be they interns, residents, or attending—were privileged above everyone else. He had an unhappy family life. His only son had just dropped out of an elite university to "find himself," and was supported in this by his mother who, with her son, demonstrated little respect for her husband.

The time was circa 1970, when young adults had raised their voices in protest against the Vietnam War and traditional institutions and their ways: "Hell no, we won't go!" "Make love, not war." The young therapist experienced himself as a conservative but "with it" member of the "new generation," and his supervisor as a dinosaur. He secretly pitied the man. The supervisor was alarmed by the disrespect, civil disobedience, and self-indulgent licentiousness of the cohort of young people. Moreover, having grown up in the Depression Era, he felt grateful to have a secure job and was frightened to leave it to try to make more money in independent practice.

Developmentally, the therapist was just emerging into truly emancipated adult life, having left his training programs "forever." He had said goodbye to his therapist of many years, married a physician, and now, with the title of "doctor," was successful in a professional role. The supervisor was in midlife crisis, exacerbated by the nature of his occupational role, his wife's dissatisfaction, and her and his adolescent son's defiance and disrespect.

Educationally, the therapist was the graduate of an elite academic program and an equally elite postdoctoral placement. He felt he had cutting-edge knowledge in object relation, on the one hand, and systems theory on the other. The supervisor had graduated from the state college, and had not pursued much lifelong education. Currently he was atheoretical, but was alienated by psychodynamic thinkers because of what he described as their rigid orthodoxy and self-righteous and dismissive arrogance. In terms of applications, the therapist had been going out on the medical wards and developing collaborative approaches. The supervisor had increasingly been doing psychological assessments of individuals referred to the department.

Our hope in telling you this story is that, as you consider these two individuals in terms of the four knowledge bases, you will sense as we do that the crisis was unavoidable. In the absence of a therapeutic third party with substantial leverage over both of them, how could it have been otherwise? You will also appreciate the lack of administrative structures, which allowed this to go so far so quickly and to stay unrepaired. You can also appreciate how the collusion of higher authorities exacerbated matters. As it turned out, about a year later the therapist left the hospital for full-time private practice. To us the real tragedy is that this occurred without either party, or the training system, having made any professional growth as a result of that experience.

Developing Supervisory Remedies

The issues in our example were fairly blatant, but the red flags that suggest the presence of conscious or unconscious expectations from a therapist's present or past life are typically more subtle and elusive. The most obvious red flag is when an individual has overresponded to a simple remark or critique. The less obvious dynamics occur when individuals underreact or are insensitive to events. Some therapists may be indifferent or calm when others would not be. They might not see or hear the obvious. Some therapists may seem immobilized by apparent confusion or anxiety.

As a supervisor, one hopes that there is enough observable evidence to help the therapist begin to see what is happening and for you to be able to make your case. However, sometimes you must patiently wait until you have enough data to get the attention of the healthiest part of the individual. For example, if a therapist shows up late for a session, it might not be prudent to suggest that the therapist is "avoiding something!" That interpretation could be too easily dismissed: "No, I got held up in traffic." You might be more persuasive if you said to that therapist, "You came late today, you keep looking at the clock, you forgot to cue up your videotape, and you keep changing the subject to tonight's basketball game. I wonder if there's something you are preoccupied about?"

We have identified three significant dilemmas and tasks for the supervisor in dealing effectively with these situations:

1. How do we as supervisors confront these underlying issues with a therapist in a supportive yet firm manner so that they can be processed within the safety of the supervisory alliance and not simply make the therapist defensive?
2. How can we accomplish some healing of these issues without crossing the line into a specifically therapeutic role with the therapist?
3. When is it appropriate to refer a therapist with such limitations to adjunctive therapy?

Reality Testing with Trainees

In supervision, as in therapy, we believe that the most effective and earliest intervention needs to be the simplest and most straightforward. This is often simply a matter of *reality testing*. For example, as a supervisor you may believe that you have evidence for an underlying distortion in your trainee's view of your role. You say to the trainee, "You seem to be furious. You are using 100 pounds of dynamite where 10 pounds might be more appropriate. You often seem to believe that I am being critical of you when I am simply raising questions with you. Can we talk about this?"

Having identified the distortion, and perhaps observed ways in which it will inhibit the therapeutic or supervisory work, the next step will be to consider its validity with the therapist.

- What evidence do you have for that?
- What keeps you from being able to make up your mind?
- What do you imagine happening if you were to do that?
- The other party maybe hesitant to accept your invitation to talk. What do you imagine happening if you were to talk about that?

The Boundaries Between Supervision and Therapy

With these issues of baggage and distortions that we have illustrated, you may be wondering where supervision crosses the line into therapy. Obviously many of our examples would warrant the need for therapeutic interventions for some of these trainees.

Supervisors differ in their opinions about where that boundary between teaching and therapy lies. It is our belief that supervisors have an obligation to help therapists recognize impediments to their therapeutic work. However, as supervisors we have boundaries which determine how far we can proceed in helping therapists recognize and process their own clinical issues. We need to be able to clearly mark those boundaries in our mind and define them for the trainee. We should be reticent to go further in our supervision than negotiating a plan that we can reasonably expect to remedy a dysfunctional dynamic's influence on clinical work. The following examples may help you think about what separates supervision from therapy.

- **Supervision:** You appear to be confusing me with someone else, perhaps someone in your family of origin.
  Therapy: Let's think about whom you are confusing me with. Is this someone you grew up with? Tell me about that person.

- **Supervision:** I am concerned that your tardiness to groups and appointments is getting in the way of your progress here.
  Therapy: Your tardiness makes me wonder if you are carrying a lot of anger around. Let's see if we can figure where that is coming from.

- **Supervision:** I have noticed that you often seem down and depressive. Do you think your mood is getting in the way of your work with clients?
  Therapy: We need to understand more about your depressive symptoms. Perhaps we need to discuss the possibility of having you evaluated for medication.

- **Supervision:** In what way do you think that accepting your client's invitation to attend her bridal shower will influence your therapy with her?
  Therapy: You seem to be reticent to say "no" to your client. Where do you think that comes from?

- **Supervision:** You said you know exactly how your client feels. Do you think that might be keeping you from understanding your client's unique experience of that situation?
  Therapy: It sounds like you've been there yourself. Tell me about that.

The Role of Adjunctive Personal Therapy in the Supervisory Process

Is personal therapy for trainees an important part of family therapy training? We believe that supervisors must be prepared to take the role of identifying a trainee's need for personal therapy and also to take the next step of making a specific referral. This is important to help a trainee resolve personal issues that get in the way of learning and practice (Reiss, 1960). It also helps trainees gain personal insights into treatment dynamics and empathy for their clients. This issue of the role of personal therapy has been hotly debated in the family therapy field for decades. Nichols (1968) and Everett (1979) have both made a strong case for what they have called the "coordinated but separate" use of psychotherapy and supervision. However, the issue remains controversial.

The early models of clinical training in all of the mental health disciplines were influenced heavily by psychoanalysis, with the embedded assumption that personal therapy was an important part of all therapists' training. This analytic view saw the therapy process as a specific ingredient of the training itself for all trainees, and not just to deal with a trainee's personal baggage when necessary. However, as the family therapy field evolved, the value of personal therapy became something of a political question. Some leaders saw the inclusion of personal therapy in training experiences as a manifestation of the old, and often ill-reputed, medical model from which many of the pioneering family therapists wanted to distance themselves. However, subsequent generations of family therapists do not seem to hold those strong views.

Another aspect of this debate has been to whom a trainee should be referred. If personal psychotherapy is indicated for a family therapy trainee, should it be provided only by another experienced family therapist or could it be offered by a clinician socialized in another field (e.g., psychiatry or social work)? Should the therapy be by someone who practices therapy from a theoretical orientation other than that of the training program or supervisor?

Despite these early and ongoing controversies, most experienced family therapy supervisors have believed that some form of adjunctive therapy is an important part of the training process (Everett, 1980a; Lee et al., in press; Nichols et al., 1990). Some supervisors do not differentiate between the two roles (see Chapter 6). However, we believe strongly that there are important boundary issues involved for the supervisor and the trainee. It has been our role as both family therapy program directors and supervisors to make sure that we have identified several supportive, effective, and affordable community therapists to whom we can refer our trainees. These community therapists, whether or not they were trained in family therapy models, should be well-experienced, clearly credentialed in their own fields, supportive of you as a supervisor and your role in a training program, and clearly separate and independent of any ties and loyalties (including contract teaching and consulting roles) with your program. The development of such resources is your professional responsibility to your trainees (Everett, 1980b).

We believe openness and flexibility are the best approaches to recommendations regarding what types and amounts of therapy are the most appropriate for family therapy trainees. Supervisors' opinions have ranged from a minimum of requiring students to develop and consider the ramification of their own family of origin genograms to asking students to participate routinely—whether or not it is indicated by symptomatic problems—in ongoing individual therapy, therapy groups, or family of origin therapy. Our belief is that there is no right form of therapy for family therapy trainees. However, when we select these referral resources for our trainees we want them to be competent clinicians *and* respectful of our family therapy roles and training programs. The goals are to facilitate the therapists' ongoing learning progress and training experience, and to get them unstuck when personal baggage and issues get in their way. Of course, certain special needs will also dictate the referral. Psychiatric symptoms may require psychiatric evaluation, ongoing management, and the introduction of medication. Substance abuse issues or addictions may require referral to a specialist in this field. On the other hand, if trainees simply need to differentiate personal and professional issues from roles in their families of origin, they should be referred to experienced family therapists.

The supervisor's ability to recognize, process, and intervene when serious issues of a trainee's emotional baggage impede his or her learning and clinical work is a critical role to success and effectiveness. It also represents a matter of a supervisor learning to develop and operationalize clear personal and professional boundaries. We hope the discussion of the relative debates, and our own views, will help you define this concern in your own philosophy of supervision. In the next chapter we discuss further pragmatic concerns that also deal with issues of boundaries for the supervisor—administrative issues and tools.

Chapter 12

Supervisory Responsibilities and Administrative Tools

When addressing problems that might arise in the supervisory system (Chapter 11), it is also important to view these issues in the context of supervisory responsibilities. As supervisors we are responsible for the maintenance of the training system. We also have an implicit contract with the community (Lee, 1994). Most communities give family therapists a protected title, a scope of practice, the right to privileged communication and, in some states, the power to certify individuals as mentally ill. In return, the community must insist on certain assurances. These include teaching family therapists their obligations under the law, ethical codes, and standards of professional practice, and holding them accountable to these. The community expects that supervisors will be fully aware of the professional conduct of therapists under our supervision, and it holds us accountable for the treatment they provide. The community trusts that our therapists will only treat cases appropriate to their individual professional development augmented by our supervisory support. As a supervisor, you will become the professional who is expected and required to monitor and enforce these standards.

To perform this role effectively, a fundamental requirement is to make sure that your therapists understand their responsibilities under the law. Most of these issues will be specified within your state's regulatory statutes (Sturkie & Bergen, 2000). Typically these statutes will specify a scope of practice, privileges within that scope of practice (e.g., privileged communication), and community responsibilities notwithstanding those privileges, such as obligations with regard to child abuse and neglect, and concerns about client harm to self or others. These statutes and their interpretive regulations will also specify what constitutes professional supervision and if a code of ethics applies in that jurisdiction. Some states reference the AAMFT Code of Ethics (2001) while others define "good moral conduct" themselves and list generic standards of professional practice. As a supervisors, you are advised to obtain these materials from your state regulatory board, be conversant with them, and make sure that your therapists are well versed in their meaning. Information about the individual regulatory boards and contacts are available on the Internet at www.amftrb.org.

A second set of supervisory responsibilities are those that are explicit or implicit in family therapy professional ethics and standards of practice derived from family therapy professional literature. These include informing therapists about their roles relative to your expectations and those of others, making careful and consistent evaluations of that performance, telling the therapists how they have done, and, on this basis, shaping their clinical responsibilities and training goals. Accordingly, we should carefully monitor our own auditing procedures, the quality of our direction, and our own ongoing capacity to listen to our therapists (Huber & Peterson, 2000).

A third set of responsibilities stems from our responsibility for the professional conduct of our trainees. This responsibility extends to all of their cases, even if we are supervising only a few, and to all of the settings in which they are practicing (Storm & Engleberg, 2000).

As supervisors we are obligated to three parties besides our therapists and ourselves:

1. The therapists' clinical families.
2. The community.
3. The institution within which the services are provided.

Our responsibilities include appropriate matching of therapists with supervisors and therapists with clinical families (Welch, 2003). We also are responsible for identifying potential areas of risk for clinical families, the community, and the agency (Hedges, 2000), and for seeing that appropriate action is taken to protect the vulnerable individuals. For example, a therapist may be colluding with a volatile client in avoiding psychotropic medication, thinking of that she or he is therapeutically offering a vote of confidence to the client. However, this action by the therapist may place the client, the client's family, the therapist, and the community at unnecessary risk. Finally, we also have an obligation to make sure that the clinical family is aware of the qualifications and training status of their therapists and what they can expect from you as the supervisor (Huber & Peterson, 2000).

A fourth set of responsibilities involves the keeping of records (AAMFT, 2002a; Welch, 1998b, 2001). Many of our therapists are obtaining supervision to satisfy regulatory boards and professional organizations. We need to be cognizant of what the relevant states and professional organizations require of these individuals, meet these requirements if we can, and document the process. This will include an accurate accounting of the number of supervisory hours provided and the nature of these hours. For example, there may be requirements that some pro-

TABLE 12.1. Supervisor's Checklist for Record Keeping

Either now or in the future you and this trainee may require documentation specific to the needs of:

—— Government
—— Accreditation body(ies)
—— Educational institution(s)
—— Your training setting

portion of a trainee's supervision be received in either individual or group formats, and that some proportion of the sessions incorporate "raw data," namely, live observation, videotape, or audiotape. The trainee's educational setting may have its own requirements for record keeping and evaluation, as may the setting in which you are offering supervision. A convenient checklist is given as Table 12.1. However, having these requirements and forms in hand is not enough. Given the administrative importance of these matters, and the need to document supervision goals and therapist progress, the supervisor must develop a documentation package that includes the following (Welch, 1998b):

- A written contract making explicit your and your trainee's expectations and needs, and the procedures to be employed.
- Supervisory progress notes containing goals of sessions, your interventions, and the trainee's response. If a professional judgment and recommendation is required—for example, in a matter of client appropriateness for this therapist, child or elder maltreatment, or potential client lethality—the supervisor should document the reasoning that takes place, the recommendations you made, and what actions were to be taken, how and when. You should also indicate if and why you and your trainee ceased taking further action, such as the police notifying you that the client was safe (see Welch, 2000a, 2000b). If you provide supervision to therapists involved with managed care settings, there may be additional considerations (Keyes, 2001; Welch, 1999). Mandated supervision also will require special care with regard to power, alliance, and reporting.
- A log of all other contacts with your therapists, including letters and telephone calls. These logs should indicate what was discussed. The documentation for matters involving professional judgment applies here as well (Welch, 1998a).
- A complete and professional compilation of all evaluative documents and supporting materials. We believe that some therapist problematic behaviors are so important that they should be documented the first time observed. These include issues such as impaired judgment and behavior contrary to professional standards, especially as these can be expected to jeopardize client welfare. (Some of these matters were discussed in Chapter 11.) The reason for your concerns should be documented in terms of the training system's welfare.

A sample supervision contract, training plan, supervision log, and supervision record form are provided in the *Approved Supervisor Designation Standards and Responsibilities Handbook* (AAMFT, 2002a).

Given our legal liability as supervisors, as well as our teaching responsibilities, we believe that supervisors should require therapists to keep similar records with regard to their clients. If suitable forms are not immediately at hand, the *Practice Management Forms* provided by the AAMFT (Hovestadt, 2001) are good resources for supervisors. These include a variety of disclosure statements, release forms, behavioral contracts (e.g., the *Contract Not to Harm Self/Others*), termination and discharge summaries, progress notes, and progress assessment forms. Perusal of these forms may alert supervisors to what they currently might be lacking.

A fifth set of responsibilities involves third-party payment systems (e.g., AAMFT, 2001; Gladding, Huber, Remley, & Remley, 2000; Woody & Woody, 2001). Supervisors must not collude in insurance fraud. This may occur when insurance companies and government medical administrators are led to believe that you, and not your therapists, are providing the services in question. Some therapists wish to protect their clients by giving them diagnoses (e.g., adjustment disorder with depressed mood) less severe than what the clinical data reflects (e.g., major depression). Other therapists may give all of their clients the same, relatively benign diagnosis. You must not collude with them in this.

Conversely, you must be alert to therapists' temptations to provide diagnoses in the absence of a diagnosable condition to qualify themselves for payment or their agencies or clients for reimbursement. Therapists, of course, also must not report that they provided covered services (individual psychotherapy) in lieu of items not covered (e.g., marital and family therapy), bill for sessions that did not occur, or bill a person with insurance coverage for those provided to someone else (e.g., a partner).

Supervisory Vulnerability

Family therapists are vulnerable in two domains of practice and so are their supervisors (Gladding, Huber, Remley, & Remley, 2000; Heath & Engelberg, 2000; Huber & Peterson, 2000; Storm & Engelberg, 2000):

1. Alleged negligence, including breaches of privileged communication.
2. Insurance fraud.

Allegations of negligence can be brought against therapists and, through them, against the supervisor. Such a claim can be made that the supervisor did not identify potential risk areas or failed to take timely and effective action to prevent the adverse events at issue. The supervisor may argue that realistically one can only control one's own behavior. However, it is generally clear that lawsuits brought in civil courts do not accept this defense.

"Negligence" is upheld when a jury believes that damage was caused by one party to another person through a breach of duty allegedly owed to that person. Therefore, a jury needs to believe that four factors were present in your training system (Stromberg, 1987):

1. A duty is owed by your trainee to the client, and you have a duty to both of them. There needs to be a credible supervisor–therapist–client relationship. A touchstone to be applied is that juries have held that even answering the telephone when someone was seeking an appointment constituted a professional relationship.
2. Your professional duty was not fulfilled in that you and your therapist's conduct fell below an acceptable standard of care. A touchstone to be applied is how a jury of your professional peers would regard what is alleged you have or have not done.
3. There is some actual injury suffered by the client.
4. There is a credible causal connection between the alleged dereliction of duty and the alleged injury to the client.

Examples of successful suits would include such issues as a therapist's sexual exploitation of a client, termination of a client against the client's wishes ("abandonment") followed by adverse consequences to the client, and unwarranted release of information that led to some loss by the other party (Heath & Engelberg, 2000; Stromberg, 1987). Notice that these same issues could also apply to supervisors' treatment of therapists. Therapists can suffer because of sexual harassment, unwanted termination, or making information about them public. Other alleged professional negligence by therapists for which their supervisors can be held culpable include homicides (Gladding et al., 2000; Monahan, 1993; VandeCreek & Knapp, 2001) and suicides (Pearson, Stanley, King, & Fisher, 2001; Schutz, 1982) considered preventable ("wrongful death"), familial consequences as a result of allegedly unfounded accusations of childhood sexual abuse (false memory syndrome: Schneider, 1994), and failure to pursue a noncompliant client (abandonment: Gladding et al., 2000; Huber & Peterson, 2000; Vesper & Brock, 1991).

We are told that the community does not necessarily expect supervisors and our trainees to always predict and protect. However, the public does expect that we will have acted *prudently* (Heath & Engelberg, 2000; Storm & Engelberg, 2000). Prudence includes having seen and thought about adverse actions in situations where our peers allegedly would have been concerned, and having made a careful decision about those potential adverse events. Therefore, in our records we need to carefully document the existence of our acts of professional judgment and their rationale, including subsequent action and nonaction (Welch, 1998a). Juries might decide later that we were wrong in our clinical recommendations but they would also know that *we used our best professional judgment.* We are told that this is an important defense (Heath & Engleberg, 2000).

As supervisors we need to cultivate and maintain a training system that is adequate to the relational needs of all of the participants. An integrative supervisory model equips us to do that. However, in our roles as teachers and administrators, we must ensure that our training systems meet very specific standards of professional practice. We have many important tools for addressing these obligations in a prudent manner. These tools include ethical codes, contracts, evaluative procedures, due process mechanisms, and performance improvement plans.

Administrative Tools

What recourse does a supervisor have when there is a concern about a therapist's or a client's well-being? The potential interventions available range from modest to extreme. At one level we can request additional supervisory sessions, more live observation, case-specific reading, reflection papers, and group discussion. We can assign co-therapists or peer mentors to be "shadowed." We can refer our therapists to personal therapy concurrent with cases that are problematic for them. We can limit our therapists' caseloads, either in number or the kinds of cases referred to them, until their problematic situation is resolved. We can recommend leaves of absence from clinical duties or from the training program. We can counsel individuals out of the training program and, probably, the profession. With regard to all of these actions, the following rules apply:

- Your trainees must never be taken by surprise, or be able to support a claim that this is so.
- Your trainees must have an adequate appeals process to respond to your judgments.
- You must be able to implement a well-conceived performance improvement plan.
- Your interventions should be parsimonious. They should be only what are needed to get the specific job done.

These guidelines make your processes appear reasonable to participants and observers and robust against legal attack. We next discuss these rules more fully in the context of the principal administrative tools available to you as a family therapy supervisor, namely, codes of ethics, contracts, evaluative processes, due process mechanisms, and performance improvement plans. These are mechanisms that protect all of the participants in training systems. They make training systems reasonable, predictable, fair, and therefore safe.

The AAMFT Code of Ethics

The AAMFT Code of Ethics (2001) is a core document in training and important in several ways. It describes responsible professional conduct in advance of undertaking professional relationships and then it guides those relationships. It can also provide immediate guidance in urgent and confusing clinical situations. When stress, conflicting emotions, and dissonant values make it hard for us to make up our minds and we need to make quick decisions, the AAMFT Code of Ethics may instruct us how to think about the diverse circumstances, prioritize them, and act. Finally, the AAMFT Code of Ethics gives us an institutionalized authority to back up our supervisory and administrative decisions.

Principle IV (Table 12.2) of the Code of Ethics governs the supervisor's relationship with trainees. Its essence is that supervisors are not to exploit the trust and dependency of those they supervise. In fact, four of the seven subprinciples

TABLE 11.2. The AAMFT Code of Ethics, Principle IV: Responsibility to Students and Supervisees

Marriage and family therapists do not exploit the trust and dependency of students and supervisees.

4.1 Marriage and family therapists are aware of their influential positions with respect to students and supervisees, and they avoid exploiting the trust and dependency of such persons. Therapists, therefore, make every effort to avoid conditions and multiple relationships that could impair professional objectivity or increase the risk of exploitation. When the risk of impairment or exploitation exists due to conditions or multiple roles, therapists take appropriate precautions.

4.2 Marriage and family therapists do not provide therapy to current students or supervisees.

4.3 Marriage and family therapists do not engage in sexual intimacy with students or supervisees during the evaluative or training relationship between the therapist and student or supervisee. Should a supervisor engage in sexual activity with a former supervisee, the burden of proof shifts to the supervisor to demonstrate that there has been no exploitation or injury to the supervisee.

4.4 Marriage and family therapists do not permit students or supervisees to perform or to hold themselves out as competent to perform professional services beyond their training, level of experience, and competence.

4.5 Marriage and family therapists take reasonable measures to ensure that services provided by supervisees are professional.

4.6 Marriage and family therapists avoid accepting as supervisees or students those individuals with whom a prior or existing relationship could compromise the therapist's objectivity. When such situations cannot be avoided, therapists take appropriate precautions to maintain objectivity. Examples of such relationships include, but are not limited to, those individuals with whom the therapist has a current or prior sexual, close personal, immediate familial, or therapeutic relationship.

4.7 Marriage and family therapists do not disclose supervisee confidences except by written authorization or waiver, or when mandated or permitted by law. In educational or training settings where there are multiple supervisors, disclosures are permitted only to other professional colleagues, administrators, or employers who share responsibility for training of the supervisee. Verbal authorization will not be sufficient except in emergency situations, unless prohibited by law.

(4.1, 4.2, 4.3, and 4.6) caution supervisors about settings and relationships with the potential to cloud professional judgment and facilitate exploitation. The remaining subprinciples inform us that therapists are only to be asked to perform within the limits of their professional competency (4.4, 4.5) and that we must act responsibly with regard to what we know about the therapists under our supervision.

Multiple Relatedness

Multiple relationships are when one person assumes more than one role at the same time with another; consequently, there may be dual agendas present for this individual (Peterson, 1992). These roles may be overtly recognized by both parties, with clear boundaries enforced, or they may be covert, with confused boundaries (Peterson, 2000). Multiple relationships have the potential to get in the way of objective reasoning by supervisors and therapists, and to facilitate exploitation. Many of us would add that conflicting multiple relationships also have the potential to inhibit free speech and self-disclosure. Few would argue that one concurrently can be a trainee's lover and a supervisor, and most would agree (see Chapters 6, 10, and 11) that one cannot simultaneously do good supervision and good therapy with the same person. In this situation, the supervisor would become privy to too much personal data about the trainee, which would likely blur and confuse professional boundaries and, therefore, judgment.

However, others have observed that many multiple relationships cannot be avoided and that they have the potential for good (Bograd, 1992; Tomm, 1992). Such relatedness, they observed, can model the complexity of real life, provide an opportunity to learn how to handle such situations productively, and promote more sensitive and egalitarian relatedness.

There are some controversies regarding dual relationship issues in the family therapy supervisory field—those who forbid multiple relationships because of the potential danger, and those who view them as potentially useful for professional development—but others observe that many of them are unavoidable. For example, participants in supervision institutes readily point out that graduate students may simultaneously be in several relationships with a faculty member. The same instructor may supervise their clinical work, teach their courses, direct their dissertation work, and employ them as teaching and research assistants. Some of these participants also work in agencies, and they observe that they may have no choice about whom their supervisors are and that the same individuals may be both their agency administrators and their clinical supervisors. Moreover, they themselves may expect to supervise therapists who will be working with court-mandated clients (e.g., families involved with the child welfare and the juvenile justice systems). Therapists also provide therapy in sociocultural settings where multiple relationships are necessary to treatment. (One supervisor pointed out that, in many Mexican American communities, one needs to be accepted by a family as fictive kin before one will be accepted as a therapist.)

Here is an exercise that may help you think through this complex dilemma. Think of situations in your work, as a supervisor or as a therapist, that could be characterized as multiple relatedness. In each occasion, what were the different roles you had relative to each other? How many of these relationships were unavoidable, or relatively unavoidable, for either party? What about each relationship enhanced your professional development? What about each relationship was detrimental to each relationship? If anything, how could that detrimental influence have been avoided or minimized?

Given the complexity of many of the settings in which family therapists are trained and work, prudent supervisors are wise to avoid the obvious traps, but also to learn how to successfully manage complex relationships (Storm, Peterson, & Tomm, 1997). You and your trainees need to mutually identify both the enhancements and the complications inherent in your proposed relationship. As we discussed in Chapter 9, all members of the training system should consider the influences of gender and the many sociocultural factors (Killian, 2000; Roberts, 2000; Turner, 2000). Supervisors and trainees should review together their respective philosophies about supervision, including how hierarchy is operationalized and evaluations completed. Both must be willing to monitor the influence of such factors (e.g., Killian, 2000) and actively listen to one another with regard to them (Roberts, 2000; Turner, 2000). Consultation outside of the training dyad should be available without penalty to both parties (Turner, 2000).

Competency and Confidentiality

We are advised that our trainees must practice in a professional manner. What does this really mean? We believe that what is "professional" might be relative to the context in which the therapy is being practiced (see Chapter 9). We appreciate that supervisors, like good coaches, encourage their trainees to take appropriate professional risks ("their growing edges") lest they stagnate. We also believe, with Minuchin and Fishman (1981), that becoming a therapist is a lifelong process. As a supervisor you will need to encourage an appropriate amount of new growth. However, you remain ethical in this process to the extent that the therapeutic challenge is based on a careful assessment of your therapists' current capabilities relative to the clinical picture and their immediate potential for limited growth (see the discussion in Chapter 5). You must be careful not to ask for too much at a time in their lives when psychological resources are not available for the challenges you have in mind (Lee et al., 2001). You also need to add to your readiness equation your own current capacity and that of the setting to support the new growth (Breunlin, Liddle, & Schwartz, 1988b).

We imagine that there have been times as a therapist when you yourself have felt in over your head. Sometimes that may have been an appropriate challenge to accomplish new learning. Sometimes it may not have been. What did you feel and think at times when what was being asked of you was not appropriate? For example, we have observed that beginning therapists often are assigned the most difficult cases because no one else wants them, such as in-home, court-mandated family therapy with marginalized families in unsympathetic settings. We would be concerned that the attendant anxiety, culture shock, logistic difficulty, unconventional therapy, and perhaps only modest apparent positive response to the treatment causes the therapists to reconsider their vocations.

The final subprinciple, 4.7, reminds us that to keep supervision safe and encourage maximum openness by the therapists, there is much that should not be shared with others. In many training settings there is more than one supervisor for each therapist, simultaneously or sequentially. Even though these differing supervisors may share responsibility for the therapists, the benefit of talking about them on each occasion must be weighed against the possibility of harm to the training alliance.

Developing Contracts

How many of you signed a written contract as a trainee with your supervisor? How many of you as supervisors currently use them? If you do not presently use written contracts, have you used an oral contract?

It has been our experience that it is critical to the supervision process to identify, clarify, and record everyone's expectations through a contract. Like a lease, contracts protect both parties! Most administrators, program directors, and supervisors believe it is prudent to develop a written contract. These can be offered to trainees unilaterally ("This is the bill of fare. Take it or leave it.") or they can be negotiated mutually. The setting in which you are working may dictate the form of such a contract. Here are some of the ingredients of supervisory contracts that we and others (AAMFT, 2002a; Lee, 2002b; Storm, 1997; Todd, 1997a, 1997b) believe are important.

- **Logistics.** The supervisor should outline in the contract the basic logistics: how long the supervision is to continue before being terminated or recontracted, the frequency with which appointments will be set, the length of the sessions, the time and place, rules about cancellations, and even a rough overall schedule. This contract should also specify how clients will be informed about the supervisory relationship.
- **The supervisory relationship.** Supervisors should address issues of fit by specifying their beliefs about hierarchy and their preferential ways of working. If there are multiple supervisors, contracts should include the respective responsibilities of each with regard to cases and the supervision process. Also if there is more than one supervisor, contracts should make clear the circumstances under which they may discuss the trainee.
- **Goals.** The contract should identify the primary goals of the supervision. For example, goals might be perceptual, executive, and technical skills—general or specific to a certain population of clients, personal growth, and support and

nurture. These goals may be different for supervisors and trainees and should be made congruent.

- **Supervision methods.** The contract should specify what modalities are to be used in supervision, in what amount, and how live supervision will be done.
- **Responsibility issues.** Because supervisors are held legally responsible for cases, how will this be facilitated? Do you expect to be notified or consulted when cases are at serious risk? If so, what clinical situations would require this and where can you be located? What contingency plans can be mutually agreed on for these emergent clinical situations? How does this reporting, consultation, and action interface with the requirements of the therapist's setting?
- **Credentialing requirements.** What needs to be done to meet the needs of accrediting bodies (AAMFT, 2002a, for Approved supervisor candidates; COAMFTE, 2002, for your therapists), licensing bodies, employers, and educational institutions? What is the trainee expecting from you in this regard? (See Table 12.1.) This section includes how the record of supervision will be kept (session notes and the supervisory log) and what therapy records will be completed by the trainee.
- **Evaluation.** The supervisor must specify evaluation procedures and criteria. This often includes issues regarding attendance, record keeping, and cooperation. There also may be some statement about what constitutes growth and what constitutes lack of growth and potential consequences. The mechanisms of due process would be summarized here. This is also a good place to consider how "safe" your supervision will be and whether therapists feel that they can challenge you.
- **Ethical considerations.** This includes what code(s) of ethics will govern the training system, and notification of the therapist's clients that the therapist is under your supervision.
- **Compensation.** What will the services cost, when is payment due, and what will be done in matters requiring collection? If payment is expected for missed sessions, the circumstances of this should be stated here.
- **Due process.** How will disagreements between you and the trainee be brought forth and resolved?
- **Termination.** Specify the circumstances under which the contract may be discontinued and how it is to be done. What summary and evaluations products are expected of both parties at the end of supervision?

Model supervisory contracts into which the discussed items can be inserted are offered by Becvar (2000) and the AAMFT (Hovestadt, 2001). The latter is given as Figure 12.1. Of course, as Todd (1997a) has pointed out, contracts need to be *real*. Contracts often suffer from two essential limitations. First, many of the issues that are important to trainees are often omitted from standard contracts. That is, the contracts tend to focus on what the supervisor expects, not on what the therapist wants or expects! Secondly, because of our own (or previous supervisors')

Sample Supervision Contract

We have decided to enter into a supervision experience together and we have gone over a number of issues in order to help us create an agreed-upon context for that experience. The purpose of this contract is to outline those issues and to serve as a resource for our work together.

Supervisor
Name: _____
Address: _____

_____

Supervisee
Name: _____
Address: _____

_____

Outline of Logistics
We have agreed to commit _____ (length of time or number of contacts) to some form of supervision contact, beginning _____ and continuing until _____. We have decided to divide up this time in the following ways: _____

In the case of a client cancellation, we have decided _____

In the case of an emergency we have discussed the following procedure:

_____
_____
_____

Note: If you think you, a client, or another individual is in imminent danger, first call the police department and then follow the procedure above.

Clarification of the Supervision Relationship

My supervision style:

_____
_____
_____

Confidentiality:

_____
_____
_____

Plan for providing feedback to one another:

_____
_____
_____

Plan for handling stumbling blocks/disagreements/etc.

_____
_____
_____

Additional clarifications:

_____
_____
_____

Identification of Goals
We have identified the following goals for our work together:

_____
_____
_____
_____

_____	_____
Therapist Signature	Supervisor Signature
_____	_____
Date	Date

From Hovestadt, A., (ed.). *Practice Management Forms: Tools for the Business of Therapy*. Reprinted with permission from the AAMFT. Copyright 2001.

FIGURE 12.1. Sample Supervision Contract

inconsistent behaviors, trainees often do not believe important aspects of the contract. For example, we may say that we value videos, but we do not ask for them or have not cared if they were not cued up to an important spot. Or we may talk about punctuality, but we have come late to supervision sessions or we have allowed interruptions.

Evaluation Processes

Some therapist evaluations need to be completed when the supervisor needs to reach an important decision about relatively recalcitrant obstacles to the learning and therapeutic process (i.e., when the problem needs to documented). More often, evaluations arc scheduled routinely at the end of training periods or a course on supervision. Sometimes, when the supervision is privately contracted, and perhaps with regard to a specific theoretical model, technique, or clinical population, the evaluation may be informal if an explicit evaluation occurs at all. This last situation seems unwise. If you have concerns about an individual's ability in some limited practice areas, there may come a time when you will wish that you had documented your concerns in writing. Moreover, a therapist who has sought your supervision may wish documentation in support of future career issues.

Here are some important issues to consider when beginning and preparing clinical evaluations for your trainees.

1. If both becoming a therapist and becoming a supervisor are lifelong processes, how is progress to be measured at any one point in time?
2. The act of evaluating often engenders anxiety for both the supervisor and the trainee. There are concerns about being evaluated and about jeopardizing the relationship. Trainees may fear being found incompetent—even to the point of being counseled out of a program.
3. In Chapter 11 we discussed baggage that interferes with learning and therapy. The process of being evaluated ("judged") can often raise fears connected to unresolved past and present hierarchical issues.
4. The very act of evaluation, with the connotation of assessing ability while reviewing the incidence and implications of mistakes, may inhibit the risk-taking that is necessary for personal and professional growth.
5. In this litigious age, negative evaluations can require the further involvement of substantial discretionary time and energy. They may even result in legal actions with the evaluator as a defendant.

The irony is that these observations apply equally to trainees and supervisors! Supervisors evaluate and judge, to be sure, but they are also judged. Has a particular trainee not developed because the trainee in some way is inadequate or disordered? Or has the supervisor been an inadequate teacher and coach?

For your evaluative processes to go best, we believe that the following guidelines will be helpful.

1. The criteria of the evaluation process should be discussed and mutually accepted in advance of the supervision. Ideally these issues would be in the supervisory contract. Kniskern and Gurman (1988) reviewed a number of questionnaires that may be used. Some criteria reflect generic aspects of consultation, including non-negotiable items such as inadequate record keeping, intoxication in the training setting, missed appointments, and inappropriate aggression or sexuality. If these prohibitions are not clearly understood in advance of the supervision, the administrative case is weakened. Because some evaluative criteria may rely on the family therapy models informing the supervision, the reader is referred to the model-specific chapters in Breunlin, Liddle and Schwartz (1988a) in which evaluation according to each major family therapy model is discussed. These insights will prove to be very important to integrative training systems.
2. Evaluation should be considered a process and not an event. The data informing the process are accrued over time from the actual therapy and supervisory sessions and reflect change. The evaluative process cannot be completed until anger, fear, and grief have been replaced by a task-oriented appreciation of what has been decided.

3. Evaluative criteria should be realistic. They should be developmentally appropriate and suited to the clinical work that was required.
4. Evaluations should be strengths-based with regard to developing competency in professional and clinical skills. Evaluations that are not based on professional competence in the situation for which the services have been contracted are inappropriate.
5. Evaluations should be mutual. The individuals should agree on the criteria for evaluation, but they should also evaluate themselves, the other party, and the relationship. Mead (2000) suggested that the clients—the consumers of the training services—should also be consulted.
6. Each party should have access to an impartial appeals process, which needs to be clearly specified.

Many of these criteria can be met in a two-stage evaluative process.

Stage 1. In the initial supervisory session, therapists may use an open-ended method to state what their personal training goals are. On a piece of lined paper they can write down their goals and prioritize them. On a line below each goal, anchored at one end by "nonexistent" and at the other end by "no improvement needed," they indicate their current status with regard to that goal. This is an excellent training tool. Supervisors and therapists can refer to it in the course of supervision to stay on track. The therapists can also use the rating scale periodically and at the end of the supervision period to make their own assessment of their growth. If supervision is privately contracted, the evaluation procedure ends here. If supervision is being provided in an institution, Stage 2 is added.

Stage 2. At the end of the supervision period, an assessment of the criteria deemed important is completed by the supervisor, such as the ability to construct systemic clinical pictures, the ability to actively listen, and the presence of warmth and concern. Both the supervisor and the therapist evaluate progress according to these criteria. The two documents then are compared and discussed. Both parties are encouraged to append a response to the other's judgments and interpretations. Both documents then become part of the therapist's training file. The therapists also have a form with which to anonymously evaluate their supervisors and these are sent to the appropriate administrator.

Evaluation forms need to be flexible to fit the professional person of the trainee (e.g., previous experience, theoretical orientation, expectations of the supervision) and the setting in which the therapy takes place. Moreover, although a formal evaluation may occur at the beginning and end of a course of supervision, it is advisable for both supervisors and trainees to frequently assess informally how they are doing. Are the goals of the supervision being met? When supervision or therapy are going well, what is the therapist doing, and what is the supervisor doing? As we suggested, the open-ended instrument described in Stage 1 above is very good for this kind of ongoing evaluation. However, supervisors and trainees are also advised to periodically assess more specific matters that may not always be present in such a simple assessment device namely, the quality of case presentations and case documents, timeliness of attendance and record keeping, adequate recognition of ethical and legal concerns emerging from supervision or the trainees' cases, the extent to which the empirical literature is informing both the supervision and therapy, and needs to modify the training goals or other aspects of the supervision contract (AAMFT, 2002a).

A number of generic-but-highly-specific trainee evaluation forms exist. They include an enumeration of the tasks of therapy: ability to join clinical families, assess and interpret cases systemically and accurately, plan and implement interventions on the basis of theory and research, assess the intervention, flexibly plan the next step, and effectively terminate the treatment. An evaluative (Likert) scale could be attached to each item, ranging from "little or no ability," through "performance at a level commensurate with peers," and ending in "mastery." A somewhat different approach to the same task is offered as Figure 12.2. The trainee and the supervisor each complete this form separately, and then meet to discuss it and (hopefully) reach consensus. Therapeutic and institutional standards of practice are given on the reverse side of the evaluation form.

Intern Name_____   **Semester** _____

The purpose of this form is to help both the trainee and the supervisor identify the areas of growth of the trainee and to identify goals for next semester. Please write a short narrative about your progress this semester in the following areas:

1. What do you see as your strengths as a therapist?

2. What do you see as your weaknesses as a therapist?

3. Evaluate your therapeutic rapport with clients.*

4. Demonstrate how you complied with the Professional Standards of Practice.**

5. Demonstrate how you followed the clinic policies and procedures.***

6. Comment on your receptiveness to the supervision process.

7. Determine a minimum of three goals you would like to work on for next semester.

8. What would be your overall rating of yourself for this semester on a scale of 0 to 5 with 0 unacceptable, 3 as competent, and 5 as outstanding?

Trainee Signature_____ Date_____

Supervisor Signature_____ Date_____

FIGURE 12.2. Sample Trainee Evaluation Form

(continues on p. 137)

*Therapeutic Rapport with Clients Includes But Is Not Limited To:
- Joins with all members of the family.
- Is sensitive to alliances and coalitions and avoids being triangled.
- Works effectively with a variety of clients and issues.
- Provides feedback in a positive and nonjudgmental way.
- Shows awareness to issues of age, gender, culture, ethnicity, sexual orientation, physical disability, socioeconomic status, and religious orientation.
- Works from a systems perspective.
- Is able to identify and separate trainee's own issues from those of the client and uses self-disclosure appropriately.
- Demonstrates a sense of caring, warmth, and concern for all family members.
- Allows the client to help direct the therapy process and solicits input from clients about the nature of the therapeutic process.

**Professional Standards of Practice Behaviors Do NOT Include:
- Physically or verbally assaulting a client.
- Dual relationships including but not limited to dating, sexual, or business relationships with clients.
- Abandoning a client or placing a client in jeopardy by negligent or unprofessional behavior.
- Violating the confidentiality of a client.
- Failure to follow legal and clinic prescriptions where a client is at risk or there is suspected child abuse or neglect.
- Failure to obtain a *fully informed* consent to treatment and clinic policy and procedures.

***Clinic Policies and Procedures for Trainees Include:
- Does not have any unapproved absences from staff meetings, supervision, or clinic sessions with clients.
- Arranges the therapy room appropriately before sessions and leaves the therapy room clean and in order for the next therapist.
- Cooperates with other trainees in use of therapy rooms.
- Dresses professionally and appropriately.
- Begins and ends therapy sessions on time.
- Videotapes all sessions for supervisory review.
- Conducts self in a manner that does not jeopardize the professional reputation of one's colleagues, the family therapy clinic and/or program, the department, or the university.
- Maintains records—i.e., closes flies in appropriate and timely manner, has supervisor sign case materials weekly, turns in completed and signed monthly logs, and responds to requests for information from supervisor and staff in a timely manner.

FIGURE 12.2. Sample Trainee Evaluation Form

A variety of trainee evaluation instruments are given in the AAMFT's collection of practice management forms (Hovestadt, 2001). However, as described in the preface and subsequent chapters of this book, we encourage integrative supervisors to assess the extent to which flexible use of conceptual and intervention tools is informed by a systems-based metatheory of relational change, the developmental levels of supervisor, therapist and client, the comfort levels and styles of all, and the clinical and diagnostic presenting problems of the family. Rigazio-DiGilio (1997) offers similar counsel.

Finally, trainees can be given an opportunity to evaluate their supervisors. COAMFTE accreditation requires such feedback (COAMFTE, 2002). Williams (1994) created the Supervision Feedback Form as a catalyst for constructive feedback. Others use instruments such as that in Figure 12.3. We believe that the

Date_____   Supervisor_____

This form was developed to provide feedback to your supervisor about your experience in supervision in accordance with COAMFTE requirements. Please type or print legibly your responses on this form and DO NOT SIGN IT. Upon completion, mail/deliver it to _____. Your responses will be consolidated with others and then shared with the supervisor when there are enough so that you cannot be identified.

1. Please comment on your overall supervision experience.
2. What are your most important expectations of supervision?
3. How well did your experience meet these expectations?
4. What are your supervisor's areas of strength?*
5. What are your supervisor's areas of weakness?
6. Please rate your overall satisfaction with his/her supervision on a scale of 0 to 5, with 0 as unacceptable, 3 as competent, and 5 as outstanding. _____
7. Additional comments:

*Possible Supervisor Strengths
• Regularly checks for at-risk clients.
• Makes supervision a safe place to admit/make mistakes and is sensitive to the trainees' issues.
• Empowers the trainees.
• Treats the trainees and the clients in a professional and respectful manner.
• Is attentive to issues of age, gender, culture, ethnicity, sexual orientation, physical disability, socioeconomic status, and religious orientation of both the trainees and the clients.
• Suggestions are clinically appropriate and in keeping with the law and AAMFT ethics.
• Completes paperwork in a timely manner and is knowledgeable and gives guidance with regard to clinic policies and procedures.
• Involves other trainees in the supervision process.
• Is flexible in theoretical approach to working with clients and is willing to let trainees explore theoretical applications.
• Assists trainees with the paperwork required (e.g., case notes and treatment plans).
• Keeps accurate records of the trainee's supervision hours.
• Regularly signs case notes.
• Structures supervision to meet the needs of the trainees.
• Is conscious of time management issues, e.g., provides enough time for everyone, as well as time for live/video supervision.

FIGURE 12.3. Supervisor Evaluation Form

survey in Figure 12.3, perhaps completed anonymously and given to an appropriate administrator, can be helpful to morale and serve as an important feedback tool.

Goal Attainment Scaling

Evaluations are desirable at all levels of the training system. Given the infinite diversity of such systems, and the relatively unique needs and concerns of their participants, evaluation instruments and processes tend to be unique to their settings. Accurate quantification and comparison across settings and individuals may not be possible. In fact, these may not be your goals. If, however, they are, the goal attainment scaling (Kiresuk & Garwick, 1975) is a method that can be used to quantitatively assess training outcomes deemed desirable by the participants on all levels of the training system. Goal attainment scaling allows individuals to specify the needs of the specific case and to use the case as its own control in the definition of "success." It also permits comparison of diverse interventions across cases, because outcomes are assessed on a similar scale. Smith (1988) has effectively applied it to individual case studies, and Daly and his associates (Barnett et al., 1999; Daly, Witt, Martens, & Dool, 1997) have found it useful in performance-based training settings.

As a supervisor, you negotiate desirable outcomes with each trainee. These can include personal training goals or desirable outcomes with regard to therapist–client relationships. As an administrator, you might focus on supervisor behaviors or supervisor–trainee relationships. Participants in the training subsystem could also focus on the climate of the training system itself.

Five or more desirable outcomes for each functional unit are typical (Smith, 1988). So that they can be quantified easily and accurately, these outcomes should be anchored in specific, observable behaviors. If a unit has improved with regard to a variable, how will we know? What will we be seeing? Ideally, the rationale for each item has a solid theoretical base, that is, an integrative model of family therapy and its supervision.

Alongside each item on these personalized lists of outcomes is placed a 5-point scale ranging from the most unfavorable training outcome (–2) thought to be likely, through the expected level of success (0), to the best possible response to training (+2). At the conclusion of training, the appropriate participant-observers determine which outcome level (–2 to +2) best describes the unit's functioning on each of the outcome scales. If it makes sense to do so, a summary score can be tallied.

A related approach, in which the participants construct their own rating scales and anchor them using personal experience, has been described by Lee and Brann (1994). Finally, because our overall discussion of evaluation has perforce touched on variables considered desirable at various levels of the training system, we would like to describe one that we and others consider very important: *resiliency*.

Resiliency

We believe that your evaluation processes should include considerations about resiliency. We have already spoken about supervision being competency based (e.g., Chapter 1, Principle 10). We believe that a focus on resiliency is an extension of this. If we extrapolate from Walsh's (1996) discussion of families, the concept of resiliency offers a useful framework to identify and fortify key processes that enable participants in training systems to cope in the presence of crises and stresses. Crises and stresses are inescapable. Training is a developmental process (see Chapter 5) and problematic circumstances typically provide our client families.

Although definitions have varied over time, there is a general consensus that resilient individuals, couples, families, businesses, and other social units—including training systems—are those with the ability to successfully adapt or maintain competent functioning despite trauma, changing situations, risk status, or other forms of stress (Cicchetti & Garmezy, 1993). Resilient social units have dispositional attributes and a supportive context that serve protective functions against stress and lead to adjustment.

We would like to extrapolate to training systems from what has been discovered about children in families (summarized in Krovetz, 1999; Seligman, 1996; Walker & Lee, 1998; Walsh, 1996). At the individual level, we hypothesize that resilient supervisors and trainees are those with the following four attributes:

1. *Social competence:* Ability to elicit positive responses from others, thus establishing positive relationships with those hierarchically above and below them and peers.
2. *Problem-solving skills:* Planning that facilitates seeing oneself in control and resourcefulness in seeking help from others.
3. *Autonomy:* A sense of one's own identity and the ability to act independently and exert some control over one's environment.
4. *A sense of purpose and future:* Goals, educational aspirations, persistence, hopefulness, and optimism with regard to these.

Supportive systemic factors in the training team's wider social context might include:

1. Permeable boundaries between the training team and its respective social contexts (e.g., training program, clinical settings of the trainees) so that external support is possible.
2. Cohesion within the wider social setting.
3. The protective influence of administrative and peer relationships. These are some of the most protective qualities in such relationships, according to researchers:
   • Stability of the attachment over time
   • Emotional accessibility of the individuals
   • A sense of warmth and acceptance as opposed to shame and blame

Finally, evaluations might focus on how the training system itself deals with stress as a functional unit. Family systems models of resilience—extrapolated here to *training systems models*—view resilience as a quality that is embedded in the process of interdependent relationships (Cohler, Stott, & Musick, 1995;

Egeland, Carlson, & Sroufe, 1993; Walsh, 1996). A training system is a developing system that is continually changing and being changed by multiple contexts. Resilient training systems adapt to stressors by using existing resources, developing new strengths, and reorganizing relationships to minimize the disruptive impact of crises. A resilient training system is one that is able to adapt to and even prosper from crises. There is remarkable consistency across studies that indicate that four characteristics are essential in facilitating basic family functioning and the well-being of constituent members. Again extrapolating from Walsh (1996), resilient training systems have:

1. Affirming belief systems. How does the training system make sense out of a crisis situation and give it meaning? Shared beliefs about who we are, how we do things, and what matters give events meaning ("chance," "personal failure"). Our shared beliefs about the past ("losers," "victims," "heroic survivors") and spiritual values and cultural heritage provide support and can give meaning to suffering.
2. Effective communication patterns. Participants have the ability to talk constructively about what is going on, in the situation and in themselves; they can consider ways of dealing with what might be occurring, and are open to feedback.
3. Relationships that are flexible, cohesive, and adaptive.
4. Awareness of external support systems and the ability and willingness to use them.

Because the abilities to withstand stress, adapt successfully to challenges, and to grow in confidence and resourcefulness are so important to therapists (e.g., reviews in Figley, 2000b) as well as to their clients (Figley, 1997), we encourage future supervisors to find ways to incorporate these factors in their trainee, supervisor, and program evaluations.

Documentation, Due Process, and Performance Improvement Plans

Whatever your skills in conflict resolution and in establishing collaborative work may be, you will find that not all of your trainees will be reasonable. Moreover, we live in a litigious age. Accordingly, your concerns about therapists' performance must be documented in writing as they occur, at an appropriate level of specificity (Welch, 1998a, 2001, 2003). We recommend that you do this according to the goal-setting methods of the solutions-focused experts (e.g., Walter & Peller, 1992). Namely, we recommend that when you document what therapists are and are not doing that is problematic that you also translate your concerns into observable behaviors easily understood by others. You also should not attribute motivations.

Logic says that the nature of the malfeasance or negligence will play a role in how much evidence a prudent individual will consider actionable. Explosive, sexually inappropriate, or intoxicated behaviors in a session should lead to faster action than incomplete or missing work documents. However, we have been consistently advised by legal counsel that when you are dissatisfied as a supervisor, your trainees must never be taken by surprise or be able to sustain a claim to that effect against you. You must not only have written documentation of your concerns about problematic behavior, but written and dated records of conferences with the therapist in question, plans for remediation, and the therapist's responses. Contemporary standards suggest that, except in cases clearly injurious to people and institutions, there must be a performance improvement plan (e.g., Langdon & Osborne, 2001). This plan specifies what behaviors, at what levels, are necessary to adequate performance. It also indicates a way of acquiring these skills, a method for assessing progress, and time limits in which specified improvements must occur. Throughout, there must be mechanisms for an appeal of your decisions and due process for the trainee.

Although the discussion and outlines in this chapter may have seemed somewhat legalistic, and perhaps even anxiety-provoking, experienced supervisors and clinical educators have learned over the years of their practices the importance of all of these issues. Most of us learned some of these issues the hard way early in our careers, simply because of naïvete or a failure to take seriously the level of animosity that can be generated by an angry trainee who believes that her or his planned career has been threatened or taken away. Please be warned that these are crucial concerns that must be a clear part of your supervisory model and role.

We saved these issues for last in our series of chapters on the practical aspects of supervision. In the next two chapters we focus on helping you pull together and begin to articulate your own integrative supervisory model and then explore some examples of the integrative approach in action.

Chapter 13

Articulating Your Personal Model for Supervision

This chapter is more personal than the others. We intend to provide you with the opportunity to actually integrate and draft your "Philosophy of Supervision Paper" (AAMFT, 2002a). If you have completed our exercises and kept notes in a journal, and now follow our guidance in this chapter, we believe that your paper will almost write itself.

At the very beginning of this book we asked you to think about your best and worst supervisory experiences. We wanted to stir up those memories in the hope that they would make your subsequent reading more relevant and remind you of how much you already know about effective supervision: As consumers of supervisory services, you have had unique experiences of the good, the bad, and the ugly. We also wanted you to start getting in touch with your "inner supervisor," because this part of you surely influences how you construct your views and identity.

Now it is time to make your inner supervisor explicit in your written philosophy of supervision. Figley (2000a) has observed that for many Approved Supervisor Candidates the philosophy of supervision paper can become a major barrier. In fact, he offered a practical outline to which you may wish to refer for accomplishing this task. However, if you have read our chapters and completed our self-discovery and reflective exercises, you have already completed, in writing, much of what must be done. The task now is to reflect on, consolidate, and reference what you already have written. Overall, as you work through this chapter, remember that the philosophy statement is meant to be a highly personal document about what you believe with regard to supervision (Storm, 2000b). The personal pronoun "I" and the possessive pronoun "my" are expected and acceptable features. For example, your paper should be characterized by this kind of language: I believe . . . I prefer . . . My reasons are . . . My experience has been. . . .

In this chapter, we invite you to do the following with considerable thought. First, we would like you to consider your philosophy about what supervision is and, in your best judgment, must be—given the respective roles and goals of the participants relative to the context in which everything is taking place. List your supervisory goals, specify your own ground rules for supervision, and describe which major family therapy theories are informing your model. Next, we ask you to specify how much time you prefer to allot to individual and group supervision, and to the live, video, and case presentation modalities. Finally, if you have been working your way through this book one chapter at a time, what you are now thinking and writing has been stimulated by contemporary supervision literature. Therefore, we ask you to review what you have just written and observe how it relates to the theory and research in supervision presented in this book and elsewhere. You then add the citations. We have summarized this process as Table 13.1

Getting Started with Your Paper

Refresh your memory by skimming back through your notes from the self-discovery exercises of Chapters 1, 6, 7, 8, and 9. Because you have had extensive experience being supervised, you have learned a great deal about what is valuable. Overall, and at various stages of development, you have experienced some things as helpful and others as unhelpful, destructive, or otherwise unappealing. Some things had to do with the nature of the supervisory relationship. Others were specific supervisor behaviors and responses. Based on this acquired knowledge over the years, it is now time for you to make some notes about the big personal picture of your philosophy of supervision.

We want you to think about who and what, ideally, you want to be. Therefore, picture yourself being *the supervisor of your dreams* with a therapist. Visualize an individual session as clearly as you can—the room, the two of you, your clothing, your posture, and your expressions. Now begin to describe the following:

TABLE 13.1. Major Ingredients of the Philosophy of Supervision Statement

1. Describe your supervisory roles and goals.
2. Specify your own ground rules for supervision.
3. Describe which major MFT theories are informing your model.
4. Define the process by which you have integrated these theories and approaches.
5. Describe your overall view of the process of supervision.
6. Specify how much time you prefer to allot to individual and group supervision.
7. Specify your expected use of live, video, and case presentation modalities.
8. Identify your awareness of cultural aspects of supervision and offer an example.
9. Identify your awareness of ethical concerns and offer an example.
10. Identify your awareness of contractual and other administrative concerns.
11. Identify your awareness of the supervisory and theoretical literature.

- What is the therapist doing?
- What are you doing?
- Is there a developmental component?
- What are each of you feeling and thinking about the supervision and about each other?
- As you consider these matters, what does the relationship look like?
- What specific behaviors continue to illustrate that both of you are on the right track?
- Do your descriptions of you and the therapist include sensitivity to who the therapist is? If not, how can you add that?

Now begin to write these reflections down. Painting in broad strokes, write down what, in your mind and heart, you want to be and do in the role of a family therapy supervisor.

Defining Your Specific Goals and Roles

In this next step we want you to once again review your notes from the self-discovery exercises of Chapters 1, 3, and 9. This time we suggest that you categorize those issues and components that you have identified as areas that define *what makes supervision go well.* You may find it helpful to have two headings, one for generic aspects of supervision (structures, techniques) and one for supervisory relationships.

Under both of these headings you probably have included some abstract concepts. Make those concepts more concrete by adding a list of specific supervisory behaviors that illustrate them. For example, if you used the word "empower," what observable, auditable things would comprise that action? If, under relationships, you perhaps wrote "supportive," what would be involved in that? Support might be demonstrated by "listening in an affirming way." However, even that statement is abstract. Therefore, you may find it helpful to next describe behaviors demonstrative of listening in an affirming way. Finally, looking at these two lists, write a summary statement of *your* supervisory goals. Again, be specific.

Next, sit back and consider the multiple roles of supervisors: teachers, social facilitators, monitors, and comforters. As teachers, supervisors help therapists cope with complexity, integrate theory into practice, address ethics and professional standards, and evaluate (Caldwell & Diamond, 2000). Supervisors perform this role in many ways, for example, by role modeling, experiential learning, didactic presentation, and coaching. Supervisors also are social facilitators. They are co-creators and monitors of the supervisory relationship and keep the training system a safe environment for learning. Finally, supervisors are administrators. We are responsible for the safety of clients, we evaluate the progress of our trainees, and we monitor adherence to ethical and administrative expectations. We must keep careful records that are required by accrediting and licensing boards, the service setting, and third-party payers.

Now, picture yourself in a variety of clinical settings. Some settings may be from your past and others predictably in your future. What are the roles of the supervisors in these settings? Make a list of all of those supervisory roles you have already experienced or might expect to perform.

Now revisit your ideal supervisory self in light of the goals, roles, and settings you have just enumerated. Once again, picture yourself with a therapist, or group of them, being the supervisor you would really like to be—teaching, coaching, social facilitating, and administering. Close your eyes, picture a setting with the most mature supervisor you can imagine in it. Now, based on that image, who and what ideally do you want to be? What do you see as your "job," and what do you see as the ways that you get that done? If negative images arise, let them linger awhile, and then ask yourself what you would like to be doing instead.

Having completed these steps, your model should be emerging more clearly now. You should have your own clear list of goals in the various roles of supervision and how you intend to implement them with therapists.

Review Superordinate Rules and Concepts

Think back to the ground rules for supervision we set forth in Chapter 1. These are basic principles that we believe are absolutely critical ingredients of effective supervision. These are so important that if an administrator suspended or interfered with them we would consider resigning our positions. In fact, one of us did just that some years ago. A trainee was terminated from a degree-granting clinical program for well-documented issues of fraudulent practice. After the dust settled between the faculty, lawyers, and administrators, the clinical director was instructed by an administrator to reinstate the trainee in the program *and* was told that a nonclinical observer/"advocate" would attend *all* of this trainee's future individual or group supervision session.

We now want you to put yourself in that serious—nonnegotiable—place. First, take a few minutes to revisit your image of yourself being the supervisor of your dreams. Let your mind drift to barriers. In your mind's eye, what sorts of things in you and around you might keep you from being that ideal supervisor? Now, based on past experiences of good and bad supervision, your supervisory goals, and all that you believe about positive and negative supervisory and social processes, make a list of *your* basic and even "nonnegotiable" rules of supervision. (Think of yourself as Martin Luther, nailing your absolute credo to the cathedral door.) These are conditions that to you are so important to the process of supervision that you would resign before accepting any amendments.

Your list of nonnegotiable rules *must include two basic components* (AAMFT, 2002a):

1. Your model must conceptualize treatment and supervision in relational terms.
2. Your model must include an awareness of patterns and sequences of replication at various system levels.

Adding Your Personal Reflections

Who are you, anyway? Because the supervision philosophy statement is meant to be a personal statement about what you believe (Storm, 2000b), you need to find a way to consider your own personal values and your unique adaptive styles, and add these to what you are writing. On the one hand, it would be good to recognize those factors that for you are matters of "moral law." You made a list of such things in Chapter 9. Examples might include how respect is demonstrated, how much anger is acceptable and in what form, or what you consider to be an infringement on privacy. On the other hand, it also would be good to appreciate how you process life and go about solving problems. Are you a detail person or someone who operates in broad strokes? Are you more cognitive or affective? Do you believe in the value of listening and nurture, or are you a doer and fixer? Is there a way to consider how others would describe you with regard to these kinds of things? Perhaps, if you have not had the fun of being profiled using a personality trait inventory such as the Myers-Briggs Type Indicator (Briggs, 1980) or the 16 Personality Factor Inventory (Karson & O'Dell, 1975), the following exercise might be helpful. Look at the personality dimensions in Figure 13.1. We created this table so that you could profile your professional self by placing an "X" on the line in between each pair that describes you as a supervisor and therapist. If you think you are "adventurous," perhaps you can prove this by also having a significant other profile you using these traits and discussing the results!

This is the place that it would be appropriate, and encouraged, to add some traits you have learned about yourself on the basis of personal life experience, experiences as a trainee, and perhaps lessons from personal therapy. What have you learned from your own family of origin genograms about past and present

Action-oriented	----------------------------------	Reflective
Reserved	----------------------------------	Effusive
Adventurous	----------------------------------	Conservative
Verbal	----------------------------------	Pictorial
Trial-and-error	----------------------------------	Analytic/systematic
Didactic	----------------------------------	Experiential
Focused on feelings	----------------------------------	Focused on thinking
Listener/nurturer	----------------------------------	Doer/fixer
Laissez faire	----------------------------------	Controlling

FIGURE 13.1. Professional Personality Profile

familial influences on your own development, therapy, and supervision? Are there things about people, especially people in therapy, to which you are very sensitive? Are there matters about which you are insensitive and perhaps rarely ask? For example, a supervisor who had been raised in a very disengaged, "proper," and nondemonstrative family rarely thought to ask his trainees about their views regarding the expressions of physical affection in clinical families. Another supervisor, who often joked that her sister was an "only child," rarely inquired with her trainees into issues of the sibling relationships in clinical families.

As you consider the multiplicity of life roles you currently occupy and will probably occupy in the future, where do you see conflicts of interest and how do you intend to resolve them? Are there nonnegotiable priorities, and, if so, what are they, and what is their relative ranking? For example, one individual wrote "In principle, my children's needs will always come first, and then—maybe—my partner's. However, if it is not a survival need of my child or my partner, and my client has a major crisis, I will attend to that first."

Integrating the Theoretical Resources

Revisit your experiential notes from Chapter 6 and envision yourself in several recent supervisory situations where things were going well. What major family therapy theories were informing your model? Which of these do you feel the most comfortable with? Pitta (1996) provided a helpful example of this in her description of initial sessions with trainees, largely informed by Intergenerational (Bowen) theory. She extended this to the course of supervision with the overall goal of supervisee empowerment:

> When working with a supervisee I want to understand his or her functioning as part of a larger whole. I want to know about the supervisee's family interactions (3 generations preferably). This is accomplished by obtaining a genogram. When the supervisee presents the genogram, I use the systemic philosophy of Bowen. . . . I explore the levels of anxiety, fusion, triangulation, differentiation, conflict, and cut-offs within the supervisee and the supervisee's family system. I identify triggers and countertransferential issues that present difficulties (stuckness). While the supervisee presents the genogram I look for contextual variables . . . such as gender, race, ethnicity, marital status, family position, geographic location, and socioeconomic factors. (p.16)

Similarly, an Approved Supervisor Candidate (Harper-Jaques, 2002) wrote:

> I ask "Am I capable of supporting the model(s) the therapist wishes to use in therapy?" To answer this question, the therapist and I talk about the models that inform each other's work. . . . [But] my framework for practice is informed by a number of family therapy models—Milan

systemic . . . the Beliefs Model . . . and the Narrative model. . . . I endeavor to incorporate the concepts of circularity, hypothesizing, neutrality, and curiosity into supervision conversations. I listen for the therapist's beliefs about the client, the client's problem, and the therapist–client relationship. I also listen for the dominant discourse about the client that may influence the therapist's view of the client and may lead to impasses in therapy. I entertain multiple realities. I enhance exposure to multiple realities through the use of reflecting teams during live supervision.

In Chapter 6 we discussed the contributions of a variety of family therapy theories and how to select relevant aspects of each in developing your integrative model. That discussion and these two examples should provide you with a good start on incorporating your own views of theory in supervision.

Defining the Modalities You Will Use

Go back to your notes from Chapter 7 and review our discussion of the unique contributions of live, video, and case presentation approaches to supervision. Also review your notes from Chapter 8 concerning the strengths and concerns of individual and group supervision. Believing what you do about the things afforded and limited by each modality of supervision, given the limits of the settings in which you are likely to practice, and given the theories that inform your supervision, what is the relative proportion of your time that you will allot to the live, video, and case presentation modalities? What percentage of your supervision would you ideally like to conduct in an individual format and what percentage in a group format? Add these decisions and a concise rationale of when you would favor one over another to your philosophy statement.

Cite the Theories and Research

Although we have been exploring the models that will define what you do as a supervisor, it is important that you observe how your supervisory goals and behaviors relate to the theory and research in supervision presented and cited in this book. Go back over what you have written and add references, where appropriate, from the current family therapy supervision literature. Be alert to linkages between what you think and what theorists and researchers have indicated are best practices. Be generous in your attributions. By way of caution, Storm (2000b) listed two "fatal flaws." She observed that often supervisory candidates cite therapy literature instead of supervision literature. She also mentioned that they may fail to recognize obvious support for their ideas in the supervision literature. Therefore, it may be helpful for you to have some colleagues review your supervisory model to see where they find linkages to current *supervision* theory and research.

Meeting AAMFT Requirements for the Supervision Philosophy Statement

The AAMFT (2002a) has indicated that your philosophy statement should be approximately three single-spaced pages. If you are writing it as part of a formal supervision class, it should be reviewed by your course instructor. In all cases, it must be discussed with your supervisory mentor. Your philosophy of supervision paper should demonstrate that you have integrated the AAMFT's nine learning objectives (AAMFT, 2002a, as identified in the preface to this book) into your theory and practice of family therapy supervision. Your supervisory mentor has been instructed to evaluate your assumptions and guiding theoretical principles according to the following criteria:

- Did you consider treatment and supervision models in relational terms?
- Did you demonstrate an awareness of patterns and sequences of replication at various system levels?
- Did you demonstrate knowledge of the family therapy supervision literature by citing recent articles, chapters, and books, and did your supervision philosophy and methods relate to the current family therapy supervision literature?
- Did you demonstrate a clear theoretical orientation by articulating your philosophies of therapy and supervision as well as the clear connection between them?
- Were you sensitive to the multilevel implications of developmental, biological, sociocultural, gender, and family of origin issues?
- Did you address how personal values, beliefs, life experiences, and theoretical assumptions impacted your philosophy and practice of supervision?
- Did you demonstrate theoretical consistency, whether from one prominent model or from an integrative perspective? If the latter, did you demonstrate a logical integration of models?
- Did you present a rationale for your choice of supervisory methods and how the methods facilitated the achievement of your supervisory goals?

Creating the Written Philosophy Paper

Based on our foregoing discussions, the many lists of issues and ingredients that we have provided you, and your own experiences of processing and integrating all of these data, it is now time for us to turn you loose and encourage you to write a first draft of your philosophy of supervision. Take time to use your mind's eye, prompted by your notes. You want to capture your best reflections, understanding, and thoughts.

In the next chapter we present some practical examples of the value and effectiveness of an integrative model of supervision in action.

Chapter 14

Integrative Supervision
in Action

W e have discussed an entry-level model of integrative supervision and a foundation for you to get started in evolving you own integrative approach. We want this to be another more personal chapter, in which Craig is going to illustrate the application of a fully developed integrative model. He tells you two supervision stories with quite different outcomes. The first example also illustrates aspects of the developmental model that we discussed in Chapter 5. Here we use a *four phase model* that represents a trainee's progression along the training continuum:

1. *The introductory phase:* Assessing the trainee's strengths and weakness in the context of getting to know one another.
2. *The early phase:* Operationalizing systemic concepts in the therapy room.
3. *The middle phase:* Learning to read the "live history" and presence of the system.
4. *The final phase:* Conceptualizing and enacting family change.

The Case of the Supervisor Being Seduced by the Trainee's Cognitive Prowess

This is one of those training cases where you look back and wonder why you ever agreed to supervise a particular therapist. You will have these experiences, too. I tend to conduct fairly exhaustive screening interviews before committing to a course of supervision, and I had done that with this therapist. Even in writing this example, I still wonder, "How could I have missed, or simply ignored, the red flags?"

The Initial Screening

Jim's goal in requesting family therapy supervision was that this was an area in which he had always been interested. However, his graduate program offered no courses or training. He also expressed an interest in eventually starting a private practice and thought that family therapy would be a good area in which to specialize. At the time of our interview, he was working at a regional mental health facility. He had completed a rather traditional internship at a Veteran's Administration hospital and he had only limited exposure to family, marital, or children's issues. Jim had a doctorate in psychology from a research-based graduate program. He had received an initial master's degree in chemistry. His transcripts reported consistently high grades.

Jim was 28 years old with less than two years of postgraduate clinical experience. He was unmarried and reported limited ties with his family of origin, who lived in another area of the country. He was also completing his private pilot's license, which was another of his lifelong goals.

Overall, Jim seemed quite motivated and rather knowledgeable of family therapy literature from his own reading and workshop attendance. He had access to a good range of family-related cases, and he had permission from his administrator to pursue external supervision and to videotape his cases as needed. Although Jim was a little "standoffish" in the two screening interviews with me, he nevertheless presented himself as bright, analytical, and adequately responsive. I agreed to supervise him, and we worked out a plan for weekly one-hour supervision sessions in my office. We agreed that my role initially would be to focus on working with him as a beginning family therapy trainee, despite the fact that Jim already had his Ph.D. and some general clinical experience. He was agreeable to this contract and seemed eager to proceed.

The Introductory Phase: Assessing the Trainee's Strengths and Weaknesses in the Context of Getting to Know One Another

Once a supervision agreement is defined, I like to give myself a few introductory sessions in which to get to know the therapist. I then translate my early impressions from the screening interview into a working plan for supervision. Because I typically share some personal reflections of my own training and experience with trainees, this introductory period also gives the therapist opportunity to learn more about me, and to anticipate my style and personal orientation. My initial supervision plan with Jim, including where and how to start, would be based on how much he seemed to really know about family therapy, the professional skills illustrated in his case descriptions, his personal skills with me, and the presence of any red flags (such an inventory is outlined in Chapter 3).

We seemed to get off to a pretty good start. Perhaps to let me know that he was not "just" a beginning family therapist, Jim used a lot of systemic language and asked many theoretical questions. However, by the conclusion of the second introductory session with Jim I began to feel tightness in my stomach. For me this is a sign that something may not be quite right or that I may be missing something. The only issues that I could seem to identify at this point were that Jim was mildly arrogant and that he needed to present his materials and reflections in a "perfect" and unblemished manner.

Jim also reminded me a little of a former trainee, a trained psychoanalyst, in his preoccupation with identifying historical details, deducing trends, and interpreting motivations. I found this orientation somewhat seductive at first, because I enjoy bantering around theoretical propositions and hypotheses. However, it was becoming clear that Jim's natural abilities to recognize, respond to, and access emotions were almost nonexistent. I recognized, now just three or four sessions into supervision, that I had been seduced by his intellectual and analytical skills, and that providing helpful supervision for him was going to become much more of a challenge than I had originally anticipated.

So far, my own supervisory checklist indicated the following:

- Jim had a fair cognitive knowledge of the family therapy field and could speak the language of systems theory.
- His knowledge was exclusively theoretical and was derived from reading books and attending workshops. He had never completed a formal family therapy course.
- He had never been asked by his former supervisors to translate his theoretical knowledge into practical clinical dynamics. For example, Jim could not speculate how certain concepts, such as boundaries, might look within a family's experience.
- Jim could not recognize or experience what these concepts really looked like while he was in the room with a live clinical family. He could define a triangle, but he was not able recognize one in a live family, even when I labeled the participants of the triangle on a videotape for him.
- Jim had never received close supervision of his work during his internship at the VA hospital, even from traditional psychologists. His training primarily had been through consultants whose roles were to make sure he made his diagnoses properly. In fact, Jim began to become uncomfortable with my close supervisory role and my requests that he define, explain, and mark the dynamics that were going on around him.
- Jim was relying on his intellectual skills to try to ward off what I am sure he was experiencing as my intrusiveness. For example, one day he brought in an annotated bibliography on triangles in family systems from family therapy literature that he had prepared and read over a weekend. (It was actually one of the better ones that I had seen.)
- In his case reports and the two videotapes that I had thus far reviewed with him, Jim had demonstrated limited clinical skills in recognizing either emotional process in a family or even basic clinical and interactive dynamics.

- Jim quickly became frustrated when, instead of allowing him to tell me about his interventions, I insisted he focus first on being able to do a thorough family assessment and convince me that he could actually see and describe the clinical dynamics that were going on in his cases. I even provided him some model written family assessments to review.

Five sessions into the supervisory relationship I had to admit to myself that Jim was bright, and even well read, but that he lacked important family therapy basics. What was becoming the most obvious to me was that Jim apparently lacked the innate ability to recognize and access his own basic emotional resources, both for himself and for his cases.

He had not yet become particularly defensive in our supervision sessions because I had indulged the analytical skills on which he was quite reliant. His intellectual prowess had allowed him to progress through graduate school easily and probably served him well in learning to pilot an airplane. However, I expected that once I began to challenge Jim's emotional deficits his resistances would arise immediately.

Therefore, my plan became somewhat more rehabilitative to help Jim develop an integrated cognitive map of family functioning. I would let Jim intellectualize matters somewhat because he needed to; but, at the same time, I would try to help him translate his theoretical model of family functioning into dynamics that actually could be recognized in a family. I would then support him in identifying these dynamics in the actual clinical process.

I decided to let the emotional deficit issues rest in my head for a while. I felt that once I triggered Jim's resistances in this area, which probably were intrinsically linked to many issues of his own personal development and distance from his family of origin, it might be hard to get him refocused again on these fundamental concepts. I also decided that, despite my growing skepticism of Jim being able to master family therapy interventions and deal with clinical process, I wanted to give him the benefit of working through a few preliminary stages so that I could judge how far he could go. This is a choice every supervisor must learn to make: How far do we continue with struggling trainees in the hope of helping them cross a sort of invisible line where they have not only learned to think systemically but can actually work systemically in clinical settings?

The Early Phase: Operationalizing Systemic Concepts in the Therapy Room

In operationalizing systemic concepts I felt that my integrative approach would be helpful. It would offer me a broad range of resources from which to choose the ones that might help get Jim better focused. If I had been operating solely from a singular approach, such as strategic or even family of origin, I believe that we would have moved too quickly into clinical data, and Jim would not have been provided with a better systemic foundation. Such a move also could very well have frustrated him further because of his discomfort with live cases.

We began with the family systems concept list (Chapter 3). I asked Jim to select three concepts that he believed were crucial to family functioning. He selected *hierarchy, boundaries,* and *triangles.* I asked him to present a videotape of a two-parent, two-child family with which he was working and asked him to focus specifically on identifying these three concepts. The following week we watched the tape for 30 minutes. At first Jim did not know what he was looking for in the family members' interactions. He was stuck, and I could not even get him to guess about dynamics because he was afraid of "being wrong." As I somewhat playfully guided him through this, Jim focused on the family hierarchy, and again he became stuck trying to decide whether the mother or the father was really in charge of the family. However, as Jim thought about this, he looked for evidence in details of what the mother and father had to say directly to him. Jim did not consider the children's interactions with their parents in the session, the children's interactions with him, or the family's overall interaction with one another.

So, as a "good systemic supervisor," I asked Jim to sit back and just watch the family on the tape. In fact, I turned the volume off. Jim was clearly perplexed and we were able to laugh about that. But even our good humor did not permit Jim to speculate about or to identify with process issues. Next, I asked Jim to review some other videotapes of his cases and to bring me one for the next appointment in which he had been able to recognize some of the family dynamics from our list. I also humorously gave him permission to "leave the volume on" in his live cases. So now I had the dual role of teaching Jim to look and think systemically while also trying to help him keep track of what he was really doing with cases on a daily basis in his office. (I was becoming very concerned about this latter issue.)

This is where integrative supervision became a real resource, because it encouraged me to focus on helping Jim acquire a foundation of systemic thinking rather than jumping right in with unformulated and contextually meaningless clinical interventions. For Jim, this was absolutely the right place to begin. If he and I were successful in this phase, he would have a foundation of systemic knowledge and thinking upon which to build his career. He would also have learned to step back and look at the bigger systemic picture of the presenting cases. Although our trainees learn various interventions and techniques over the course of their careers, what they learn here in these early stages of integrative training will shape the way they see all of their cases and impact their relative future success as clinicians.

Jim's assignments with the tapes and my focus of supervision continued for the next eight weeks. Because he continued to struggle to identify dynamics within his own cases, I recommended that he review some of Minuchin's clinical tapes—the ones in which Minuchin interviewed families and then discussed the dynamics he had observed. This helped Jim briefly. Apparently, because this exercise did not involve his personal involvement with a case, he was less anxious and could be more objective. However, when we returned to the first videotape of Jim's clinical family, Jim still struggled to define the hierarchy.

Jim was becoming very frustrated with himself because his normally good analytical skills seemed to be failing him. There was somewhat of a breakthrough when I suggested to him that he was not objectively looking at the bigger picture. However, he still did not fully understand this, so I pointed out that perhaps the power in this family was not really with one of the parents, the people he had focused exclusively on, but with the older, parentified child. After nearly 15 minutes of puzzled looks and trying to fathom this, Jim began to get it. This was his first step at not only beginning to think systemically but realizing that he could learn a lot from the clinical data in front of him and not just rely on what his head—based on his reading—told him to find. Shifting his focus to the child seemed to make sense and opened a door, at least cognitively.

Over the next eight weeks Jim made progress slowly, but at least he was looking at the clinical dynamics. He was focusing on what was really going on within the clinical families and not just on what he should be doing to the family. We gradually expanded the list of systemic concepts until he was able to identify all of them on family tapes. This was a big accomplishment for him. He seemed delighted when he made a presentation that involved recognizing dynamics contributed by multiple family members.

For me, reaching this goal concluded the initial phase of supervision. Although Jim's progress was somewhat limited to his cognitive functioning, he now had a foundation for thinking systemically. If I had focused more on clinical interventions Jim would not have had this critical learning experience. In fact, I believe he would have become quite frustrated and even potentially self-destructive, as a trainee, due to frustrations with trying to make something happen clinically. I could have seen him become a therapist who applies a multitude of interventions with clients but lacks the ability to make informed, integrated decisions about what a particular case needs over the short-term and long-term. I have observed other beginning therapists, including family therapists, who practice in that fashion. To me, such a nonintegrative approach is akin to going to your family physician for a lingering stomachache and being prescribed antibiotics, then steroids, then antidepressants, and then an antianxiety agent, all without the benefit of a clear diagnostic procedure.

For the supervisor teaching from an integrative model, the primary goal is to lay a solid foundation of systemic concepts and systemic thinking. This foundation is used in the assessment/diagnostic process, and from these judgments come the selection of informed subsequent interventions.

The Middle Phase: Learning to Read the "Live History" and Presence of the System

For me, the middle phase of supervision focuses on teaching, prodding, confronting, and cajoling the therapist to experience the presence of the family system. I

see this as, in part, what Ackerman (1968) discussed when he encouraged therapists to "let the live history of the family emerge." But it is a lot more than that.
This step involves learning to engage (join) the family as a system. Many beginning therapists fail here. They must now put into action their internal checklist of
systemic concepts, appreciate how a clinical family is put together, and recognize
what is unique about its structure and process, where the power lies, and how to
engage each member. *This is the first step of integrating theory and practice.*

The therapist learns to move between *structure* (the interactional organization of the system) and *process* (the interactional data and emotions of the system). Teaching beginning therapists to experience and connect with another living
system is always an interesting process because, as we have discussed previously,
it elicits the unique qualities of their own family of origin experiences.

For Jim, this was the most difficult phase of his supervision. He was from a
moderately disengaging family of origin. Affection and caring were not expressed
demonstratively during his growing up years. He was not close to either of his
parents or his two sisters. He had learned quite well to use his cognitive skills to
get along in his family, but he did not learn to use his emotions. This pattern can
be a serious deficit for potential therapists because it leaves them without internal
models of how emotions are shared among family members. These unlucky therapists not only have trouble with the expression and understanding of their own
emotions, and those of their clients, but they also are uncomfortable when clinical
families become emotional. This translates into the therapist becoming standoffish, only cognitively available, and usually very analytical. Isomorphically, these
were the same traits (red flags) that I had sensed even in the early screening interviews. Jim demonstrated all of these traits with his cases, both individuals and
families, so where would we start?

Jim could visualize structural issues well because cognitively he had integrated the early systemic concepts. Of course, he had trouble recognizing these
features in the actual course of therapy because he was not able to identify with or
experience the emotional process within a family. It was as if there were a path-
way missing between what happened in front of him in his office and the knowledge he had in his head. Usually he would ask too many questions in sessions.
Even as he overcame the anxiety experienced by most beginning therapists, he
would continue to ask too many cognitive questions because he did not know how
to experience the family or how to allow them to show him what they were experiencing.

I explored some family of origin experiences and roles with Jim in the hope
that he could integrate aspects of this slightly more cognitive approach. I thought
that if he could at least do some "coaching," even cognitively, he would find a
start. But this was to little avail: There was simply very little personal family of
origin data from which he could draw and begin to apply to his work. I considered
referring Jim for adjunctive personal therapy. However, I decided that if I could
not access many emotional reflections in supervision, a therapist for Jim probably
would not fare any better.

When I reach this place of feeling stuck with a therapist, I try to look into the therapist's own broader system of life experiences for some help. Unfortunately, Jim had not been in a serious personal relationship for a year or more. If he had been, I might have referred him for couples therapy. That would at least have provided some live data for him to process. I even found myself wishing that Jim might have had some pets. I have been able to use pets with therapists and families to identify and explore personal models of interaction.

I turned my focus to the only interactive experiences that Jim could report in his current life situation, namely, his clinical cases. We began watching videotapes of his therapy sessions as well as some of the teaching tapes from other family therapists. As I often do with trainees who rely too often on cognitive/analytical styles, I turned off the volume, sat patiently with Jim, and speculated about what was happening in the nonverbal process we were observing. It probably took five hours of watching tapes like this before Jim was able to even feel some enthusiasm about this supervisory intervention. Without his and the clients' words to define his place within the family, he simply did not know what to do.

Simultaneously, I asked Jim to take his time with his clinical families. His only task was to talk casually and try to get to know them, the same way he would if he were in a social context. Jim had more success with this exercise than with the videotape process. Because he was not working in a setting where we could do live supervision, I finally offered to sit in on a few ongoing sessions with a couple and two family therapy cases. Following his cases through verbal reports and videotapes was not proving to be very helpful, so I decided to model dealing with process issues in a variety of his cases.

When I do this kind of live work with trainees, I like to identify myself to the clinical family as the therapist's supervisor and a consultant. Personally I am not comfortable being a silent supervisor who sits in sessions as an observer—my experience has been that it makes clinical families uncomfortable. I also do not like the role of co-therapist, even though many training programs use this model, because I believe that it diminishes a trainee's necessary role as the therapist.

Sometimes it is helpful for beginning therapists to observe the interviewing skills of their supervisors, but I have always used that sparingly, and usually just at the beginning of a training sequence. I believe it is more helpful to the professional growth of a trainee when I use the identity of a consultant because it gives me an identified role adjunctive to the ongoing role of the therapist while giving me permission to interact directly with the family. In any work like this it is always important for the supervisor to make every effort to support and empower the trainee therapist for the clinical family.

I must admit that I am often appalled when I see supervisors enter a case with a trainee and simply *take* over. The therapist is often pushed aside! I believe these are clear ego issues for the supervisors and not at all productive for the therapists. I can vividly remember observing such an experience at the site of a large doctoral program's clinic where I was consulting. I watched silently behind the one-way mirror as the supervisor was intrusively taking over the session while the members of the family tried desperately to keep eye contact with their therapist with whom they had been identified for three months. They almost seemed to be nonverbally pleading with the therapist to stand up to the supervisor. I felt sorry for the therapist whose authority and future role with this family were being undermined right before my eyes.

My preparation with Jim did not differ from when I do live work with other therapists. I carefully plan and rehearse potential issues with the trainee in the supervisory session just before the live interview. This is much like the football coach who scripts the first eight or ten offensive plays of a game. I do this to carefully support the therapist's role and authority with the family, and to give the trainee the first couple of "plays" so that she or he begins the session with a sense of authority. I do not want the therapist looking over her or his shoulder toward me for support or being worried about criticism.

In the rehearsal, I asked Jim to begin the interviews by introducing me as his supervisor and a consultant—again, to reinforce his role as the therapist. We scripted the next two exchanges (not interventions). His first task was to simply tell the family "It's nice to see you this week." He was to watch me for nonverbal cues as to whether I felt that he was following our plan and that he was listening to the family. He knew that I would not say anything, other than greeting the family, unless I felt he was going astray. He had been instructed to let the family offer the initial data and reply to his greeting.

Unfortunately, because of this family's prior experience with Jim, they expected him to take the lead. So they lacked spontaneity and waited to "answer" his questions. As Jim looked to me for help, I decided I needed to jump in. I was not willing to give up my goal of showing Jim how to allow the family to begin a session with their own data. (I am sure I had quoted Ackerman to him about the "live history" a dozen times.)

I had said a few playful things to the 8-year-old girl, the youngest in the family, as we walked into the session together. So I continued Jim's introductory remarks by asking the child about how school was going this week. She was eager to respond, and I imagined that Jim had probably never really addressed her personally in the prior sessions. She seemed pleased that I had talked to her first before her older brother or parents. She said she was going on a field trip but was worried that her parents would not let her go. I responded, "Oh," and she volunteered that her parents had a "bad fight" the other night and she was "grounded" because she had locked the door to her room and would not come out.

Of course, this was great stuff! I glanced at Jim and he seemed surprised. The parents were squirming in their chairs because they had neither planned for their conflict to be brought out so blatantly, nor expected that their daughter would make them look like the bad guys in the family.

I looked over to Jim again to give him a chance to jump in, but he had a hopeless look on his face and would not budge. I said to the little girl, "Well, tell me more." This opened up the entire session. Jim never got to use his second scripted exchange, which would have been, simply, "Tell me what's been happening this week." I really believe that he was still looking for a chance to make this statement, no matter how irrelevant, at the end of the session. He did interact with the parents a little bit on his own while they were trying to explain and defend their "fight." However, all of his interactions took the form of asking clarifying questions to each parent individually. He never followed my lead to continue the interaction with the child.

I always schedule a 30- to 60-minute review and debriefing session to take place immediately after such interviews. In fact, I will not schedule live supervision unless the therapists can be present for an immediate follow-up session, as too much data and too many reflections can be lost by waiting even a few hours. Jim was a mixture of emotions that he could not sort out. He was amazed by how much emotional data had been shared by the family in the absence of any direct questions. He talked with unusual animation about the way "the child" opened things up and he seemed pleased that he was able to "help" the parents "clarify" what had happened. I asked him if he felt sorry for the parents and he acknowledged that he did, but he could not say exactly why. However, it had not occurred to him that he had failed to interact with either of the children. He understood what I had done, but he could not see himself interacting so casually with this child.

Jim was also quite hard on himself for not doing more. I asked what he would have liked to have done differently. He responded, "I wanted to find out more about what the parents' fight was about and how long they had been fighting like this." He still could not step back and see the richness and drama of the here-and-now emotional process and dynamics of this family and the therapy session.

The middle phase of supervision concludes when students can show me videotapes of themselves sitting calming within the initial second or third family interview, engaging the system pleasantly, and reflecting clearly and succinctly on the dynamics, structure, and process of the system. Such demonstrations tell me that the therapists have made progress in integrating their own personal comfort and resources with the ability to recognize the dynamics of the family. This is the foundation upon which integrative therapy is based. If therapists cannot acquire this fundamental resource of listening and experiencing the structure and process of a family, then all of their future interventions will be at best random and haphazard. At worst, their future interventions will be determined by the therapists' unconscious personal needs. Sadly, Jim was not going to progress past this phase.

The Final Phase: Conceptualizing and Enacting Family Change

The final piece of the puzzle to be integrated involves the trainee's ability to select and effectively enact certain clinical interventions that are appropriate to the timing of the therapy process and the make up of the family system. This should not be confused with the process of integrating or, more accurately, blending aspects of major theoretical approaches (e.g., structural and psychoanalytical, or structural and strategic), as we discussed in Chapter 6. It is my belief that these efforts to blend differing theoretical approaches into a reasonable and effective clinical intervention can be accomplished effectively only by family therapists who have had at least five years of clinical experience. However, from an integrative approach, such a task is never necessary!

The final supervisory phase involves the therapists' ability to sort through their assessment checklists and to target specific dynamics (not just symptoms) within the context of the family system that would create the most meaningful changes for their clinical families. From an integrative perspective, this does not mean simply attempting interesting interventions that one saw demonstrated at a weekend conference to see if they will work. Nor does this mean plodding through extensive histories, unless you are looking for a specific pattern that reinforces a symptom. It means recognizing who you are as a therapist and what you think will evoke some change (first or second order) for the family, whether that is in the form of a structural, historical, or experiential approach.

So, if you are going to teach therapists to integrate their personal intervention styles with what they have learned from and are seeing in a clinical family, where do you start? Let's return to Jim. I was now into the fifth month of our supervision. I decided to take one more half-step to see if he could be moved a little farther toward the applied aspects of this phase. My own supervisory checklist told me that he was still at the beginning of the prior phase and he was not showing any evidence that he possessed the personal skills that would allow him to progress. However, on a few occasions I have jumped ahead with certain trainees who, once they actually experienced being able to "accomplish" interventions, were able to become more reflective and actually get in touch with clinical families' processes.

I selected Jim's case that I previously discussed. I had met them once and had a good feeling for them. With beginning-level family therapists, I usually start by recommending a straightforward structural intervention. I have found over the years that students can visualize changing a structure and, if they are successful, they will feel somewhat empowered. I reviewed our joint interview of that family with Jim and we discussed the powerful role of the daughter who spilled the beans about her parents' big fight. He had learned in subsequent interviews with this family that the girl often took the role of intervening in the parents' fights. She would even place herself physically between them. Jim agreed that this was an unhealthy family dynamic.

I suggested that, for the next therapy session, we develop a structural strategy through which Jim would engage the girl and her brother. The idea was to reinforce the sibling subsystem while subtly creating some boundaries for them apart from the parents. We expected that this development might expose issues in the marital subsystem. So, I predicted that Jim might observe some anxiety or discomfort on the part of the parents or even direct actions by them to sabotage his intervention with the children. This was all theoretical reasoning, so Jim enthusiastically discussed it with me and actually looked forward to the next family session. However, when I asked him how he thought he might engage the children, he seemed to have a hard time coming up with ideas. After a time he suggested, "I could ask them what their rooms look like."

Finally, I laid out a scenario for Jim to simply rearrange the family structurally in his office, after they had arrived and taken their seats, so that he would have the two children sitting together on one side of the room and the parents somewhat separated from them in chairs on the other side of the room. This involved moving the girl away from sitting next to the parents. He asked, "Do you mean that I just ask them to move their chairs?" I suggested that he just make up a reason for wanting to talk to the children separately.

The second goal I gave him, after he had accomplished the first, was to interact, playfully if he could, with the children for about 10 minutes. After this, I suggested that he gently change his position physically in his chair so that he could turn away from the children slightly and address the parents. Again, I explained how this subtle interaction that he was initiating and controlling in the family was a way of marking clearer boundaries in the system. This rang a bell and he understood what the goal was. However, Jim looked petrified: It seemed to me that he was clearly out of his element. He could not rely on his words, and, although he had the concepts in his head and the intervention had been laid out step by step for him, he did not appear to have the personal resources to integrate his cognitive knowledge with the actual process of interacting and changing family behaviors.

I offered Jim the chance to back-off of this intervention until he was more comfortable, but he said he wanted to try it. He brought the videotape of the session in for review at the next supervision meeting. It showed that right from the family's entrance into his office Jim was nervous and unsettled. The family had sat down with the girl seated, as predicted, next to the mother and the boy across the office by himself. Jim was so nervous that he did not even greet the family or offer any pleasantries. There were several minutes of awkward silence before the father began to complain about some financial issues. Jim then lost his chance for the intervention by becoming comfortably engaged with the father in the financial discussion.

In reviewing the videotape of this segment of the session, Jim explained, "My mind went blank." He added that he was relieved when the father finally spoke to him. The rest of his goals were lost and the session went downhill from there. Jim felt bad and confused. I told him that I believed him when he said that his mind genuinely went blank.

I had considered over the past month about how much longer I could legitimately supervise Jim. It was apparent that he did not have the personal resources to be an effective clinician or family therapist. In the next supervision session I apologized to him for promoting interventions that he could not handle. He seemed somewhat relieved but discouraged. I told him of my concern that he might not be well-suited to clinical work. We discussed his last interviews and reviewed his struggles, frustration, and discouragement. Jim was neither as surprised nor as upset as I had expected. I think he felt somewhat relieved but had trouble accepting a sense of failure, which he had never experienced in the pure academic world of concepts and words.

We discussed again the option of adjunctive psychotherapy. I told him that I would be happy to make a referral but that I would nevertheless discontinue supervision. I was not optimistic that personal therapy would instill resources that Jim just did not seem to possess, and I did not want to appear to be leading him on to continuing in the clinical field. After another supervision session, we agreed to discontinue supervision. I encouraged Jim to consider teaching in a nonclinical format because he was drawn to ideas, theories, and analytical thinking. Happily, he decided to take a position teaching marriage and family relations classes at a large junior college.

The Therapist Who Could Not Stop Fixing People

This next illustration describes a therapist that we join in the important middle phase of her supervision with me. Cathy was a 26-year-old second-year master's student in a COAMFTE-accredited family therapy program. She was the eldest daughter of an intact ethnic minority family. She had an older brother and a younger sister and brother. She described her family of origin as "very enmeshing" and she recognized that she had often played a caretaker role with her alcoholic parents. She had divorced two years before entering the family therapy program after a brief marriage to her high school sweetheart. She was bright, reasonably mature, and engaged well with her clients and other students.

Cathy had no trouble with the early and middle phases of supervision. She integrated well her systemic concepts with a good ability to observe the family's interaction and make effective assessments. In fact, she was ahead of the other trainees that I was supervising. I was impressed that, by the end of the first month in which I had been supervising her, she was able to define her own interventions which appropriately targeted clinical dynamics. The challenge in supervising her in this phase was to help her in an ongoing struggle with objectivity. Cathy brought to her therapy an underlying need, learned from her family of origin, to fix or take care of her clients.

As I observed her videotapes and live interviews, I continually pointed out to Cathy that she was allowing herself to be pulled too far into the internal dynamics and interactions of her clinical families. I worked with her on monitoring issues of *closeness* and *separateness*. She would typically get pulled into the role of a sympathizing caretaker with certain family members or with the entire family system. For example, the parents of one family were arguing in a therapy session over the intrusive role of the father's mother. Cathy actually left the session and placed a telephone call to the grandmother to explain how her behaviors and telephone calls had created a problem for the family.

This fix-it orientation created two specific problems for Cathy in therapy. First, it truncated what were often creative and on-target interventions. Cathy had the ability to easily create structural changes and to effectively use gentle strategic interventions. However, because she inevitably got pulled into the family's issues prematurely, she rarely gave her well-conceived interventions time to develop. Secondly, this fix-it trait made Cathy chronically susceptible to unnecessarily taking sides in arguments, be it one spouse against the other, or a child against a parent. In fact, two families had dropped out of treatment with her, and in each of the cases the fathers allegedly had refused to return. One of them said that the therapist and his wife had ganged-up against him.

In my experience, therapists who come from highly enmeshing families of origin like Cathy's, but lack her confidence and energy, have a tendency to get lost within the interaction of powerful systems. (Note the difference between Cathy's baggage from her enmeshing family of origin and Jim's struggles with the deficits from his disengaging family of origin.) Admittedly, I have observed that therapists who were parentified in their families of origin tend to bring a little more sense of control to their work with enmeshing systems. Nevertheless, I have seen some dramatic instances where the therapeutic skills of fairly objective and controlling parentified children were completely swallowed up in a highly enmeshing clinical family.

I have a training tape in which I sent a female/male team of second-year doctoral students into an initial session with a large family that included two parents, an adolescent, and two young adult children. The family was dominated by a verbally controlling and passive-aggressive father. I often show this tape to trainees and play the initial 10 minutes of the interview. I ask them, "Tell me if you can pick out the two therapists who are in this room." In most cases they cannot— both therapists were completely swallowed up by this powerful enmeshing system. One of the therapists had been a parentified child in her own enmeshing family of origin and the other (the male) was from a more disengaging family of origin. I had actually expected the male therapist to be able to remain somewhat aloof (which was an aspect of his own learning issues) and not become seduced by this family.

Cathy acknowledged my supervisory concerns but seemed compelled to continue her rescuing and fixing. She had been in personal therapy for six months following her divorce and reported that she learned through that experience that she had probably married her former partner to "take care of him . . . he had a drinking problem." As part of the training program, she had also completed a personal family of origin genogram. I asked her to bring the genogram to the next supervision session. In discussing her genogram, Cathy was able to identify her family of origin as quite enmeshing, and she had already labeled her role in the family as the parentified child. She had made progress personally in differentiating from her rather closed, highly enmeshing family system. She was also able to recognize how some of her family of origin experiences and roles were able to help her recognize familiar patterns and dynamics with her clinical families.

Cathy demonstrated good objectivity about these family of origin dynamics and some ease in discussing them. I decided not to struggle directly with trying to help Cathy back off her fix-it role (this was the metaphor I had begun to use, somewhat humorously, to characterize it). I also decided that there was no need to refer her at this time to adjunctive therapy, because she had already reported a good therapy experience and she seemed to recognize her personal dynamics fairly objectively from her genogram work.

This is where the integrative supervisor benefits from a broad range of possible resources. The integrative supervisor is not wedded to a singular model of intervention, so she or he can help trainees decide not only on what treatment intervention might be appropriate to the clinical family, but also on what approach would be the most useful and successful for the therapist. Cathy's demonstrated skills with structural and strategic interventions had not helped her remain objective or manage her own fix-it tendencies. In fact, I sensed that her success, particularly with structural interventions, had actually reinforced the fix-it role. So I decided to focus her on integrating a more historical model in her therapeutic role. She was active and liked to "do" things (unlike Jim, who liked to talk about things), so I thought that a less active, more historical and reflective perspective might help her gain some objectivity over her inherent skills and predilection for caretaking.

I asked Cathy to review some of the works of Framo and Bowen to see how they had defined differentiation issues as a part of improving family and marital functioning. Of course, my other strategy here was that, by giving Cathy permission to focus on clinical history in order to define differentiation issues, I was also laying the groundwork for her to recognize and learn to integrate her own differentiation issues into her model of therapy (parallel process and isomorphism, again). I believe that supervisors need to appreciate that many of the inherent traits of our trainees can provide both positive and negative attributes for their roles as therapists. We should not assume that all personal baggage is dysfunctional. That is why this process of integrating personal resources with knowledge and clinical skills is so important.

I offered to do a live observation with some of Cathy's next sessions because I suspected she would struggle somewhat in making the recommended shift in her therapeutic role. Just 10 minutes into one of these sessions with a couple, Cathy began sympathizing with the wife about her husband's work schedule. When we consulted later in mid-session, Cathy recognized what she had been doing. She returned to the therapy session determined to gather family of origin history equally from both spouses. I had suggested Cathy pretend that she was developing her own genogram, and that she should simply try to collect more data for it. This artifice worked and she was able to start with and stay focused on some historical information with her next case, too.

Several weeks later, Cathy indicated that she now felt comfortable and objective about her former need to fix clients. She understood where that need came from and how it got in her way without her realizing it. She believed that our supervisory experience provided her with a valuable intervention resource that she could integrate into her clinical work.

This recognition became a turning point for Cathy. By learning to integrate historical data into her therapeutic interviews she was able to create more objectivity for herself. She could also experience herself as helping/fixing aspects of the family without becoming too personally enmeshed in the family's emotional system. The important integrative step for Cathy was learning to utilize a certain clinical approach (in this case, family of origin) that not only helped her remain focused in her direct clinical role, but also served to integrate aspects of her own personal issues and resources with her developing therapeutic model.

We hope the struggles with Jim's training and the use of a broad range of integrative resources have illustrated the value of this approach even with a difficult trainee. The positive outcomes in Cathy' supervision, we believe, could only have been accomplished this efficiently by being able to use multiple resources and helping her to integrate the most helpful ones for her personal style.

Chapter 15

Bringing the First Stage of Our Journey to a Close

Because the first half of this final chapter is very personal, it is characterized by a lack of citations. We wish to summarize where we hope we have been together with you, and share some personal thoughts about the lifelong process of becoming a family therapy supervisor. In the second half, we discuss the supervision of supervision.

Recapitulation and Final Thoughts

We have written an introductory textbook on family therapy supervision. One of our prepublication reviewers observed the paradox inherent in this. On the one hand, our goal is to provide something very basic and simple. We want to eschew esoteric concepts and jargon. We want fundamental concepts to be clear and not obscured by sophisticated splitting of hairs. On the other hand, we are writing to an audience of experienced clinicians and, in many cases, experienced supervisors. Because we are painting in broad strokes and eschewing jargon, some highly educated and experienced individuals may at first glance perceive our work as simplistic. It is not. We believe that, as you have traveled along with us, you have seen how this work is informed by a wealth of clinical experience, book knowledge, and research. Nevertheless, if your experience with us through this book is a journey, we understand that the departure point and destination will differ for each of you. Our approach has been designed to meet each of you where you currently stand, and to facilitate your progress to your uniquely personal next step.

We are also aware that there are two other excellent treatises on family therapy supervision on library shelves. Why have we offered a new one? In working with the last two generations of supervisors, our approach has evolved in response to the changing practice of marital and family therapy, defined by the diversity of its professionals, its theories and interventions, and the settings in which it is practiced. As we noted from the outset, we have come to recognize that a "one size fits all" approach is no longer a viable way to operate. If supervisors perceive themselves as hammers, then their trainees must all be nails. Just as therapy must not be a procrustean couch, neither should its supervision. Moreover, the participants in our workshops and classes often spoke of their frustration in educational pursuits dominated by one theoretical school. They complained that their learning objectives were not being met—namely, to be able to provide supervision specific to their practice settings and clientele. They also did not feel that their experience and their unique stories were respected. Through verbal and nonverbal communication they emphasized that they wanted a collaborative learning experience that began with their definition of who they were, and that included their own unique learning objectives. They did not want this process to be a voyage into narcissism, however. They wanted their journey to be informed by the major family therapy theoretical influences and the best supervisory academic lore. Many also wanted it to satisfy the educational requirements for the AAMFT Approved Supervisor credential.

Throughout this book we have spoken about our concerns with eclecticism and intuitive approaches. We believe that insight is as important, along with behavioral change. The latter brings relief, but the cognitive learning that takes place is expected to become part of the supervisor's clinical resources and to be used whenever problematic circumstances again arise. Moreover, although many effective teachers of family therapy have written eloquently about the practice of therapy as an "art" and a "dance," it is in reality an artistry informed by a (perhaps implicit) metatheory of human relational behavior formed by many years of education, training, and clinical experience. The "artists" in fact are scientist-practitioners who appreciate the cybernetics of cybernetics. Actions that may seem intuitive to the observers of master sessions in fact are not. We also are reminded of the admonishment of a supervisory consultant (Joseph Dreyer) many years ago. When a therapist or a supervisor "shoots from the hip," that is, acts on intuition, it creates substantial room for the influence of his or her unconscious processes. The unconscious may be a powerful source of creativity, but it requires the mediation of our conscious, sophisticated, mature, and problem-oriented faculties. *We should know why we are doing what we are doing.*

With all of these goals in mind, we began our journey with you with "generic" family therapy supervision. But because we respect who you are and what you ultimately will need as family therapy supervisors, we tried to stay relevant to the unique contexts in which you may now or later be practicing. Therefore, we set out some fundamental ideas while also giving you solution-focused exercises to remind you of your own experiences and to help you sort through them. In this way we intended to get you started (a) consolidating your experience if you were already doing supervision, or (b) doing supervision if you were just beginning. We described those things—rules and methods—all family therapy supervisory settings require. We described an introductory model for integrative supervision that incorporated the developmental features of the entire training system. We looked at what the major family therapy theories had to contribute to the supervision process. We discussed the tools of supervision: live, videotape, and case presentation approaches, and the unique contributions of individual and group supervisory formats. We offered an overview of how to regard contextual issues throughout the training system. We discussed troubleshooting and administrative tools and resources. These preparatory chapters then culminated in exercises in which you constructed your own personal models of supervision—with the understanding that your models would be dynamic constructs that would evolve over time and context. Throughout, we tried to have a dialogue with you about family therapy supervision focused on the practical, day-to-day application of scholarship in contemporary supervision settings.

In this endeavor, except for our 13 Principles (Table 1.1) we do not believe that we are bringing you "sacred scripture." We see ourselves as facilitators who have value because of our own experiences as lifelong learners to be therapists and supervisors. We also believe that sophisticated integrative models of therapy and supervision are not explicitly taught or imposed from the outside. We believe that your models of therapy and supervision are internal constructions that will emerge and evolve. Years of reading and appreciative reflection on the events of your practice will percolate down though your thought processes and come forth as internalized convictions about what family therapy and its supervision are, these will become your guidelines about how to train therapists. Our models are ways that we have found to make sense out of the supervisory setting. Like all such models, they alert you to some things and blind you to others. Their ultimate value is the extent to which they are useful to you.

However, as much as we view becoming a supervisor as being a lifelong process in which the evolving person of the supervisor is an integral component, at the conclusion of this book we expect that you would have accomplished the content objectives set forth in the *Approved Supervisor Designation: Standards and Responsibilities Handbook* (AAMFT, 2002a). You are familiar with the major models of family therapy and their philosophical assumptions about and pragmatic implications for family therapy supervision. You have articulated your own personal model of supervision, drawn from existing models of supervision and from your preferred styles of therapy. Having considered the implications of the supervisor–therapist–client system, you can facilitate the co-evolving therapist–client and supervisor–therapist–client relationships, and be able to identify and evaluate problems in therapist–client and supervisor–therapist–client relationships. You can structure supervision, solve problems, and implement supervisory interventions within a range of supervisory modalities (e.g., live and videotaped, and individual and group supervision). Finally, you are sensitive to contextual variables such as culture, gender, ethnicity, and economics, and knowledgeable of ethical and legal issues in supervision.

The Process of Becoming a Family Therapy Supervisor

We have said that we view becoming a family therapy supervisor as a lifelong process in which the evolving person of the supervisor is an integral component. Our hope is that it is a *self-conscious* process that appreciates the interdependency of clinical experience (both therapy and supervision, as a consumer and a practitioner), formal learning experiences (continuing involvement with family therapy and supervision theory and research), and one's personal and professional developmental trajectory. Out of this multivariate equation, and the "facts" of the training system, come models and interventions that must be evaluated with regard to auditable outcomes. Your supervisory self should accommodate to the results of these assessments.

We recognize that this is a kind of case study or field research in which individuals may serve as their own controls. Although not always satisfactory for formal research, it may be the best that we can do, and the least that we should do. (For a thorough discussion of these matters, see Moon & Trepper, 1996.)

Our enthusiasm for educational experiences throughout supervisors' professional lives is dampened by two areas of concern. First, research in family therapy reminds us that no one theory has demonstrated its superiority over another (Pinsof & Wynne, 1995). Some therapists get better results using a given theory than do others, and some clients "do better" than others. We well may wonder how much positive change is attributable to who the therapist is and who the client is. We also may wonder if the specifics of a given theory are important to a given clinical situation, or if there are growth-inducing elements common to all of them (Sprenkle, 2002; Sprenkle, Blow, & Dickey, 1999). Generalizing from research in therapy to research in supervision, it is reasonable to hypothesize that who the supervisor is and who the therapist is may be more important than the theory that informs their interaction. Research also may uncover factors common to successful supervision, for example, the *13 Principles* given as Table 1.1. Moreover, supervisors may wish to pursue outcomes beyond those specified by traditional family therapy theories. For example, they may wish to inculcate those aspects facilitative of resiliency in their training settings, with the goals of increasing the resourcefulness and hardiness of their trainees.

Second, we recommend that family therapy supervisors be wary of training in models and interventions of which the validity is "proven" by anecdotal evidence, testimonials, or their own personal reaction to it when demonstrated. Presenters usually select cases that illustrate success. We rarely are given examples where applications do not work, and presenters often do not discuss the indications and contraindications of their models. We rarely are told about those who dropped out of the training process or who expressed unhappiness with it. We have no way of knowing whether trainees would have done equally well or better with another supervisor or a different supervisory process. In some cases, the presenter makes no reference to a body of work (theory, practice, or research) other than his or her own. Master sessions by revered supervisors bring their wisdom to a single event, on a stage, that may be far removed from the context and course of actual supervision. Attendance at master sessions and participation in circumscribed workshops also may trigger personal emotional issues that may not be linked to the needs of one's immediate clinical practice.

Finally, we encourage our readers to develop supervision courses themselves. Active, cooperative learning is more efficacious than passive and didactic learning (Johnson, Johnson, & Holubec, 1994). By teaching supervision to others, you have an opportunity to consolidate what you know and to benefit from the critique and diverse experiences of others. As we try to convey ideas to others, free of jargon, we often come to understand the content area and process better ourselves.

Supervision of Supervision

Candidacy Requirements

Many readers are using this book in connection with obtaining Approved Supervisor status through the AAMFT. The requirements for this credential have been changed (October, 2002). The current policies and procedures, along with helpful forms and checklists, are given in the *Approved Supervisor Designation: Standards and Responsibilities Handbook* (AAMFT, 2002a; hereafter referred to as the *Handbook*). This resource is available online at www.aamft.org; a booklet copy also is available:

> Approved Supervisor Specialist
> The American Association for Marriage and Family Therapy
> 112 South Alfred Street
> Alexandria, Virginia 22314
> Phone: (703) 838-9808

The *Handbook* is indispensable to serious candidates. We will briefly summarize the principal features of the credentialing process. Specific policies and recommendations are given in the *Handbook*.

1. You will identify an Approved Supervisor at the time you wish to begin training and contract with that person to be your supervisory mentor. Together, you will develop a plan for your training. Your supervisory mentor will guide and monitor your progress and eventually will make the recommendation that you be designated an Approved Supervisor.

2. You will complete the training requirements, including a supervision fundamentals course approved by the AAMFT, provide supervision to marriage and family therapy trainees, and receive supervision mentoring.
3. If not one already, you will become an AAMFT clinical member or demonstrate that you have been offered clinical membership.
4. Once you have met all of the training and experience requirements for the Approved Supervisor designation, you will make a formal application.
5. Every five years you will need to renew your Approved Supervisor designation.

Whatever other responsibilities you may have, Approved Supervisors and Approved Supervisor candidates are expected to train individuals who are seeking AAMFT clinical membership. Often AAMFT Approved Supervisors are invited to provide clinical supervision of those seeking state practice credentials or holding a limited license. Whether its purpose is to meet the credentialing requirements of AAMFT or of legal statutes, supervision of marital and family therapy is expected to have the following characteristics (AAMFT, 2002a):

- There is weekly face-to-face conversation between trainee and supervisor, usually in periods of one hour each.
- The learning process is sustained and intense and focuses on raw data from the trainee's ongoing clinical practice.
- It is a process that is different from personal psychotherapy.
- It is normally completed over a period of at least one year.

Supervisory mentoring, in turn, is also a sustained and intense process (AAMFT, 2002a). There is an overarching aspect to it, wherein the supervisory mentor assumes responsibility for overseeing a candidate's work, provides supervision mentoring, evaluates the candidate's progress, and assists the candidate in making final application for the Approved Supervisor designation. The supervision mentoring sessions must meet certain standards:

- They must focus primarily on live or videotaped supervision sessions.
- They must consist of face-to-face conversation between the mentor and the trainees, and are typically an hour in length.
- There may be no more than two supervision candidates present in a mentoring session.
- The focus of the mentoring sessions is to be on the candidates' development of supervisory skills.

Again, for specific details about policies and procedures, and for information about special candidacy circumstances, the reader is referred to the *Handbook*.

The Process of Supervision of Supervision

Some experts have observed that supervision of supervisors is different from supervising therapists (Storm, Todd, McDowell, & Sutherland, 1997). We are not persuaded that this is so. Supervisory mentors, supervisors, therapists, and clinical families all must establish a working alliance (a collaborative relationship in pursuit of mutual goals). Supervisory mentors, supervisors, and therapists must be attentive to and manage all four levels of the training system (Figure 4.1, Chapter 4), including their own unique perceptions of and contributions to it. All three parties are responsible for co-creating a developmentally and task appropriate learning experience at each level, oriented toward developmentally appropriate outcomes. Supervisory candidates, therapists, and client families must all move from appropriate identification and dependency to individuation/emancipation (Bardill, 2000). All three parties also have troubleshooting, evaluative, and gatekeeping functions, best understood in the context of the four-dimensional training system model and the four knowledge bases (Figure 11.1, Chapter 11).

Because of isomorphism on the one hand, and family system and developmental dynamics on the other, we believe that supervision of supervision is indissoluble from the dynamics at and between all levels of the training system. Our introductory integrative model (Chapters 3 to 5) subsumes supervision of supervision, and we believe that yours should as well.

Supervision of supervision must be appreciative of contextual issues, professional responsibilities, and standards of ethical practice at all levels of the training system. Just as therapists attend to the person of the client, and supervisors to the person of the therapist, supervisory mentoring should include attention to the person of the supervisor in terms of transgenerational legacies and contextual factors influencing personal and professional development (Le Roux, 2000). Supervisory mentors co-create a safe training and therapeutic environment by dint of their expectations, mood, and interventions. Also, because of their own administrative responsibilities, supervisory mentors must be aware of the responsibilities of the other members of the training system and use the best administrative tools available. The administrative responsibilities, ethics, standards of practice, and the administrative resources and tools discussed in Chapter 12 apply to supervision of supervision. For example, supervisory candidates should practice within the scope of competence of the training system and within its contextual requirements (including auditing, record keeping, and reports). Moreover, supervisory mentors can be expected to prepare supervisors for the business side of their work and to interface their professional work with other areas of their lives (Storm, 2000c).

References

Ackerman, N. W. (1968). *Psychodynamics of family life.* New York: Basic Books.

Ackerman, N. W., & Behrens, M. (1956). The family group and family therapy: The practical application of family diagnosis. *International Journal of Sociometry, 1,* 52–54.

Akinyela, M. M. (2001). Sometimes I rage: Black men, therapy, and resilience. Presentation to the 59th annual conference, American Association for Marriage and Family Therapy, Nashville, TN.

Allen, W. D., & Olson, D. H. (2001). Five types of African-American marriages. *Journal of Marital and Family Therapy, 27,* 301–314.

American Association for Marriage and Family Therapy. (2001). *AAMFT Code of Ethics.* Washington, DC: Author.

American Association for Marriage and Family Therapy. (2002a). *Approved supervisor designation: Standards and responsibilities handbook.* Washington, DC: Author.

American Association for Marriage and Family Therapy. (2002b). International supervisees: A different perspective on cultural competency. *Family Therapy Magazine, 12,* 44–45.

Andersen, T. (1991). *The reflecting team.* New York: Norton.

Andersen, T. (1993). See and hear, and be seen and heard. In S. Friedman (Ed.), *The new language of change: Constructive collaboration in psychotherapy* (pp. 303–322). New York: Guilford.

Anderson, H. (1993). On a roller coaster: A collaborative systems approach to therapy. In S. Friedman (Ed.), *The new language of change: Constructive collaboration in psychotherapy* (pp. 323–344). New York: Guilford.

Anderson, H. (2000). "Supervision" as a collaborative learning community. In *Readings in family therapy supervision* (pp. 8–11). Washington, DC: American Association for Marriage and Family Therapy.

Anderson, J. (2000). Supervising in an urban multi-cultural agency. In *Readings in family therapy supervision* (pp. 202–203). Washington, DC: American Association for Marriage and Family Therapy.

Anderson, S. A., Rigazio-DiGilio, S. A., Schlossberg, M., & Meredith, S. (2000). Four dimensions deemed essential to quality supervision: Theoretical, personal, and empirical account. In *Readings in family therapy supervision* (pp. 64–66). Washington, DC: American Association for Marriage and Family Therapy.

Anderson, S. A., Schlossberg, M., & Rigazio-DiGilio, S. (2000). Family therapy trainees' evaluations of their best and worst supervisory experiences. *Journal of Marital and Family Therapy, 26,* 79–91.

Aponte, H. J. (1994). How personal can training get? *Journal of Marital and Family Therapy, 20,* 3–15.

Ard, B. N. (1973) Providing clinical supervision for marriage counselors: A model for supervisor and supervisee. *Family Coordinator, 22*(1), 91–97.

Bardill, D. R. (2000). Fostering creativity in the supervisory process. In *Readings in family therapy supervision* (pp. 229–231). Washington, DC: American Association for Marriage and Family Therapy.

Barnett, D. W., Daly, E. J., Hampshire, E. M., Rovak Hines, N., Maples, K. A., Ostrom, J. K., & Van Buren, A. E. (1999). Meeting performance-based training demands: Accountability in an intervention-based practicum. *School Psychology Quarterly, 14,* 357–379.

Bean, R. A., Perry, B. J., & Bedell, T. M. (2002). Developing culturally competent marriage and family therapists: Treatment guidelines for non-African-American therapists working with African-American families. *Journal of Marital and Family Therapy, 28,* 153–164.

Becvar, D. S. (2000). Professional boundaries and ethics: Ongoing considerations. In *Readings in family therapy supervision* (pp. 157–159). Washington, DC: American Association for Marriage and Family Therapy.

Becvar, D. S., & Becvar, R. J. (2003). *Family therapy: A systemic integration* (5th ed.). Boston: Allyn & Bacon.

Berg, I. K., & DeShazer, S. (1993). Making numbers talk: A solution-focused approach. In S. Friedman (Ed.), *The new language of change* (pp. 5–24). New York: Guilford.

Bernard, J. M., & Goodyear, R. K. (1998). *Fundamentals of clinical supervision* (2nd ed.). Boston: Allyn & Bacon.

Bischoff, R. J., McKeel, A. J., Moon, S., & Sprenkle, D. H. (1996). Therapist-conducted consultation: Using clients as consultants to their own therapy. *Journal of Marital and Family Therapy, 22,* 359–379.

Black, L., & Piercy, F. P. (1991). A feminist family therapy scale. *Journal of Marital and Family Therapy, 17,* 111–120.

Blow, A. J., & Sprenkle, D. H. (2001). Common factors across theories of marriage and family therapy: A modified Delphi study. *Journal of Marital and Family Therapy, 27,* 385–401.

Bograd, M. (1992). The duel over dual relationships. *The Psychotherapy Networker, 16,* 33–37.

Bordin, E. S. (1979). The generalizability of the psychoanalytic concept of the working alliance. *Psychotherapy: Theory, Research, and Practice, 16,* 252–260.

Bowen, M. (1978). *Family theory in clinical practice.* New York: Aronson.

Boyd-Franklin, N. (1989). Five key factors in the treatment of Black families. *Journal of Psychotherapy and the Family, 6,* 53–69.

Breunlin, D. C., Karrer, B. M., McGuire, D. E., & Cimmarusti, R. A. (1988). Cybernetics of videotape supervision. In H. A. Liddle, D. C. Breunlin, & R. C. Schwartz, (Eds.), *Handbook of family therapy training and supervision* (pp. 194–206). New York: Guilford.

Breunlin, D. C., Liddle, H. A., & Schwartz, R. C. (Eds.). (1988a). *Handbook of family therapy training and supervision.* New York: Guilford.

Breunlin, D. C., Liddle, H. A., & Schwartz, R. C. (1988b). Concurrent training of supervisors and therapists. In H. A. Liddle, D. C. Breunlin, & R. C. Schwartz, (Eds.). *Handbook of family therapy training and supervision* (pp. 207–224). New York: Guilford.

Breunlin, D., Schwartz, R., & Mac Kune-Karrer, B. (1992). *Metaframeworks: Transcending the models of family therapy.* San Francisco: Jossey-Bass.

Briggs, I. B. (1980). *Gifts differing: Understanding personality type.* Palo Alto, CA: Consulting Psychologists Press.

Bronfenbrenner, U. (1992). Ecological systems theory. In R. Vasta (Ed.), *Six theories of child development* (pp. 187–249). London: Jessica Kingsley.

Caldwell, K., & Diamond, D. (2000). In the cauldron: A case study of training for clinical supervisors. In *Readings in family therapy supervision* (pp. 241–243). Washington, DC: American Association for Marriage and Family Therapy.

Carlson, T. D., & Erickson, M. J. (2001). Honoring the privileging personal experience and knowledge: Ideas for a narrative therapy approach to the training and supervision of new therapists. *Contemporary Family Therapy: An International Journal, 23,* 199–220.

Carolan, M. T. (1999). Integrating gender into the practice of supervising marriage and family therapists. In R. E. Lee & S. Emerson (Eds.), *The eclectic trainer* (pp. 17–37). Galena, IL: Geist & Russell.

Carter, B., & McGoldrick, M. (Eds.). (1998). *The expanded family life cycle: Individual, family, and social perspectives* (3rd ed.). Boston: Allyn & Bacon.

Caust, B. L., Libow, J. A., & Raskin, P. A. (1981). Challenges and promises of training women as family systems supervisees. *Family Process, 20,* 439–447.

Chaney, S. E., & Piercy, F. P. (1988). A feminist family therapist behavior checklist. *American Journal of Family Therapy, 16,* 305–318.

Cicchetti, D., & Garmezy, N. (1993). Propsects and promises in the study of resilience. *Development and Psychopathology, 5,* 497–502.

Cohler, B. J., Stott, F. M., & Musick, J. S. (1995). Adversity, vulnerability, and resilience: Cultural and developmental perspectives. In D. Cicchetti & D. Cohen (Eds.), *Developmental pathology, Vol. 2: Risk, disorder, and adaptation* (pp. 753–800). New York: Wiley.

Colapinto, J. (1988). Teaching the structural way. In H. A. Liddle, D. C. Breunlin, & R. C. Schwartz, (Eds.), *Handbook of family therapy training and supervision* (pp. 17–37). New York: Guilford.

Commission on Accreditation for Marriage and Family Therapy Education (2002). *Standards of Accreditation* (version 10.1). Washington, DC: Author.

Constantine, M. G., Juby, H. L., & Liang, J. J-C. (2001). Examining multicultural counseling competence and race-related attitudes among white marital and family therapists. *Journal of Marital and Family Therapy, 27,* 353–362.

Corey, G., Corey, M., & Callanan, P. (1988). *Issues and ethics in the helping professions.* Pacific Grove, CA: Brooks/Cole.

Daly, E. J., Witt, J. C., Martens, B. K., & Dool, E. J. (1997). A model for conducting a functional analysis of academic performance problems. *School Psychology Review, 26,* 554–574.

Daniels, H. (1996). *An introduction to Vygotsky.* New York: Routledge.

Dicks, H. V. (1967). *Marital tensions.* New York: Basic Books.

Di Nicola, V. (1997). *A stranger in the family: Culture, families, and therapy.* New York: Norton.

Doehrman, M. (1976). Parallel process in supervision and psychotherapy. *Bulletin of the Menninger Clinic, 40,* 9–104.

Doherty, W. J., & Simmons, D. S. (1996). Clinical practice patterns of marital and family therapists: A national survey of therapists and their clients. *Journal of Marital and Family Therapy, 22,* 9–25.

Dumka, L. E., Martin, P., & Sprenkle, D. H. (1995). Development of brief scales to monitor clients' constructions of change. *Journal of Family Psychology, 9,* 385–401.

Dwyer, T. F. (1999). Barging in. In R. E. Lee & S. Emerson (Eds.), *The eclectic trainer* (pp. 133–143). Galena, IL: Geist & Russell.

Dwyer, T. F., & Lee, R. E. (1999). A picture is worth a thousand words: Exploring metaphors in training. In R. E. Lee & S. Emerson (Eds.), *The eclectic trainer* (pp. 88–104). Galena, IL: Geist & Russell.

Egeland, B., Carlson, E., & Sroufe, L. A. (1993). Resilience as process. *Development and Psychopathology, 5,* 517–528.

Elliot, R. (1986). Interpersonal process recall (IPR) as a psychotherapy process research method. In L. Greenberg & W. Pinsoff (Eds.), *The psychotherapy process: A research handbook* (pp. 503–527). New York: Guilford.

Ekstein, R., & Wallerstein, R. S. (1958). *The teaching and learning of psychotherapy.* New York: Basic Books.

Emerson, S. (1999). Creating a safe place for growth in supervision. In R. E. Lee & S. Emerson (Eds.), *The eclectic trainer* (pp. 3–12). Galena, IL: Geist & Russell.

Everett, C. A. (1979). The masters degree in marriage and family therapy. *Journal of Marital and Family Therapy, 5,* 7–13.

Everett, C. A. (1980a). An analysis of AAMFT supervisors: Their identities, roles, and resources. *Journal of Marital and Family Therapy, 6,* 215–226.

Everett, C. A. (1980b). Supervision of marriage and family therapy. In Allen Hess (Ed.), *Psychotherapy supervision: Theory, research, and practice.* New York: Wiley.

Everett, C. A. (Ed.). (2000). *Family therapy glossary* (3rd ed.). Washington, DC: American Association for Marriage and Family Therapy.

Everett, C. A. (in press). Family therapy for Parental Alienation Syndrome: Understanding the interlocking pathologies. In R. Gardner & R. Sauber (Eds.), *International handbook of Parental Alienation Syndrome: Legal and clinical issues.* New York: Haworth Press.

Everett, C. A., & Everett, S. V. (1994). *Healthy divorce.* San Francisco: Jossey-Bass.

Everett, C. A., & Everett, S. V. (1999). *Family therapy for ADHD.* New York: Guilford.

Everett, C. A., & Everett, S. V. (1998). *Short term family therapy with borderline patients.* Galena, IL: Geist & Russell.

Everett, C. A., Halperin, S., Volgy, S., & Wissler, A. (1989). *Treating the borderline family.* Boston: Allyn & Bacon.

Fairbairn, W. R. D. (1963). Synopsis of an object-relations theory of the personality, *International Journal of Psycho-Analysis, 44,* 224–225.

Falicov, C. (1988). Learning to think culturally. In H. A. Liddle, D. C. Breunlin, & R. C. Schwartz, (Eds.), *Handbook of family therapy training and supervision* (pp. 335–357). New York: Guilford.

Falicov, C. (1995). Training to think culturally: A multidimensional comparative framework. *Family Process, 34,* 373–388.

Figley, C. R. (1997). *Burnout in families: The systemic costs of caring.* Boca Raton, FL: CRC.

Figley, C. R. (2000a). Helping our supervisors-in-training (SITs) write their supervision philosophy statement. In *Readings in family therapy supervision* (pp. 46–48). Washington, DC: American Association for Marriage and Family Therapy.

Figley, C. R. (Ed.). (2000b). *Treating compassion fatigue.* New York: Brunner-Mazel.

Foley, V., & Everett, C. A. (1982). *Family therapy glossary.* Washington, DC: American Association for Marriage and Family Therapy.

Framo, J. (1976). Family of origin as a therapeutic resource for adults in marital and family therapy: You can and should go home again. *Family Process, 15,* 193–210.

Friedman, E. (1991). Changing the line: An interview with Edwin Friedman. *The Commission on Supervision Bulletin, 4*(3), 1–2.

Friedman, S. (Ed.). (1993). *The new language of change: Constructive collaboration in psychotherapy.* New York: Guilford.

Gladding, S. T., Huber, C. H., Remley, T. P., & Remley, T. P., Jr. (2000). *Ethical, legal, and professional issues in the practice of marriage and family therapy.* Upper Saddle River, NJ: Pearson Education.

Goldenthal, P. (2000). A matter of balance: Challenging and supporting supervisees. In *Readings in family therapy supervision* (pp. 61–62). Washington, DC: American Association for Marriage and Family Therapy.

Goolishian, H., & Anderson, H. (1992). Strategy and intervention versus nonintervention: A matter of theory? *Journal of Marital and Family Therapy, 18,* 5–15.

Grant, B. (2000). Supervisory power as an asset. In *Readings in family therapy supervision* (p. 63). Washington, DC: American Association for Marriage and Family Therapy.

Grunebaum, J. (1987). Multidirected partiality and the "parental imperative" [Special Issue: Psychotherapy with Families]. *Psychotherapy: Theory, Research, Practice, and Training, 24,* 646–656.

Haber, R. (2000). Supervision as an ethical gym. In *Readings in family therapy supervision* (pp. 167–168). Washington, DC: American Association for Marriage and Family Therapy.

Haley, J. (Ed.). (1971). *Changing families: A family therapy reader.* New York: Grune & Stratton.

Haley, J. (1976). *Problem-solving therapy.* San Francisco: Jossey-Bass.

Hardy, K. (1990). The theoretical myth of sameness: A critical issue in family training and treatment. In G. Saba, B. Karrer, & K. Hardy (Eds.), *Minorities and family therapy* (pp. 17–33). New York: Haworth.

Hardy, K. V. (1993). Live supervision in the postmodern era of family therapy. Issues, reflections, and questions. *Contemporary Family Therapy: An International Journal, 15,* 9–20.

Hardy, K. V., & Laszloffy, T. A. (1995). The cultural genogram: Key to training culturally competent family therapists. *Journal of Marital and Family Therapy, 21,* 227–237.

Harper-Jaques, S. (2002). *Supervision philosophy statement.* Unpublished document submitted in partial fulfillment of an AAMFT-sponsored supervision course.

Hastings, C. (2002). So, how do you become culturally competent? *Family Therapy Magazine, 1*(2), 18–24.

Heath, A., & Engleberg, S. (2000). Legal liability in supervision: An interview with AAMFT legal counsel. In *Readings in family therapy supervision* (pp. 162–164). Washington, DC: American Association for Marriage and Family Therapy.

Hedges, L. E. (2000). *Facing the challenge of liability in psychotherapy: Practicing defensively*. Northvale, NJ: Aronson.

Hoffman, L. (1981). *Foundations of family therapy*. New York: Basic Books.

Hoffman, L. (1997). Deconstructing family therapy. Presentation to the 55th annual conference, American Association for Marriage and Family Therapy, Atlanta, GA.

Holloway, E. (1995). *Clinical supervision: A systems approach*. Thousand Oaks, CA: Sage.

Hovestadt, A. (Ed.). (2001). *Practice management forms: Tools for the business of therapy*. Washington, DC: American Association for Marriage and Family Therapy.

Huber, C., & Peterson, C. M. (2000). MFT supervision: Evaluating and managing critical issues. In *Readings in family therapy supervision* (pp. 160–161). Washington, DC: American Association for Marriage and Family Therapy.

Isaacs, M. R., & Benjamin, M. P. (1991). Towards a culturally competent system of care. Washington, DC: CASSP Technical Assistance Center, Georgetown University.

Johnson, D. W., Johnson, R. T., & Holubec, E. J. (1994). New circles of learning: Cooperation in the classroom and school. Alexandria, VA: Association for Supervision and Curriculum Development.

Jordan, K. B. (2000). Live supervision of all therapy sessions: A must for beginning therapists in clinical practica. In *Readings in family therapy supervision* (p. 116). Washington, DC: American Association for Marriage and Family Therapy.

Karson, S., & O'Dell, J. W. (1975). A new automated interpretation system for the 16 PF. *Journal of Personality Assessment, 39*, 256–260.

Keeney, B., & Ray, W. (2000). Shifting from supervision to superaudition. In *Readings in family therapy supervision* (p. 55). Washington, DC: American Association for Marriage and Family Therapy.

Keiley, M. K., Dolbin, M., Hill, J. Karuppaswami, N., Liu, T., Natrajan, R., Poulsen, S., Robbins, N., & Robinson, P. (2002). The cultural genogram: Experiences from within a marriage and family therapy training program. *Journal of Marital and Family Therapy, 28*, 165–178.

Keiley, M. K., & Piercy, F. P. (1999). The consulting-your-consultants interview: A final narrative conversation with graduating family therapy masters students. *Journal of Marital and Family Therapy, 25*, 461–468.

Keyes, C. (2001). Risk management issues for clinicians who treat suicidal patients in managed systems. In J. M. Ellison (Ed.), *Treatment of suicidal patients in managed care* (pp. 153–172). Washington, DC: American Psychiatric Association.

Killian, K. D. (2000). Locating self in relation to "other": Supervision and white privilege. In *Readings in family therapy supervision* (pp. 188–190). Washington, DC: American Association for Marriage and Family Therapy.

Kiresuk, T. J., & Garwick, G. (1975). Basic goal attainment scaling procedures. In B. E. Compton & B. C. Galaway (Eds.), *Social work processes* (pp. 47–66). Homewood, IL: Dorsey.

Kniskern, D. P., & Gurman, A. S. (1988) Research. In H. A. Liddle, D. C. Breunlin, & R. C. Schwartz, (Eds.), *Handbook of family therapy training and supervision* (pp. 368–378). New York: Guilford.

Kohls, L. R., & Knight, J. M. (1994). *Developing intercultural awareness: A cross-cultural training handbook.* Yarmouth, ME: Intercultural Press.

Kostelnik, M. J. (1999). Everyone has a culture. In R. E. Lee & S. Emerson (Eds.), *The eclectic trainer* (pp. 147–163). Galena, IL: Geist & Russell.

Krovetz, M. L. (1999). *Fostering resilience: Expecting all students to use their minds and hearts well.* Thousand Oaks, CA: Sage.

Langdon, K., & Osborne, C. (2001). *Performance reviews.* New York: DK Publishing.

Langs, R. (1994). *Doing supervision and being supervised.* London: Karnac.

Laszloffy, T. A. (2000). The implications of client satisfaction feedback for beginning family therapists: Back to the basics. *Journal of Marital and Family Therapy, 26,* 391–197.

Lawless, J. (2002). A Caucasian male's journey toward cultural competence. *Family Therapy Magazine, 1*(2), 26–29.

Leaf, M. (1975). Baking and roasting. In J. P. Spradley & M. A. Rynkiewich (Eds.), *The Nacirema: Readings on American culture* (pp. 19–20). Boston: Little, Brown.

Lebow, J. (1987). Developing a personal integration in family therapy: Principles for model construction and practice. *Journal of Marital and Family Therapy, 13,* 1–14.

Lebow, J. (1997a). The integrative revolution in couple and family therapy. *Family Process, 36,* 1–17.

Lebow, J. (1997b). Rejoinder: Why integration is so important in couple and family therapy. *Family Process, 36,* 23–24.

Lee R. E. (1994). The marriage and family therapy examination program. *Contemporary Family Therapy, 15,* 347–368.

Lee, R. E. (1999a). Seeing and hearing in therapy and supervision: A clinical example of isomorphism. In R. E. Lee & S. Emerson (Eds.), *The eclectic trainer* (pp. 81–87). Galena, IL: Geist & Russell.

Lee, R. E. (1999b). Getting started. In R. E. Lee & S. Emerson (Eds.), *The eclectic trainer* (pp. 33–44). Galena, IL: Geist & Russell.

Lee, R. E. (2002a). *Who is being licensed?* Unpublished report to the Association of Marital and Family Therapy Regulatory Boards, Cincinnati, OH.

Lee, R. E. (2002b, October 27). Ethical issues and responsibilities for supervisors. Presentation to the 60th annual conference, American Association for Marriage and Family Therapy, Cincinnati, OH.

Lee, R. E., & Brann, D. (1994). Women retrospectively identify and weigh the emotional events of their lives: Exploration of a scaling technique. *Psychological Reports, 74,* 1307–1311.

Lee, R. E., Emerson, S., & Kochka, P. B. (1999). Using the Michigan State University Family Therapy Questionnaire for training. In R. E. Lee & S. Emerson (Eds.), *The eclectic trainer* (pp. 107–119). Galena, IL: Geist & Russell.

Lee, R. E., Eppler, C. S., Kendal, N., & Latty, C. R. (2001). Critical incidents in the lives of 1st year MFT students. *Contemporary Family Therapy: An International Journal, 23,* 51–61.

Lee, R. E., Nichols, D. P., Nichols, W. C., & Odom, T. (in press). Supervision in family therapy: Trends over 25 years. *Journal of Marital and Family Therapy.*

Lee, R. E., & Sturkie, K. (1997). The national marital and family therapy examination program. *Journal of Marital and Family Therapy, 23*(3), 255–269.

Lerner, R.M. (1991). Changing organism-context relations as the basic process of development: A developmental contextual perspective. *Developmental Psychology 27*, 27–32.

Lerner, R. M. (2001). *Concepts and theories of human development* (3rd ed.). Mahwah, NJ: Erlbaum.

Le Roux, P. (2000). Developing the person of the supervisor: An approach to training. In *Readings in family therapy supervision* (pp. 227–228). Washington, DC: American Association for Marriage and Family Therapy.

Liddle, H. A. (1982). Family therapy training: current issues, future trends. *International Journal of Family Therapy, 4,* 81–97.

Liddle, H. A. (1984). Toward a dialectical-contextual-coevolutionary translation of structural-strategic family therapy. *Journal of Strategic and Systemic Therapies, 3*(3), 66–79.

Liddle, H. A. (1988). Systemic supervision: Conceptual overlays and pragmatic guidelines. In H. A. Liddle, D. C. Breunlin, & R. C. Schwartz, (Eds.), *Handbook of family therapy training and supervision* (pp. 153–171). New York: Guilford.

Liddle, H. A., Breunlin, D. C., & Schwartz, R. C. (1988a). Family therapy training and supervision: An introduction. In H. A. Liddle, D. C. Breunlin, & R. C. Schwartz (Eds.), *Handbook of family therapy training and supervision* (pp. 3–9). New York: Guilford.

Liddle, H. A., Breunlin, D. C., & Schwartz, R. C. (Eds.). (1988b). *Handbook of family therapy training and supervision.* New York: Guilford.

Liddle, H. A., Davidson, G. S., & Barrett, M. J. (1988). Outcomes of live supervision: Trainee perspectives. In H. A. Liddle, D. C. Breunlin, & R. C. Schwartz, (Eds.), *Handbook of family therapy training and supervision* (pp. 386–398). New York: Guilford.

Lowe, R. (2000). Supervising self-supervision: Constructive inquiry and embedded narratives in case consultation. *Journal of Marital and Family Therapy, 26*, 511–521.

Mazza, J. (1988). Training strategic therapists: The use of indirect techniques. In H. A. Liddle, D. C. Breunlin, & R. C. Schwartz (Eds.), *Handbook of family therapy training and supervision* (pp. 93–109). New York: Guilford.

McAdoo, H. (2002). The ever expanding African tapestry in America. Presentation to the 60th annual conference, American Association for Marriage and Family Therapy, Cincinnati, OH.

McCollum, E. E., & Wetchler, J. L. (1995). In defense of case consultation: Maybe "dead" supervision isn't dead at all. *Journal of Marital and Family Therapy, 21*, 155–166.

Mead, E. E. (2000). Assessing supervision: Social validity and invalidity of evaluation. In *Readings in family therapy supervision* (pp. 85–86). Washington, DC: American Association for Marriage and Family Therapy.

Midori Hanna, S., & Brown, J. H. (1995). *The practice of family therapy: Key elements across models.* Pacific Grove, CA: Brooks/Cole.

Minuchin, S., & Fishman, H. C. (1981). *Family therapy techniques.* Cambridge, MA: Harvard University Press.

Monahan, J. (1993). Limiting therapist exposure to Tarasoff liability: Guidelines for risk containment. *American Psychologist, 48*, 242–250.

Montalvo, B. (1997). Live supervision: Restrained and sequence-centered. In T. C. Todd

& C. L. Storm (Eds.), *The complete systemic supervisor: Context, philosophy, and pragmatics* (pp. 289–297). Boston: Allyn & Bacon.

Moon, S. M., & Trepper, T. S. (1996). Case study research. In D. H. Sprenkle & S. M. Moon (Eds.), *Research methods in family therapy* (pp. 393–410). New York: Guilford.

Moultrop, D. J. (1986). Integration: A coming of age. *Contemporary Family Therapy, 8,* 157–167.

Nazario, A. (2000). Latina/os, Latino/a families, therapy and supervision. In *Readings in family therapy supervision* (pp. 194–197). Washington, DC: American Association for Marriage and Family Therapy.

Nelson, K. W., Brendel, J. M., Mize, L. K., Lad, K., Hancock, C. C., & Pinjala, A. (2001). Therapist perceptions of ethnicity issues in family therapy: A qualitative inquiry. *Journal of Marital and Family Therapy, 27,* 363–375.

Newfield, N., Sells, S. P., Smith, T. E., Newfield, S, & Newfield, F. (1996). Ethnographic research methods: Creating a clinical science of the humanities. In D. H. Sprenkle & S. M. Moon (Eds.), *Research methods in family therapy* (pp. 25–63). New York: Guilford.

Newman, B. M., Newman, P. R., & Morgan, K. (2002). *Development through life: A psychosocial approach.* Pacific Grove, CA: Brooks/Cole.

Nichols, W. C. (1968). Personal psychotherapy for marital therapists. *Family Coordinator, 17,* 83–88.

Nichols, W. C. (1975). *Training and supervision* [cassette recording no. 123]. Claremont, CA: American Association for Marriage and Family Therapy.

Nichols, W. C. (1988). An integrative psychodynamics and systems approach. In H. A. Liddle, D. C. Breunlin, & R. C. Schwartz, (Eds.), *Handbook of family therapy training and supervision* (pp. 110–127). New York: Guilford.

Nichols, W. C. (1992). *The AAMFT: Fifty years of marital and family therapy.* Washington, DC: American Association for Marriage and Family Therapy.

Nichols, W. C. (1995). *Treating people in families.* New York: Guilford.

Nichols, W. C. (1997). The maturing of family therapy. Invited presentation to the 55th annual conference, American Association for Marriage and Family Therapy, Atlanta, GA.

Nichols, W. C., & Everett, C. A. (1986). *Systemic family therapy: An integrative approach.* New York: Guilford.

Nichols, W. C., & Lee, R. E. (1999). Mirrors, cameras, and blackboards: Modalities of supervision. In R. E. Lee & S. Emerson (Eds.), *The eclectic trainer* (pp. 45–61). Galena, IL: Geist & Russell.

Nichols, W. C., Nichols, D. P., & Hardy, K. V. (1990). Supervision in family therapy: A decade review. *Journal of Marital and Family Therapy, 16,* 275–285.

Northey, W. F. (2002). Characteristics and clinical practices of marriage and family therapists: A national survey. *Journal of Marital and Family Therapy, 28,* 487–494.

O'Hanlon, W. H., & Weiner-Davis, M. (1989). *In search of solutions: A new direction in psychotherapy.* New York: Norton.

Papero, D. V. (1988). Training in Bowen theory. In H. A. Liddle, D. C. Breunlin, & R. C. Schwartz (Eds.), *Handbook of family therapy training and supervision* (pp. 62–77). New York: Guilford.

Pearson, J. L., Stanley, B., King, C. A., & Fisher, C. B. (2001). Intervention research with persons at high risk for suicidality: Safety and ethical considerations. *Journal of Clinical Psychiatry, 62*, 17–26.

Perlesz, A. J., Stolk, Y., & Firestone, A. F. (1990). Patterns of learning in family therapy training. *Family Process, 29*, 29–44.

Perlesz, A. J., Young, J., Paterson, R., & Bridge, S. (1994). The reflecting team as a reflection of second order therapeutic ideals. *Australian and New Zealand Journal of Family Therapy, 15*, 117–127.

Peterson, M. (1992). *At personal risk: Boundary violations in professional-client relationships.* New York: Norton.

Peterson, M. (2000). Covert agendas in supervision: Identifying the real culprit. In *Readings in family therapy supervision* (pp. 169–170). Washington, DC: American Association for Marriage and Family Therapy.

Pike-Urlacher, R. A. (1996). Towards the development of the Supervisee Developmental Needs Scale (SDNS): An instrument for assessing the developmental needs of family therapy supervisees (Doctoral dissertation, Purdue University, 1995). Dissertation Abstracts International, 56(9-B), 5220.

Pinsof, W. M. (1983). Integrative problem centered therapy: Toward the synthesis of family and individual psychotherapies. *Journal of Marital and Family Therapy, 9*, 19–35.

Pinsof, W. M., & Wynne, L. C. (1995). The efficacy of marital and family therapy: An empirical overview, conclusions, and recommendations. *Journal of Marital and Family Therapy, 21*, 585–613.

Pitta, P. (1996) An integrated supervisory model. *The Family Psychologist*, Winter, 16–18.

Proctor, B. (2000). *Group supervision: A guide to creative practice.* Thousand Oaks, CA: Sage.

Protinsky, H. (1997). Dismounting the tiger: Using tape in supervision. In T. C. Todd & C. L. Storm (Eds.), *The complete systemic supervisor: Context, philosophy, and pragmatics* (pp. 298–307). Boston: Allyn & Bacon.

Protinsky, H., & Preli, R. (1987). Intervention in strategic supervision. *Journal of Strategic and Systemic Therapies, 6*, 18–23.

Quinn, W. H. (1996). The client speaks out: Three domains of meaning. *Journal of Family Psychotherapy, 7*(2), 71–83.

Quinn, W. H., & Nagirreddy, C. (1999). Utilizing clients' voices in clinical supervision: The Interpersonal Process Recall method. In R. E. Lee & S. Emerson (Eds.), *The eclectic trainer* (pp. 120–132). Galena, IL: Geist & Russell.

Quinn, W. H., Nagirreddy, C., Lawless, J., & Bagley, R. (2000). Utilizing clients' voices in clinical supervision. In *Readings in family therapy supervision* (pp. 98–100). Washington, DC: American Association for Marriage and Family Therapy.

Rambo, A. H., & Shilts, L. (1997). Four supervisory practices that foster respect for diversity. In T. C. Todd & C. L. Storm (Eds.), *The complete systemic supervisor: Context, philosophy, and pragmatics* (pp. 83–92). Boston: Allyn & Bacon.

Reimers, S. (2001). Understanding alliances: How can research inform user-friendly practice? *Journal of Family Therapy, 23*, 46–62.

Reiner, P. A. (1997). Psychoanalytic approaches to supervising couple and family therapy. In T. C. Todd & C. L. Storm (Eds.), *The complete systemic supervisor: Context, philosophy, and pragmatics* (pp. 135–155). Boston: Allyn & Bacon.

Reiss, B. (1960). The selection and supervision of psychotherapists. In N. Dellis & H. Stone (Eds.), *The training of psychotherapists.* Baton Rouge: Louisiana State University.

Rigazio-DiGilio, S. A. (1997). Integrative supervision: Approaches to tailoring the supervisory process. In T. C. Todd & C. L. Storm (Eds.), *The complete systemic supervisor: Context, philosophy, and pragmatics* (pp. 195–216). Boston: Allyn & Bacon.

Rita, E. S. (1998). Solution-focused supervision. *Clinical Supervisor, 17*(2), 127–139.

Roberto, L. G. (1997). Supervision: The transgenerational models. In T. C. Todd & C. L. Storm (Eds.), *The complete systemic supervisor: Context, philosophy, and pragmatics* (pp. 156–172). Boston: Allyn & Bacon.

Roberts, H. (2000). Contextual supervision involves continuous dialogue with supervisees. In *Readings in family therapy supervision* (pp. 183–187). Washington, DC: American Association for Marriage and Family Therapy.

Roberts, J. (1997). Reflecting processes and "supervision": Looking at ourselves as we work with others. In T. C. Todd & C. L. Storm (Eds.), *The complete systemic supervisor: Context, philosophy, and pragmatics* (pp. 334–348). Boston: Allyn & Bacon.

Scharff, J. S., & Scharff, D. E. (1995*). A primer of object relations theory*. Northville, NJ: Aronson.

Schneider, J. G. (1994). *Legal issues involving "repressed memory" of childhood sexual abuse.* Washington, DC: National Register of Health Service Providers in Psychology.

Schutz, B. M. (1982). *Legal liability in psychotherapy: A practitioner's guide to risk management.* San Francisco: Jossey-Bass.

Schwartz, I. S., & Baer, D. M. (1991). Social validity assessments: Is current practice state of the art? *Journal of Applied Behavior Analysis, 24*, 189–204.

Schwartz, R. C., Liddle, H. A., & Breunlin, D. C. (1988), Muddles in live supervision. In H. A. Liddle, D. C. Breunlin, & R. C. Schwartz, (Eds.), *Handbook of family therapy training and supervision* (pp. 183–193). New York: Guilford.

Selekman, M., & Todd, T. (1995). Co-creating a context for change in the supervisory system: The solution-focused supervision model. *Journal of Systemic Therapies, 14*, 21–33.

Seligman, M. (1996). *The optimistic child: A proven program to safeguard children against depression and build lifelong resilience.* New York: HarperPerennial.

Sells, S. P., Smith, T. E., & Moon, S. (1996), An ethnographic study of client and therapist perceptions of therapy effectiveness in a university-based training clinic. *Journal of Marital and Family Therapy, 22*, 321–342.

Simon, F. B., Steirlin, H., & Wynne, L. C. (1985). *Language of family therapy: A systemic vocabulary and sourcebook.* New York: Family Process.

Smith, R. E. (1988). The logic and design of case study research. *The Sport Psychologist, 2*, 1–12.

Solomon, M. F. (1992). *Narcissism and intimacy: Love and marriage in an age of uncertainty.* New York: Norton.

Sprenkle, D. H. (2002). A therapeutic Hail Mary. In D. A. Baptiste (Ed.), *Clinical epiphanies in marital and family therapy: A practitioner's casebook of therapeutic insights, perceptions, and breakthroughs* (pp. 20–28). New York: Haworth.

Sprenkle, D. H., Blow, A. J., & Dickey, H. M. (1999). Common factors and other nontechnique variables in marriage and family therapy. In M. A. Hubble, B. L. Duncan, & S. Miller (Eds.), *The heart and soul of change: What works in therapy* (pp. 329–359) Washington, DC. American Psychological Association.

Storm, C. L. (1997). The blueprint for supervision relationships: Contracts. In T. C. Todd

& C. L. Storm (Eds.), *The complete systemic supervisor: Context, philosophy, and pragmatics* (pp. 272–282). Boston: Allyn & Bacon.

Storm, C. L. (2000a). Live supervision as a window: An interview with Braulio Montalvo. In *Readings in family therapy supervision* (pp. 109–110). Washington, DC: American Association for Marriage and Family Therapy.

Storm, C. L. (2000b). Greasing your pen: Showing you know the literature. In *Readings in family therapy supervision* (pp. 43–45). Washington, DC: American Association for Marriage and Family Therapy.

Storm, C. L. (2000c). Increased responsibility for preparing supervisors: Preventing supervisees from experiencing the kiss of death. In *Readings in family therapy supervision* (pp. 225–226). Washington, DC: American Association for Marriage and Family Therapy.

Storm, C. L., & Engleberg, S. (2000). Supervising defensively: Advice from legal counsel. In *Readings in family therapy supervision* (pp. 165–166). Washington, DC: American Association for Marriage and Family Therapy.

Storm, C. L., & Minuchin, S. (2000). Supervisors as social engineers: Creating family therapy-friendly organizations. An interview with Salvador Minuchin. In *Readings in family therapy supervision* (pp. 59–60). Washington, DC: American Association for Marriage and Family Therapy.

Storm, C. L., Peterson, M., & Tomm, K. (1997). Multiple relationships in supervision: Stepping up to complexity. In T. C. Todd & C. L. Storm (Eds.), *The complete systemic supervisor: Context, philosophy, and pragmatics* (pp. 253–271) .Boston: Allyn & Bacon.

Storm, C. L., Todd, T. C., McDowell, T., & Sutherland, T. (1997). Supervising supervisors. In T. C. Todd & C. L. Storm (Eds.), *The complete systemic supervisor: Context, philosophy, and pragmatics* (pp. 373–388). Boston: Allyn & Bacon.

Stromberg, C. D. (1987). Managing the risk of practice. *Register Report: The Newsletter for Psychologist Health Service Providers, 1,* 349.

Sturkie, D. K., & Bergen, L. P. (2000). *Professional regulation in marital and family therapy.* New York: Pearson Education.

Sturkie, K., & Lee, R. E. (2001). Assessing professional competence: Marital and family therapy examination programs. In K. Sturkie (Ed.), *Professional regulation in marriage and family therapy.* Boston: Allyn & Bacon.

Szapocznik, J., Kurtines, W., Santisteban, D. A., & Pantin, H. (1997). The evolution of structural ecosystemic theory for working with Latino families. In J. G. Garcia & M. C. Zea (Eds.), *Psychological interventions and research with Latino populations* (pp. 166–190). Needham Heights, MA: Allyn & Bacon.

Taibbi, R. (1995). *Clinical supervision: A four-stage process of growth and discovery.* Milwaukee, WI: Families International.

Todd, T. C. (1997a). Problems in supervision: Lessons from supervisees. In T. C. Todd & C. L. Storm (Eds.), *The complete systemic supervisor: Context, philosophy, and pragmatics* (pp. 241-252). Boston: Allyn & Bacon.

Todd, T. C. (1997b). Purposive systemic supervision models. In T. C. Todd & C. L. Storm (Eds.), *The complete systemic supervisor: Context, philosophy, and pragmatics* (pp. 173–194). Boston: Allyn & Bacon.

Todd, T. C. (1997c). Privately contracted supervision. In T. C. Todd & C. L. Storm (Eds.),

The complete systemic supervisor: Context, philosophy, and pragmatics (pp. 125–134). Boston: Allyn & Bacon.

Todd, T. C., & Storm, C. L. (1997). Thoughts on the evolution of MFT supervision. In T. C. Todd & C. L. Storm (Eds.), *The complete systemic supervisor: Context, philosophy, and pragmatics* (pp. 1–16). Boston: Allyn & Bacon.

Tomm, K. (1984). One perspective on the Milan systemic approach: Part II. Description of session format, interviewing style and interventions. *Journal of Marital and Family Therapy, 10*, 253–271.

Tomm, K. (1992). The ethics of dual relationships. *The Calgary Participator: A Family Therapy Newsletter, 1*, 11–15.

Tucker, B., Hart, G., & Liddle, H. A. (1976). Supervision in family therapy: A developmental perspective. *Journal of Marriage and Family Counseling, 2*, 269–276.

Turner, J. (2000). Males supervising females: The risk of gender-power blindness. In *Readings in family therapy supervision* (pp. 185–187). Washington, DC: American Association for Marriage and Family Therapy.

Turner, J., & Fine, M. (1997). Gender and supervision: Evolving debates. In T. C. Todd & C. L. Storm (Eds.), *The complete systemic supervisor: Context, philosophy, and pragmatics* (pp. 72–82). Boston: Allyn & Bacon.

VandeCreek, L., & Knapp, S. (2001). *Tarasoff and beyond: Legal and clinical considerations in the treatment of life-endangering patients* (3rd ed.) Sarasota, FL: Professional Resource Press.

Vesper, J. H., & Brock, G. W. (1991). *Ethics, legalities, and professional practice issues in marriage and family therapy*. Boston: Allyn & Bacon.

Von Bertalanffy, L. (1980). *General system theory* (rev. ed.). New York: George Braziller.

Walker, J. P., & Lee, R. E. (1998). Uncovering strengths of children of alcoholic parents. *Contemporary Family Therapy, 20*, 521–538.

Walsh, F. (1996). Family resilience: A concept and its application. *Family Process, 35*, 261–281.

Walter, J. L., & Peller, J. E. (1992). *Becoming solution-focused in brief therapy*. New York: Brunner-Mazel.

Wark, L. (2000). Research: Trainees talk about effective live supervision. In *Readings in family therapy supervision* (p. 119). Washington, DC: American Association for Marriage and Family Therapy.

Warr, P. B., & Knapper, C. (1968). *The perception of people and events*. New York: Wiley.

Watson, M. F. (1993). Supervising the person of the therapist: Issues, challenges, and dilemmas. *Contemporary Family Therapy, 15*, 21–23.

Watzlawick, P., & Weakland, J. H. (Eds.). (1993). *The interactional view: Studies at the Mental Research Institute, Palo Alto, 1965-1974*. New York: Norton.

Wedge, M. (1996). *In the therapist's mirror: Reality in the making*. New York: Norton.

Welch, B. L. (1998a). Reducing liability in a litigious era. *Insight: Guarding psychologists against liability risks* (Ed. 1). Simsbury, CT: American Professional Agency

Welch, B. L. (1998b). Walking the documentation tightrope. *Insight: Guarding psychologists against liability risks* (Ed. 2). Simsbury, CT: American Professional Agency.

Welch, B. L. (1999). Protecting you from the managed care tinderbox. *Insight: Guarding psychologists against liability risks* (Ed. 2). Simsbury, CT: American Professional Agency.

Welch, B. L. (2000a). Reducing your suicide liability. *Insight: Guarding psychologists against liability risks* (Ed. 1). Simsbury, CT: American Professional Agency.

Welch, B. L. (2000b). Borderline patients: Danger ahead. *Insight: Guarding psychologists against liability risks* (Ed. 2). Simsbury, CT: American Professional Agency.

Welch, B. L. (2001). Caution: State licensing board ahead. *Insight: Guarding psychologists against liability risks* (Ed. 1). Simsbury, CT: American Professional Agency.

Welch, B. L. (2003). Supervising with liability in mind. *Insight: Guarding psychologists against liability risks* (Ed. 1). Simsbury, CT: American Professional Agency.

Westheafer, C. (1984). An aspect of live supervision: The pathological triangle. *Australian Journal of Family Therapy, 5*(3), 169–175.

Wetchler, J. L. (1990). Solution-focused supervision. *Family Therapy, 27*(2), 129–138.

Wetchler, J. L., & McCollum, E. E. (1999). Case consultation: The cornerstone of supervision. In R. E. Lee & S. Emerson (Eds.), *The eclectic trainer* (pp. 62–75). Galena, IL: Geist & Russell.

Wheeler, D., Avis, J. M., Miller, L. A., & Chaney, S. (1986). Rethinking family therapy education and supervision: A feminist model. In F. P. Piercy (Ed.), *Family therapy education and supervision* (pp. 53–71). New York: Haworth.

When supervision is mandated: Education or punishment? 2000). In *Readings in family therapy supervision* (pp. 176–177). Washington, DC: American Association for Marriage and Family Therapy.

Whitaker, C., & Ryan, M. O. (Eds.) (1990). *Midnight musings of a family therapist.* New York: Norton.

White, M., & Epston, D. (1990). *Narrative means to therapeutic ends.* New York: Norton.

White, M. B., & Russell, C. S. (1995). The essential elements of supervisory systems: A modified Delphi study. *Journal of Marital and Family Therapy, 21*, 33–53.

White, M. B., & Russell, C. S. (1997). Examining the multifaceted notion of isomorphism in marriage and family therapy supervision: A quest for conceptual clarity. *Journal of Marital and Family Therapy, 23*, 315–333.

Willi, J. (1982). *Couples in collusion.* New York: Aronson.

Willi, J. (1984). *Dynamics of couples therapy.* New York: Aronson.

Williams, L. (1994). A tool for training supervisors: Using the supervision feedback form (SFF). *Contemporary Family Therapy, 20*, 311–315.

Williams, L. M., & Dombeck, H. J. (1999). To speak or not to speak: Guidelines for self-disclosure in supervision. In R. E. Lee & S. Emerson (Eds.), *The eclectic trainer* (pp. 22–30). Galena, IL: Geist & Russell.

Woodside, D. B. (2000). Reverse live supervision: Leveling the supervisory playing field. In *Readings in family therapy supervision* (pp. 113–114). Washington, DC: American Association for Marriage and Family Therapy.

Woody, R. H., & Woody, J. D. (Eds.). (2001). *Ethics in marriage and family therapy.* Washington, DC: American Association for Marriage and Family Therapy.

York, C. D. (1997). Selecting and constructing supervision structures: Individuals, dyads, co-therapists, groups, and teams. In T. C. Todd & C. L. Storm (Eds.), *The complete systemic supervisor: Context, philosophy, and pragmatics* (pp. 320–333). Boston: Allyn & Bacon.

Young, J., Perlesz, A., Paterson, R., & O'Hanlon, B. (1989). The reflecting team process in training. *Australian and New Zealand Journal of Family Therapy, 10*(2), 69–74.

Index